JEAN ANOUILH
THE COLLECTED PLAYS
VOLUME 2

Jean Anouilh

THE COLLECTED PLAYS

VOLUME 2

Time Remembered

Point of Departure

Antigone

Romeo and Jeannette

Medea

METHUEN · LONDON

First published in Great Britain in 1967
by Methuen & Co Ltd, 11 New Fetter Lane, EC4

Printed in Great Britain by W. & J. Mackay & Co Ltd, Chatham

Contents

Time Remembered

Characters

AMANDA
(*a Milliner*)

THE DUCHESS OF PONT-AU-BRONC

PRINCE ALBERT TROUBISCOI

LORD HECTOR

THEOPHILUS
(*a Butler*)

FERDINAND
(*a Head Waiter*)

THE TAXI-DRIVER

THE GHILLY

THE ICE-CREAM MAN

THE LANDLORD

THE CLOAKROOM ATTENDANT

FOOTMEN, WAITERS
AND GIPSIES

Original Title: Léocadia

Translator: Patricia Moyes

First produced in 1939

Act One

SCENE: *A drawing-room of stupefying elegance. In the midst of the splendour sits a young girl,* AMANDA, *with a little cardboard suit-case at her feet. She yawns, fidgets, then finally gets up and begins to examine a Venetian ebony figure of a negro, who proffers his tray of glass fruit ingratiatingly from a marble pedestal. Suddenly she starts guiltily as the door opens, and a little old lady enters with immense dignity, preceded by her lorgnette. It is the* DUCHESS. *She pauses before the negro, adjusts his position to her satisfaction, and then bears down upon* AMANDA.

DUCHESS: So, you've arrived, have you?
AMANDA: Yes, madame . . . I think so.
DUCHESS: Stand up straight, child. Chest over toes.

AMANDA, *bewildered, straightens her back.*

(*Severe.*) How do you contrive to be so absurdly small?
AMANDA: I don't know, madame, I do my best. . . .
DUCHESS: Not good enough. You must make a serious effort.

AMANDA *looks at her.*

My child, I am sixty. I have improved upon nature all my life, and intend to go on doing so.

She extends her foot, showing that she is wearing elegant high-heeled shoes.

You must wear shoes, child, shoes . . . not plimsolls like an all-in wrestler. How tall do you think I am in bare feet?
AMANDA: About five foot two, I should say, madame.
DUCHESS (*annoyed*): Not a bad guess. I am five foot one and three-quarters. However, it is of no consequence, as you will never see me in bare feet. I am glad to say nobody has ever

seen me in bare feet, except the dear duke, of course. But he was as blind as a bat.

She goes up to AMANDA.

(*Severe.*) And what have you got there?

AMANDA (*taken aback*): Gloves, madame.

DUCHESS (*with a disapproving snort*): Give them to the cat!

AMANDA: The cat?

DUCHESS: I spoke metaphorically. The cat would be horrified. I have a profound aversion to green, which is shared by my Siamese kitten. The sensitive little creature would sooner be made into a meat pie than sit on a green cushion. I may say that she has never seen a green cushion. There is not one single green object in this house – except for your gloves.

She throws them in the fire. AMANDA *cannot suppress a cry of protest.*

AMANDA: Madame! I paid a lot for those gloves!

DUCHESS: You were swindled.

She takes AMANDA'S *hand.*

Good. You have pretty hands. As I thought. They may be accustomed to making hats, but they have a certain air about them. In any case, who hasn't had to make hats these days? I haven't, of course. But then I belong to a different world altogether. Now, I trust that my telegram explained quite clearly why I want you here.

AMANDA: I gathered you had a situation here in the household, madame.

DUCHESS: A situation . . . what a delicious expression. The child is quite enchanting.

She thrusts her face to within an inch of AMANDA'S *and repeats:*

Enchanting.

Without taking her eyes off AMANDA, *she adds:*

Is she not, Gaston?

Since there is nobody else in the room, AMANDA *looks round in some surprise.*

I was talking to the duke. He died in 1923, but I have never been able to break myself of the habit of talking to him.

She studies AMANDA *again, then sits down beside her.*

Enchanting.

Suddenly she adopts a coaxing tone, as though speaking to a pampered lap-dog.

And is the little girl pleased to have found a situation then?

AMANDA: Oh, yes, madame. You see, two days ago – I don't mind telling you, because they gave me an excellent reference – but two days ago I lost my job at Madame Rensada's, and—

DUCHESS: I know all about that, dear. I arranged it.

AMANDA (*jumping up in angry astonishment*): You did! Well, of all the cheek!

The DUCHESS *laughs delightedly and sweeps out of the room, saying:*

DUCHESS: Cheek! Cheek, she says! Gaston, didn't I tell you she was adorable . . . ?

She has gone. AMANDA *sits down again abruptly. She grasps her little suitcase and looks desperately around, on the verge of tears. A* BUTLER *comes in and bows to her elaborately.*

BUTLER: Her Grace the Duchess wishes me to inquire whether it will be convenient for mademoiselle to partake of a cold collation while awaiting Her Grace's return.

AMANDA: I'm not hungry, thank you.

BUTLER: I beg mademoiselle's pardon, but my inquiry was merely rhetorical. Her Grace has given orders that the cold collation will be served. (*He claps his hands.*)

To the accompaniment of lilting music, a procession of FOOTMEN *stream into the room, bearing dish after elaborate dish amidst a dazzling welter of silver, cut glass and gleaming napery.* AMANDA *is confronted by a display of cakes, fruits and sweetmeats extravagant enough to daunt the staunchest appetite.*

FIRST FOOTMAN: Smoked salmon, mademoiselle?
SECOND FOOTMAN: Chicken in aspic?
THIRD FOOTMAN: A little lobster?
FOURTH FOOTMAN: Pâtè de fois gras?
FIRST FOOTMAN: Iced melon?
SECOND FOOTMAN: A peach?
THIRD FOOTMAN: An éclair?
FOURTH FOOTMAN: A tangerine?
FIRST FOOTMAN: Chocolate gateau?
SECOND FOOTMAN: Wild strawberries and cream?
THIRD FOOTMAN: Lemon soufflé?
AMANDA (*angry*): Stop! Please stop! Honestly, I'm not hungry. I'll just have a tangerine. . . .

She takes a tangerine and begins to peel it. The DUCHESS *returns like a whirlwind, followed by* LORD HECTOR, *a tall, thin and tweedy individual redolent of the countryside and its pursuits. The* DUCHESS *bears down upon* AMANDA, *snatches the tangerine away from her, and throws it into the fire.*

DUCHESS: No tangerines, no oranges or lemons. They make you thin, and you cannot afford to lose a single ounce. Now, look at her, Hector. Would she not be quite striking . . .
HECTOR: Striking. . . .
DUCHESS: . . . if we could fill her out a little?

HECTOR, *who has placed a monocle in his eye the better to study* AMANDA, *has no time to reply. The* DUCHESS *sweeps on relentlessly.*

Eggs and pastry, pastry and eggs. (*Calls.*) Theophilus!

The BUTLER *materializes discreetly.*

BUTLER: Your Grace?
DUCHESS: Remove all this paraphernalia and bring the young lady an egg.

AMANDA *jumps up, pale but determined.*

AMANDA: No, madame!
DUCHESS (*turning to her, astounded*): Did I understand you to say 'No'? Explain yourself, miss.
AMANDA (*desperately bold*): I'm not hungry and I don't like eggs!
DUCHESS (*to* HECTOR): I told you so. Adorable.

She turns and sweeps out, followed by HECTOR, *who echoes:*

HECTOR: Adorable.

They have gone. AMANDA *can stand no more. She grabs her suit-case, and seems on the point of either smashing something or else bursting into tears. She shouts at the* FOOTMEN *who have arrived to take away the dishes.*

AMANDA: What's happening! Why won't anybody tell me? Why was I brought here?
BUTLER (*as he goes, bringing up the rear of the procession of* FOOTMEN): Mademoiselle must excuse us, but these matters are not confided to the domestic staff. To obtain a reply, mademoiselle must address herself directly to Her Grace – or, as a last resort, to Lord Hector.

He goes. AMANDA, *left alone, throws her case down on the ground and stamps her foot in fury.*

AMANDA: Bother, bother, bother, bother!
DUCHESS (*coming in by another door*): What a hideously inelegant word! Say 'Confound it', my dear. That is a fine old full-blooded oath which you can be proud to utter. Bother is not only insipid; it is also ugly.

She sits down, and addresses AMANDA *in a sophisticated drawl.*

I must apologize, my dear, for keeping you here so long – you must be simply *dying* to see your room and have a little rest after your journey – but the fact is that there is a certain person whom I am particularly anxious should not see you, and he is due back from his walk at any moment. It might jeopardize all my plans should you meet him just now.

AMANDA (*sitting down and making an effort to clarify the situation*): I received a telegram from you this morning, madame, saying that you might have a job for me – but I am beginning to think that I must have misunderstood it.

DUCHESS: I am quite convinced that you misunderstood it, child.

AMANDA: I thought so. You see, I'm a milliner, madame. I only know about making hats—

DUCHESS: And you have deduced that I am not the type of woman who has her hats remodelled at home? A good point.

AMANDA: Well, I'd rather tell you straight out, madame, that if the vacancy is for a housemaid, or even a lady's maid . . . I . . . well, I'm a skilled worker, madame, and even though it has put me in an awkward position, losing my job at Madame Rensada's, still I'm determined to carry on with my profession.

DUCHESS: You were quite right, Gaston. The girl has spirit.

She gets up and goes to the door, saying to AMANDA *as she passes:*

Another good point!

AMANDA (*jumping up*): No, madame! This time I'm not going to let you go!

DUCHESS: Not let me go? Did you hear that, Gaston? We are to be prisoners in our own home – just as we were under Francis the First.

AMANDA (*a little taken aback*): Francis the First?

DUCHESS: Yes, we were confined to our estates after an abortive attempt to seize power. Apparently we died of boredom.

AMANDA: I promise you, madame, I have no intention of keeping you prisoner. But I arrived here on the 2.17 train, and it's nearly five o'clock now, and the last train back to Paris tonight is the 6.19. If I'm not going to be of any use to you here, I really must catch it.

DUCHESS: No, child, you will not travel by that train.

AMANDA: Why not, madame?

DUCHESS: Because it is not running.

AMANDA: But I looked it up in the timetable!

DUCHESS: I have no doubt that it appears in the timetable. Nevertheless, it is not running – as from yesterday.

AMANDA (*to whom anything seems possible by now*): You stopped it running so that I couldn't get away. Didn't you?

DUCHESS: A hundred years ago, my dear, I would most certainly have done so. No, it was not I who cancelled the train. (*Darkly.*) It was the Freemasons.

She sits down.

They realized, you see, how useful that train was to people visiting this house. We've opened it to the public, you know. Twice a week, ten till six, fifty francs admission. And very nicely we were doing – picture postcards for sale, cups of coffee on the terrace, a tour of the dungeons extra – oh, yes, I move with the times. I realize the value of publicity. And then – out of a blue sky, before I could lift a finger – (*she snaps her fingers*) – they cancelled my train. Just like that. Ah, but I'm too clever for them. Do you know what I'm going to do? (*In a confidential whisper.*) Motor coaches! What do you think of that?

On this triumphant note, she gets up to go. AMANDA, *at the end of her tether, follows her tearfully.*

AMANDA: But I don't understand, madame. I don't know what you're talking about – dungeons and trains and Freemasons. I've been waiting for over two hours and I didn't even have time for any lunch before I left home—

DUCHESS: No lunch? No lunch? What can have happened to that egg? I will go and investigate.

She makes as if to go again. AMANDA *raises her voice in a wail of desperation.*

AMANDA: Oh, madame, please, please don't go away again without explaining things to me, or I'll go mad!

The DUCHESS *stops in the doorway.*

DUCHESS (*serious*): You are cleverer than you look, child. I will make a confession to you. I am not sixty. I am sixty-seven. I have survived the birth of the aeroplane, the death of the corset, short hair and two World Wars. So if I say that I'm an old woman who has seen many bizarre and exciting things in her time, you will agree with me, won't you?

AMANDA (*at a loss*): Yes, madame. . . .

DUCHESS: Well, then, you must take my word for it that the reason I have been popping in and out of this room like a jack-in-the-box for the last ten minutes is simply that I cannot summon up the courage to tell you the truth of why I made you come here.

She goes out, leaving AMANDA *more dumbfounded than ever.* AMANDA *picks up her case, half tearful, half angry, and announces almost hysterically to the empty room:*

AMANDA: Mad! They're all stark staring mad! I'll . . . I'll *walk* back to Paris!

She opens the french window, looks round anxiously to see if she is observed, and then runs out into the garden. The orchestra strikes a mysterious chord. The stage is empty for a moment. Then the DUCHESS *comes in, followed by* HECTOR.

DUCHESS: Hector! Hector, where is she? I have a most curious presentiment—

HECTOR (*looking stupidly round the empty room*): For once your presentiment seems to be correct. She's evaporated.

DUCHESS: She's what?

HECTOR: She's gone.

DUCHESS: Well, obviously. Hector! If she meets him in the park, we are lost! Hurry! Hurry!

They rush out into the garden. The lights dim. The music swells up under a chorus of birdsong. When the lights go up again, we are in a clearing in the park. It is wild and overgrown. There is a small obelisk surrounded by a circular stone bench. At one side of the scene, pulled up near a large tree, stands an ancient taxi. Two legs stick out from under it. A closer inspection reveals that this is a mere caricature of a taxi – filthy and antiquated, and overgrown with ivy and honeysuckle. A cock crows from the vantage-point of its roof. Not far away stands an ice-cream cart displaying its gaudy pictorial representations of strawberry and vanilla cones and bars. Two legs are also visible under the cart. AMANDA *runs in, carrying her suitcase. When she sees the taxi, she stops, and exclaims joyfully:*

AMANDA: Oh, thank heavens! A taxi!

She looks round, sees no one, and then notices the legs.

Oh . . . excuse me . . .
A VOICE: Who are you talking to?
AMANDA: I . . . I don't know . . . are these your legs?

A benevolent OLD MAN *appears from behind the ice-cream cart. He adjusts his spectacles, and says:*

ICE-CREAM MAN: Which legs?

AMANDA, *mute with embarrassment, indicates the legs which protrude from under the taxi.*

(*Simply.*) No. Those aren't mine.

He disappears behind his cart again, newspaper in hand.

AMANDA (*as he goes*): Oh, sir . . . please. . . .

He reappears.

Am I still in the park? I've been walking for ever so long.
ICE-CREAM MAN (*lugubrious*): Yes, miss. You can walk as long as you like and you'll still be in the park.

A mocking-bird's song shrills out as though to taunt AMANDA. *Suddenly she snatches up her case and runs to the taxi.*

AMANDA: Taxi! Taxi! Driver, are you free?

At these words, the DRIVER *emerges from under his cab, furious.*

DRIVER: Of course I am free. Am I not a Socialist?
AMANDA: Oh, thank goodness, I am saved.

She opens the door of the taxi and jumps in, crying:

Take me to the railway station, please! As fast as you can!

The DRIVER *watches her get into the taxi with mingled astonishment and amusement. She emerges almost immediately from the door on the other side.*

Driver!

DRIVER: Yes?
AMANDA (*angry*): There are rabbits in your taxi!
DRIVER: Of course there are rabbits in my taxi!

He grows very angry.

So now I'm not allowed to keep rabbits, is that it? Eh? Have I or have I not a right to keep rabbits if I want to?

AMANDA (*retreating a step*): Of course you have a right to keep rabbits. . . .
DRIVER (*advancing angrily*): Am I a human being or am I not? I'm only asking. Getting at me just because they pay me thirty thousand francs a month for doing nothing? Well, I'm not denying it, am I? That has absolutely nothing to do with it. Anyway, I always said I'd never be a private chauffeur . . . that's what they call me. Huh! Well?
AMANDA (*retreating rapidly*): I assure you I never meant—
DRIVER: All right then.

AMANDA *takes another step back and trips. She cries out, for by now everything scares her. Then she smiles timidly at the* DRIVER, *as if to excuse her exclamation.*

AMANDA: I'm sorry . . . I'm a bit nervy today. . . .

She sees what she has tripped over, and breathes again.

Oh . . . it's only a bit of ivy. . . .

DRIVER (*calmer*): Of course it's ivy. Any objection?

He goes back to his motor.

It's easy to grow, ivy is. I tried rambler roses once, pruned 'em, watered 'em every day – no good. Wouldn't grow. So now I stick to ivy; it's pretty and it grows quick.

AMANDA: It must be awkward when you want to drive away.

DRIVER: What d'you mean, awkward?

AMANDA: Well . . . the . . . the ivy. . . .

By now anything seems possible. She asks with a timid smile:

Do you . . . take it with you?

DRIVER (*delighted at the idea*): You're a comic, you are. What d'you think the ivy's made of then – elastic?

He calls:

Hey! Giuseppe!

The ICE-CREAM MAN *reappears.*

D'you know what she just said? Asked me if the ivy follows me around! She's a proper scream, she is. Can't you just see me taking it out for a walk every day. (*Calls, as if to a dog.*) Come along, then! (*Whistles.*) There's a good little ivy . . . heel, sir, heel! (*He roars with laughter.*)

AMANDA (*continuing her inspection*): But your taxi can't possibly go at all! There are creepers growing all over it!

DRIVER: What's that? My taxi not go! D'you hear that, Giuseppe? So my taxi won't go, won't it?

He rushes to the taxi, livid, and turns the handle viciously. A hiccough, and the motor starts.

There! Now who says it won't go!

AMANDA: No! No, please! Don't make it move! Not with the ivy! I couldn't bear it! I think I'm going mad . . . everything is absolutely crazy today . . . (*To the* ICE-CREAM MAN.) You . . . are you really an ice-cream man?

ICE-CREAM MAN: 'Course I am, miss.

AMANDA: Well, sell me an ice-cream then. I'm terribly thirsty.

ICE-CREAM MAN: An ice-cream! My dear young lady, it's two years since I last made an ice-cream. I doubt if I could remember how.

AMANDA: Just as I expected. Thank you. You've set my mind at rest. I'm beginning to see a mad sort of sense in all this. I'd only have been worried if you'd *had* an ice-cream to sell – a real, freezing ice-cream. Will you do one more thing for me?

She hands him something.

ICE-CREAM MAN: What's this? A pin? What d'you expect me to do with a pin?

AMANDA: Prick me, please – not too hard, just enough to make sure I'm not dreaming.

ICE-CREAM MAN (*pricking her*): She's a character all right.

DRIVER (*lugubrious*): She's worse than a character. She's looney.

AMANDA: Ow! Thank you. May I have my pin back, please?

She takes the pin, and pricks her own hand, gently, experimentally, as if to confirm her previous opinion that she is awake. Having done so, she suddenly turns to the two men, desperately defiant.

I *am* awake – and alive! D'you hear? I'm alive and when I'm pricked with a pin, I feel it. I've got two legs and two feet, and I can walk on them. I'm not even going to ask you the way to the railway station. I'm going to walk straight ahead and follow my nose till I find the main road. And on the road I'll find a signpost – because in the world I come from – the real world – there are real signposts on the road, pointing to real places! And I'll read it with my own two eyes and then I'll walk to the station, and I'll find the station master – and he'll be a real live station master, made of flesh and blood!

She picks up her case with a sigh which is very close to tears, and adds:

I hope.

As she goes off, she collides with the DUCHESS, *who arrives at a canter, followed by the faithful* HECTOR.

DUCHESS: Oh, thank heaven, we've found her!

She sits heavily on the circular bench.

Oh, child, what a fright you gave me! I nearly died . . . and I am prostrate with exhaustion.

AMANDA: Don't try to make me feel sorry for you. What about me? *I'm* exhausted too, and *I* nearly died of fright.

DUCHESS: Fright? What on earth is there for you to be frightened of?

AMANDA: Everything, madame – especially you.

DUCHESS: Me? What an extraordinary notion. D'you hear that, Hector?

AMANDA (*lively*): Yes – you! And the taxi-driver whose taxi is overgrown with ivy, and the ice-cream man who hasn't sold an ice-cream for two years, and this awful park with no way out of it . . . Where am I? What do you want of me? Why did you get me dismissed from Madame Rensada? Why did you entice me out here by promising me a job – what sort of job could I possibly do in this madhouse? I suppose you want a milliner who doesn't make hats! (*Determined.*) Well, I'm not frightened of you any more. Which is the way to the station? I demand that you tell me the way to the station!

DUCHESS: Hector, she is adorable.

HECTOR: Adorable.

AMANDA, *worn out, sinks on to the bench, crying amidst her sobs:*

AMANDA: Tell me the way to the station!

DUCHESS (*taking her hand*): No, no! You must on no account cry! I appreciate your confusion and your curiosity, child. The moment has come for plain speaking, however painful. I will be brief. I have a nephew, mademoiselle. A nephew whom I idolize above everything else in the world. His name is Albert. The poor boy is the victim of a most strange melancholia, which—

She stops.

The story is so poignant to me that I really cannot bear to repeat it. Hector, you go on.

HECTOR *stands up, ceremoniously. The* DUCHESS *introduces him in a brisk tone.*

Allow me to present my cousin, Baron Andinet of Andaine.

HECTOR *bows.* AMANDA *drops a little curtsy.* HECTOR *is about to speak, but the* DUCHESS *forestalls him.*

Lord Hector. He is not to be confused with Lord Jerome, who is first secretary at the consulate in Honolulu, nor with Lord Jasper, the General's son. (*With a gesture.*) Lord Hector.

HECTOR *bows again, and opens his mouth to speak. Once more he is too late.*

There is very little likelihood of your confusing him with Lord Jasper. He has been dead for some years, poor fellow.

HECTOR: Poor fellow!

DUCHESS: Go on, Hector.

HECTOR: Well, mademoiselle, my cousin, Prince Troubiscoi . . .

DUCHESS: Yes, my sister became a Troubiscoi by her second marriage, the silly girl. The Tsar was visiting Paris at the time – Slavonic charm, I am afraid, quite fatal – however, we've been into all that . . . go on, Hector.

HECTOR: My cousin, Prince Troubiscoi—

DUCHESS: Call him Prince Albert, or she may think you are referring to the other one – that imbecile who married the Englishwoman – Patrick Troubiscoi. (*To* AMANDA, *perfectly naturally.*) You may have met him?

AMANDA: No, madame.

DUCHESS: You amaze me. One meets him absolutely everywhere. Go on, Hector.

HECTOR: Well, mademoiselle, some years ago my cousin, the Prince Albert, visited Dinard, where he met a young woman who—

DUCHESS (*interrupting*): No, no, no! Be quiet, Hector. You manage to invest the story of this exquisite romance with such a flat-footed platitudinous boredom that I prefer to make the sacrifice and tell it myself. Two years ago, mademoiselle, my beloved Albert became deliriously enamoured of a lady of incomparable beauty and impeccable aristocracy . . . a lady of whom you will certainly have heard. I will tell you her name. Léocadia Gardi.

AMANDA: The ballerina?

DUCHESS: Yes, child. The great and glorious ballerina. The divine Gardi, as they called her. Ah, the exquisite, ethereal grace of that first entry of hers in *Lac des Cygnes.*

She dances a few steps, then stops.

Unhappily I am no dancer. When I was a girl I was as light as thistledown on my feet – but thirty years of waltzing with the dear duke proved too much for my delicate talent . . . a pity, but there it is. Where was I?

HECTOR: In the *Lac des Cygnes.*

DUCHESS: Oh, yes . . . Léocadia. Dear Léocadia. You say you knew her well. That will be the greatest help to us.

AMANDA: Oh, no, I didn't know her at all. I just read about her death in the newspapers.

DUCHESS: Alas, yes! You know how she died?

AMANDA: I think they said it was an accident.

DUCHESS: Yes. The poor darling always wore a scarf of immense length; she had a different one for every costume she possessed . . . very becoming they were, too . . . they became quite a legend, Léocadia's scarves. As she said good-bye to you, she would fling her scarf around her lovely neck, and knot it in her own inimitable way. . . . Well, one evening she was leaving the house of some friends after a most interesting discussion on the thirty-two *fouettés.* On the doorstep, saying good-bye, she knotted her scarf with a magnificent, characteristic gesture. (*She demonstrates.*) Alas, she flung her arm too wide . . . strangled herself. She let out a single cry – a strangled one, of course – and fell, dead.

She sniffs.

Finish it, Hector. I can't go on.

HECTOR (*who is under the impression that it is already finished, merely repeats*): Dead. . . .

DUCHESS: It was only three days before this tragedy that poor Albert fell in love with her. He has never recovered from those three days. Now do you begin to understand?

AMANDA: No.

DUCHESS: Very well, I will proceed. When he heard the ghastly news, his first thought was to fling himself from his balcony. For more than an hour I held him back by his coat-tails with my own hands. But that was merely a temporary danger. I had to think of the future. I decided that he must travel. We went on a most expensive and enthralling cruise – one and a half times round the world – but all in vain. One hundred and twenty-two days we spent on that peregrination – Albert sitting in his cabin gazing at a photograph of his dear departed, and me sitting in mine gazing at him through the intervening keyhole, to make sure he did not jump overboard. Do you wish me to describe to you in detail the agonies of my long martyrdom?

AMANDA (*who is beginning to be fed up*): No, madame.

DUCHESS: No. You are right. It would be too long and too painful. Suffice it to say that I, the very soul of curiosity, travelled one and a half times round the world with one eye shut and the other glued to a keyhole. Now and then, when we were in harbour, my gipsy nature became too strong for me, and I would snatch a peep through the porthole. Once I caught a glimpse of a turban – that was India. Another time, a pigtail – China, of course. The smoke of a volcano told me we were approaching Italy . . . only when we were on French soil once more did I dare to think of myself again. . . . I found I had lost two stone through worry and anxiety . . . fortunately, however, the lack of exercise had put it on again . . . we are now in Marseilles. Are you following me, or am I going too fast for you?

AMANDA: No, madame. I'm with you.

DUCHESS: Good. We returned home with all speed – we both needed a rest. At last I seemed to detect a lessening of Albert's grief . . . but his melancholy was still deep enough to worry me. I set my spies on him, to report on his every movement. I learnt that he spent his days in Dinard, chatting sometimes with a taxi-driver, sometimes with an ice-cream merchant, sometimes with the landlord of a wretched little inn called the Chime of Bells. As for his evenings, he invariably went to a certain Viennese nightclub, sat always at the same table, and was served always by the same waiter. September came . . . Dinard was deserted.

HECTOR: Always is in September.

DUCHESS: All the cafés closed for the winter – except that one. It remained open, and night after night Albert sat there in solitary state. Soon I discovered that he was financing the place, which otherwise would have been bankrupt long ago – simply for the pleasure of being able to sit at that particular table every night. Frankly, I was baffled. I could not understand – and then, suddenly, I saw the light!

AMANDA (*who is beginning to take an interest in the love story*): Was it there that they first discovered that they loved each other?

DUCHESS (*regarding her admiringly*): Oh, Hector! What a splendid thing it is to have a plebeian soul! The girl has understood instinctively what we, with our intelligence, took months to grasp. Yes, child, you are right. The taxi-driver, the ice-cream man, the Chime of Bells, the gipsy café . . . all of them formed the background of poor Albert's love affair with his divine Léocadia, and every day for three long months he returned to their enchantment, like a man possessed.

AMANDA (*dreamy*): It must be wonderful to love someone as much as all that. . . .

DUCHESS: I dare say. But think of my position. Albert is not only a Troubiscoi, but – far more important – he is an Andinet of Andaine, on his mother's side. Please don't think I am simply a reactionary old fossil – nothing could be farther from the truth. In the first war, I signed on to the nursing reserve without making any stipulation whatsoever about the social status of my patients . . . I felt I must set an example. But all the same . . . all the same . . . you must admit that it is scarcely worth going to the trouble and expense of gaining control of half the kingdom in the reign of Louis the Great, if a mere seven hundred years later one is going to have one's nephew gossiping on street corners with taxi-drivers and ice-cream men. However . . . where was I?

HECTOR: You'd suddenly seen the light.

DUCHESS (*picking up the thread*): Ah, yes. I realized suddenly that these people were merely the souvenirs of dear Albert's great love. Well, I am a collector at heart. I bought the taxi, the ice-cream cart, the park benches upon which they sat . . . these benches were the most difficult of all. . . . I had to go to court over them – but I got them. As for the inn and the Viennese nightclub, I had them rebuilt stone by stone in the park.

AMANDA: It's . . . it's like a fairy story . . .

DUCHESS: Nonsense. It was the least I could do. I confess I am thankful that the poor children did not visit the Eiffel Tower. . . .

AMANDA: How you must love your nephew, madame!

DUCHESS: My dear, I worship him – and so will you, when you meet him. In any case, Albert and I are both stay-at-homes by nature, and so I have arranged that the dear boy shall have his precious souvenirs within easy reach.

AMANDA: But I still don't understand where I fit in, madame. I promise you I've never set eyes on your nephew at any time – let alone during those three fatal days – I can't possibly be one of his souvenirs. I've never set foot in Dinard in my life. Why, when Léocadia Gardi died, I was working for Madame Rensada from nine till six every day. It was my first year, and I didn't have a holiday at all that summer – I can prove it! I had no chance to go to the seaside!

DUCHESS (*to* HECTOR): Hector, I find her quite delightful.

HECTOR: I must admit she's rather pretty.

DUCHESS: She is far more than just pretty. She has spirit.

HECTOR: That's what I meant.

DUCHESS: Hector, you're pathetic. (*To* AMANDA.) Pay no attention to him, dear. You have spirit. A quality all too rare these days.

AMANDA (*lively*): I am well aware that I have spirit, madame. But I was not aware that my reputation for it had spread all the way down here from the Rue de la Paix. Don't try to tell me that *that's* why you sent for me!

DUCHESS: No, child.

She suddenly seems uneasy.

What time is it? Here we are, chattering away . . . it must be quite late. . . .

She starts to rise.

AMANDA (*desperate, pushing her down again*): No, madame. Sit down and give me a straight answer for once. I don't know what time it is, and I don't care. I've missed my train back anyway, thanks to you. . . .

DUCHESS: Nobody has ever dared to use that tone with me – not even the dear duke!

AMANDA: Well, nobody has ever dared to lure me into the wilds of Brittany by promising me a job, and then refused to tell me what the job is!

DUCHESS (*to* HECTOR): This is painful for us, Hector, but we have asked for it. (*Resolute.*) Hector, we must tell her.

HECTOR (*unenthusiastic*): Yes, we must.

DUCHESS: We must.

A long pause. They stare into the distance, deeply embarrassed.

(*Suddenly.*) Hector.

HECTOR: Yes.

DUCHESS: Are you a man or a mouse?

HECTOR (*without hesitation*): A mouse.

DUCHESS: What?

HECTOR (*pathetic but firm*): A mouse. You're always telling me so.

DUCHESS (*annoyed*): Only in fun, Hector. Of course, you're a man. Tell the girl the truth, before she begins to suspect the worst.

AMANDA: I suspect the worst already, madame.

DUCHESS: My dear child, what you call the worst is the least of your worries. It is far worse than the worst. Go on, Hector. We are waiting.

HECTOR (*after much preliminary clearing of the throat*): Well . . . the fact is . . .

Pause. In a strangled voice:

No, I can't say it! It was your idea, anyway!

DUCHESS: Very well. I will meet you half-way. Let us speak in unison.

HECTOR: In unison?

DUCHESS (*ironic*): Unless you feel up to the descant. We will recite together the speech we prepared this morning.

HECTOR: Word for word?

DUCHESS: Word for word. Watch my hand. One, two, three . . . ready?

HECTOR: Yes, I suppose so.

DUCHESS: Go!

They take a step forward, and begin, together:

DUCHESS AND HECTOR: Mademoiselle . . . or rather . . . dear child, if we may presume so to address you. . . .

They look at each other, and take a breath in unison. Then they continue.

Dear child . . . what we have to say may shock you, coming as it does from such irreproachably respectable lips as ours. . . .

HECTOR'S *voice has trailed off miserably. The* DUCHESS *gives him an admonitory look.*

DUCHESS: Hector, where are you?

HECTOR: It's no good . . . I can't say it . . . not even in unison!

DUCHESS (*sad*): To think that an ancestor of yours once defended a bridge single-handed against the entire Albanian army.

HECTOR (*stung*): That has nothing to do with it! Show me the Albanian army, and I'll defend a bridge against it with pleasure. But this is a different kettle of fish altogether, and I want no part of it.

DUCHESS: Very well. In that case, go away. Since the head or my family turns tail at the first whiff of grapeshot, I shall have to carry the banner alone! Leave us!

HECTOR *goes, his head bowed in shame. The* DUCHESS *abandons her belligerent attitude, and draws* AMANDA *to her, speaking more quietly and with less buffoonery than before, a genuine sensitivity shining under the raillery which makes her suddenly warm and human.*

Well, child. I suppose you think I'm a mad old woman . . . no, no, don't deny it . . . but I do assure you that I'm not. I know perfectly well that you will be offended by what I'm going to say. You will stand up in adorable affronted dignity, clutching your little cardboard suitcase, and slip away through my fingers into the dusk.

She looks at AMANDA, *then goes on:*

And the tragic thing is that if you were my daughter, that is just what I would want you to do . . . and yet . . . my dear . . . no one can overhear us . . . and even you and I are beginning to grow dim to each other, as the violet velvet of the evening falls tactfully between us, until your face is only a glimmer of whiteness in the twilight. . . .

She stops, and dreams a little.

If you were my daughter . . . but I have no daughter. I could never have a child. Was it poor Gaston's fault or mine? I never knew. And when he died it was too late for me to find out. I have no daughter. But I have a nephew. Perhaps it is naughty of me to be so indulgent with him . . . but it is only because I love him too well . . . and in any case, I am extravagant by nature.

A little pause. She looks at AMANDA *again.*

If you were my daughter . . . but there it is. Providence sends us good fortune and bad – burdens we feel we shall never be able to bear, and blessings we forget too soon. Sometimes we have bitter roles to play, believe me. And here I am, near the final curtain of my life, playing a ridiculously unsuitable part for a woman in my position . . . but you . . . you are so young . . . standing in the wings of your life . . . waiting to make your entrance, tremulous on the brink of adventure . . . it would be so easy for you to come to the rescue of a poor old woman who is at her wit's end.

AMANDA (*a murmur*): I don't understand what you mean, madame.

DUCHESS: I did not intend that you should, my dear. I am only talking to myself – rambling on to spin out the tardy time until the dusk deepens to hide my blushes. How strange it feels to blush. I have not blushed since I was a little girl in a crinoline and frilly pantaloons, made to stand in the corner because I refused to kiss a Field Marshal with a black beard.

Pause. It grows darker.

AMANDA (*a whisper*): It is almost dark now, madame . . .

DUCHESS (*a sudden brisk voice from the gathering gloom*): Tell me, then, child – have you had many lovers?

AMANDA (*taken aback*): Lovers?

DUCHESS: Flirtations, I mean. Nothing serious. Snatched kisses in the shrubbery after a croquet party – oh, what am I saying! I simply cannot get my epochs right! I should say, of course, snatched kisses in the darkness of the cinema, or behind the springboard at the lido.

AMANDA *is silent. Pause.*

(*A little weary.*) Now I've frightened you. Or even disgusted you. I don't want to know whether you have ever been in love, child. I wouldn't pry into your secret heart. I am simply talking about flirtations.

AMANDA (*soft, after a pause*): Yes, madame. I have had flirtations, but I have never been in love.

DUCHESS: Life is full of delicious surprises, child. One day love will burst upon you out of a clear sky in a sudden golden glory. Until then, you must live as intelligently as you can from day to day, and when your moment of happiness comes . . . seize it with both hands – be greedy – don't waste it, for it will never come again.

Pause.

But I did not mean to speak of love.

Pause

Albert is a fine, handsome boy – but all his youth and gaiety have been numbed by his sorrow. One day he will take his own life, tomorrow perhaps, perhaps the day after . . . I don't know. But one day he will do it, unless he can find some echo of Léocadia, something more satisfying than the bricks and mortar which sheltered her, or the fools who knew her when she lived, but haven't the wit to conjure up her spirit for him now that she is dead. I am a very influential old woman, even in these democratic days, and ludicrously rich, and yet I cannot lift a finger to save his life . . . and afterwards I shall be alone, and as useless as a pile of dead ashes on a windy day.

AMANDA: How can I help him, madame? I dare not think that you mean . . . well . . . in any case, why me? I'm not very pretty. And even if I was, how could anybody come between him and his memories?

DUCHESS: Nobody could – except you.

AMANDA (*amazed*): Me?

DUCHESS: The first time I saw you in Madame Rensada's shop, child – I wept. Because, to anyone who knew her as she really was, you are the living image of Léocadia.

Silence. The nightbirds have taken over from the day-time songsters. The park is vibrant with rustling leaves and chasing shadows.

AMANDA (*very soft*): Even so, I'm afraid I can't do it, madame. I may be poor and insignificant, but at least my flirtations have been my own. . . .

DUCHESS (*soft and very sad*): Of course. I beg your pardon.

She gets up slowly. For the first time, we realize what a very old lady she is. Suddenly there is the sound of a bicycle bell. The DUCHESS *trembles.*

Listen! There he is! Oh, let him see you standing beside the obelisk, where he first met her! Let him see you just once – and cry out, be horrified, anything! I swear I will tell him tomorrow that it was a trick I played on him, even though he may hate me for it. It's worth it, if only I can see him stung into feeling again by something alive – by anything except that relentless ghost who is forever beckoning, enticing him to join her in the shadows.

She grasps AMANDA'S *arm.*

I beg you, mademoiselle . . . on my knees. Take pity on me.

She looks at her imploringly, then adds quickly:

And you will see him, too. And . . . great heavens, I'm blushing again . . . the third time in sixty years and the second time in ten minutes . . . how gloriously illogical life is. My dear, he is handsome, he is charming. Why shouldn't he be one of your very own flirtations – for a moment?

The bicycle bell sounds again, closer.

AMANDA (*a whisper*): What shall I say to him?

DUCHESS (*embracing her*): Just say, 'Excuse me, can you tell me the way to the sea?'

She disappears into the deep shadows under the trees – just in time. Out of the darkness, the shadow which is the PRINCE *on his bicycle passes close to the shadow which is* AMANDA *standing by the obelisk.*

AMANDA: Excuse me. . . .

The PRINCE *stops, gets off his bicycle, and sees her.*

PRINCE: Yes, mademoiselle?
AMANDA: Can you tell me the way to the sea?
PRINCE: The second turning on the left, mademoiselle.

He bows stiffly and sadly, remounts and cycles off. The bell sounds again, receding into the distance. The DUCHESS *emerges from the shadows. Pause.*

AMANDA (*soft*): He didn't recognize me. . . .
DUCHESS: It is very dark . . . and then he may remember her differently after all this time. (*Pause, then she says, almost shyly.*) The last train has gone, mademoiselle. Won't you change your mind and stay with us tonight?
AMANDA (*after a pause, softly*): Thank you, madame. . . .

The darkness has really closed in now, and the figures of the two women can no longer be distinguished in the gloom. Only the wind can be heard sighing in the tall trees. The curtain falls.

Act Two

The DUCHESS'S *drawing-room. Morning. The* BUTLER *stands there, like a statue. He appears to be waiting for something. The door opens and a man comes in. In dress, deportment and manner, he is as like the* BUTLER *as two peas in a pod. He is the* HEAD WAITER. *The two regard each other with hostility.*

HEAD WAITER: Good morning.
BUTLER: Good morning.

Pause. They look each other up and down. The BUTLER *straightens his bow-tie. In spite of himself, the* HEAD WAITER *does the same.*

May one ask to what we owe the pleasure of your company?
HEAD WAITER: Her Grace requested me to wait upon her here at nine o'clock, in order to discuss certain details relating to the entirely imaginary Viennese nightclub which I run in the park.
BUTLER (*with a tinge of bitterness which he takes pains to conceal*): In that case, won't you take a seat?
HEAD WAITER: I am much obliged to you.

He sits down, stiffly. The BUTLER *makes as if to leave the room, pausing as he goes to adjust the position of the Venetian negro, with an authority calculated to drive home the fact that this is his domain. At the door, however, he changes his mind and comes back.*

BUTLER: I wonder if I may have a word in your ear?
HEAD WAITER: You may.
BUTLER: I myself have been in service all my life with high-class families – representing, I flatter myself, all that is best in the upper reaches of society. But I have a brother-in-law who has elected to pursue his profession in the hotel and restaurant side of our calling – for the sake of money. He

has been employed at the Waldorf, the Savoy, the Excelsior . . . perhaps you may have heard of these establishments?

HEAD WAITER: I have heard of them.

BUTLER: Now, I must confess that in him, and in his colleagues, I have always detected a certain slackness . . . a tendency towards familiarity, which invariably characterizes those who habitually serve a customer rather than a master.

HEAD WAITER (*inscrutable*): I fear I cannot follow your train of thought.

BUTLER: I will elucidate. I have failed, to my great astonishment, to observe in you any sign of this degeneracy. I understand you used to work in Dinard, in a short-lived establishment which, if I may say so, could not in the nature of things have been . . . shall we say . . . five star.

HEAD WAITER (*pale*): It was an excellent restaurant of its kind . . . excellent . . . but five star, no. Three, say. But not five.

BUTLER: As I thought. So I would like to put a question to you. Did you not spend long years of service in a private household before—

HEAD WAITER (*bowing his head, with a stifled sob*): Yes, you are right. I did . . . before . . . but then one day—

BUTLER (*silencing him with a gesture*): Please. Please. Far be it from me to pry into the reasons for your downfall. I merely wished to verify my contention that a butler who is worthy of the name can always be distinguished by a standard of etiquette which no degradation can eradicate.

HEAD WAITER (*raising his head*): Thank you.

BUTLER (*affable and superior*): Think nothing of it, my dear fellow. You must forgive me if I have twisted the knife in an old wound. The subject will never be mentioned again. (*Formal.*) I will inform Her Grace of your arrival.

He goes. The DUCHESS *enters in a whirl as usual, followed by* HECTOR *and* AMANDA. *The latter is dressed in the flamboyant style which one would associate with Léocadia.*

DUCHESS (*to the* HEAD WAITER): Ah, there you are, Ferdinand.

HEAD WAITER (*rising precipitately*): Good morning, Your Grace.

DUCHESS (*a cry*): Don't say good morning to me yet! Look at this young lady. Study her from every angle! Well, what have you to say to me now?

The HEAD WAITER *looks at* AMANDA, *somewhat bewildered at first, and not understanding what the fuss is about. Then suddenly, realization breaks upon him.*

HEAD WAITER: Great heavens!

The DUCHESS *forgets herself to the point of seizing his hand in her enthusiasm.*

DUCHESS: Thank you! Oh, thank you for that! (*To* AMANDA.) We have succeeded, child. Come and kiss me.

She kisses AMANDA. *Then she turns to the* HEAD WAITER *again.*

Now you may wish me good morning.

HEAD WAITER: Good morning, Your Grace.

DUCHESS (*in her usual, aloof tone*): Good morning, Ferdinand.

She indicates AMANDA.

Well? Is it not truly amazing?

HEAD WAITER: It's . . . it's phantasmagoric, Your Grace.

DUCHESS (*a cry*): Phantasmagoric! The very word I have been searching for since yesterday! Phantasmagoric! That is exactly it. Where did you find it?

HEAD WAITER: What, Your Grace?

DUCHESS: That word! Where did you find it?

HEAD WAITER: I really don't know, Your Grace . . . in a newspaper, I think . . .

DUCHESS: Ah, I never read the newspapers. That accounts for it. All the same, it is the exact word I want. Phantasmagoric. (*She is delighted.*) Phantasmagoric! You are phantasmagoric, child!

AMANDA: I don't much like the sound of it, madame.

DUCHESS: Oh, what a quaint girl it is! Don't worry, child, you may appear phantasmagoric to us, but in reality you are a Greuze. A little living Greuze.

HECTOR: I'd say she has more of the piquant, provocative quality of a Boucher.

DUCHESS: Fiddlesticks. Don't talk nonsense, Hector. She is not at all a Boucher, she is a Greuze. When she smiles, I will grant you a fleeting glimpse – no more – of a Le Nain shepherdess . . . (*To* AMANDA.) Has nobody ever remarked on it before?

AMANDA (*simply*): No, madame. I've never heard of any of those people.

DUCHESS: She is adorable, Hector.

HECTOR: Adorable.

DUCHESS (*to* AMANDA, *as though explaining to an imbecile child*): They are painters, dear. Great artists who lived long ago, and painted pictures . . . with paint brushes . . .

AMANDA (*a little smile*): Yes, I know what a painter is.

DUCHESS (*off-hand*): I have a couple of dozen of their best canvases in the picture gallery. That will settle the argument. But meanwhile, we have work to do.

She approaches the HEAD WAITER.

Ferdinand, we need your help. That is why I asked you to come here. The Prince has not yet had the opportunity of being presented to this young lady, and I am determined that when he sees her, he shall be thunderstruck. Absolutely thunderstruck! But, alas, we cannot work miracles. It would be so much easier if we could – frankly, we need one.

AMANDA: Oh, don't say that, madame! I'm scared enough as it is!

DUCHESS: There's no sense in minimizing the difficulties of our task, dear. We have a physical resemblance. That goes a long way, but not far enough, especially in the case of a woman like Léocadia. We must create an atmosphere. First of all – (*to* HECTOR) – where are the orchids?

HECTOR (*jumping up, as though afraid that he might have been sitting on them*): The orchids!

DUCHESS: Have you forgotten that Léocadia never went anywhere without a sheaf of orchids? I must telephone Dinard and have a selection sent along immediately.

She goes out. He follows. AMANDA *is left alone with the* HEAD WAITER. *They look at each other for a moment, embarrassed. Then she says, with a smile:*

AMANDA: Phantasmagoric, am I . . . ?

He hesitates, as though unsure what attitude to take – then makes a vague and non-committal gesture.

We've got a funny profession, you and I, haven't we?

HEAD WAITER (*stiff and formal*): There is no such thing as a funny profession, mademoiselle.

AMANDA (*gently*): No, I suppose there isn't. (*Pause.*) Well, we all have to eat, don't we? How long have you been at it?

HEAD WAITER: At what, mademoiselle?

AMANDA: Being a memory.

HEAD WAITER: Nearly two years now, mademoiselle.

AMANDA: D'you get decent pay?

The HEAD WAITER *is shocked by this question. He makes a gesture reminiscent of a butler refusing a tip.*

HEAD WAITER: Mademoiselle!

Then, abashed by AMANDA'S *clear gaze, he adds:*

Yes, mademoiselle, very good pay. . . .

At once he is overcome with remorse at having given away forbidden secrets of his profession. He adds shamefacedly:

Well . . . that is . . . when I say 'good' . . . I don't mean . . .

AMANDA (*amused at his embarrassment*): Is it tiring?

HEAD WAITER: What, mademoiselle?

AMANDA: Being a memory.

The HEAD WAITER *makes a negative gesture.*

What do you do all day?

HEAD WAITER: Nothing. I just wait. I wait for him to come. I walk about among the empty tables. I think.

He adds, in a burst of confidence:

It's strange, isn't it, when you consider it. Strange, and a bit sad, really.

AMANDA: I only saw him for a moment last night – and it was very dark. What's he like? Is he nice?

HEAD WAITER: He's neither nice nor not nice. He just doesn't seem to be there at all, if you know what I mean.

AMANDA: What does he do when he comes into your restaurant?

HEAD WAITER: He sits down at a table – always the same one – the table they had that night. Then he orders what they ordered then – a bottle of Pommery '47. I bring the champagne and two glasses. Then he sits and stares at the empty chair opposite him, without saying a word. Sometimes all night. And then he goes away.

AMANDA (*dreamy*): Poor chap.

HEAD WAITER: And we drink the champagne.

AMANDA (*ingenuous*): Ooh! Aren't you lucky!

HEAD WAITER: I don't know so much about that, mademoiselle. It's beginning to affect my liver. . . .

AMANDA (*after a pause*): What's so funny is that they only knew each other for three days. I should have thought it took longer than that to fall in love . . . properly, I mean. . . .

Suddenly she demands of the HEAD WAITER:

Were they lovers?

HEAD WAITER (*after his first shocked reaction*): That I can't say, mademoiselle. They certainly didn't spend the night together in *my* establishment.

Pause. Unbending a little . . .

The people who run the Chime of Bells – they've been brought here too, you know – they maintain . . . but then I have reason to believe that they circulate the story simply to try to look important themselves . . .

AMANDA (*very soft*): And even if they were lovers . . . they had so little time together . . . just one night. . . . (*Urgent again.*) Do you think he's *really* heartbroken, really and truly?

The HEAD WAITER *indicates by a gesture that he does not intend to commit himself.*

I know people do suffer terribly from broken hearts. But I always thought that they either bottled it all up so that nobody knew about it, or else went really crazy. I've never known anyone behave as he does.

HEAD WAITER (*infinitely lofty and patronizing*): How can one presume to analyse the grief of the aristocracy, mademoiselle? I remember before the war at Monte Carlo seeing the Grand Duke Sosthène, in an excess of neurasthenia, empty three hundred magnums of Veuve Cliquot, chateau-bottled, on the floor of his private sitting-room in the hotel, and force all the members of the staff to wash their feet in it. Then he burst into tears, beat his breast, and begged our pardon most profusely.

AMANDA (*soft*): I don't believe that was real grief. . . .

The DUCHESS *has returned, followed by* HECTOR.

DUCHESS: There! Two hundred orchids will be here in ten minutes.

AMANDA (*smiling*): Surely that's far too many?

DUCHESS (*turning, surprised*): What do you mean, too many?

AMANDA: I may not know much about painters, madame, but I do know about flowers. I used to work for a florist before I went into millinery.

DUCHESS: Too many? I very much doubt whether it will be enough. Léocadia used to nibble them ceaselessly. How long do you think it takes a person of sensitivity to nibble the heart out of an orchid – naturally, she discarded the outside petals?

AMANDA: I've no idea. If I wanted to eat flowers, I'd buy daisies. They're cheaper.

DUCHESS (*not even hearing this last remark*): Now, we must plan. I have decided to reconstruct a specific incident for the child. I think that the arrival of Léocadia at the Blue Danube restaurant would be the most vivid.

She seizes a chair.

First of all, we must set the scene. (*To* AMANDA.) Sit there for a moment. (*To* HECTOR.) Isn't she ravishing? And she is getting the idea of it already.

She inspects AMANDA'S *face at very close quarters, and adds:*

Ravishing!

AMANDA: I suppose I'd better try to look distinguished.

DUCHESS (*bustling away*): No, no. Don't try to look anything. We will tell you what to do. (*To the* HEAD WAITER.) I don't want to rehearse in your café, because Albert is in the park and he might come in and catch us at it. Here we are perfectly safe. He never comes into the house in the morning, and in any case Theophilus is keeping watch at the door. Right.

She goes to AMANDA.

Now, child, I have come to the conclusion that the secret of Léocadia's fascination lay in her eyes. She had a way of looking at one – something like this – which was absolutely irresistible. Between ourselves, she was extremely short-sighted. While we are arranging the furniture, I want you to practise screwing up your eyes, as I showed you. . . . (*To the* HEAD WAITER.) You can help me move this negro. Léocadia loved him. She always called him her coal-black Ariel, as fickle and insubstantial as a fugitive shadow. . . .

She lifts the figure with the aid of the HEAD WAITER.

Heavens, what a heavy brute he is.

As she passes AMANDA, *she says:*

Screw up your eyes, child. Screw up your eyes and incline your head slightly forward. That's better. You're coming on splendidly.

The door half opens noiselessly, the BUTLER *peeps in, and is shattered to see that his rival, aided by the* DUCHESS, *is flaunting the most sacred conventions of the drawing-room by moving the statue, while in a corner the strange young person is screwing up her eyes and bowing her head incessantly, and for no apparent reason. He trembles with horror and disappears.*

(*Rearranging the furniture.*) If this is the stage where the orchestra is, then the table where they sat should go here. Is that right?

HEAD WAITER: Approximately, yes, Your Grace.

DUCHESS: Well done. (*As the* HEAD WAITER *looks up in surprise.*) I was talking to myself. (*To* AMANDA.) Stop screwing up your eyes now, child, you'll get cramp, and the knack will desert you when you need it most. (*To the* HEAD WAITER.) Now I will tell you what I want you to do. I knew Léocadia too well. It would be of the greatest value to us if you, as a stranger, would describe to the young lady your instinctive, overwhelming impression of the divine Léocadia when she entered the Blue Danube nightclub for the first time.

HEAD WAITER (*delighted to be asked to play such an important role*): My impression?

DUCHESS: Your instinctive impression. Don't be afraid. Take your time. We are all comrades here, seeking only to unearth the truth, the whole truth and nothing but the truth.

HEAD WAITER (*instinctively raising his hand*): So help me God.

DUCHESS: What's that?

HEAD WAITER (*blushing*): Nothing, Your Grace. Forgive me.

DUCHESS: Very well. We are waiting. (*To* AMANDA.) I said stop screwing up your eyes, girl. For heaven's sake, stop!

AMANDA (*whose eyes are screwed up in a desperate effort to hide her laughter*): I didn't know I was doing it, madame.

DUCHESS (*delighted*): Excellent! You are really beginning to feel like Léocadia. In that case, screw them up by all means, dear. (*To the* HEAD WAITER.) We are still waiting.

HEAD WAITER (*who has had time to think it over*): Very well then. To be honest, Your Grace, when Mademoiselle Léocadia Gardi first came into the Blue Danube, I think I am speaking for all of us there when I say that we received a profound shock.

DUCHESS: A shock? How very interesting. A shock. (*To* AMANDA.) Remember that, child. Have you a pencil?

AMANDA (*who can hardly suppress her mirth*): No, but I'll remember. (*Imitating the* HEAD WAITER.) A shock.

DUCHESS (*repeats, entranced*): A shock.

HEAD WAITER: A shock. First of all, Mademoiselle Léocadia was beautiful – very beautiful indeed. And then, she had a most disturbing way of looking you straight in the eyes, walking right up to you, and then looking away at the very moment when you expected her to speak to you . . . she did it with an air of arrogance, of distinction . . . which reminded me more than anything of . . . may I speak frankly, Your Grace?

DUCHESS: Please do.

HEAD WAITER: A dog! A mad dog! A demented Borzoi!

DUCHESS (*enthusiastic*): A demented Borzoi! (*To* AMANDA.) Remember all that. It is surprisingly accurate. This fellow has a rare and courageous gift of observation. It's quite true – the whole of Léocadia's character was revealed in that particular and inimitable manner of walking.

She demonstrates.

Holding your eyes with hers until your noses were in imminent danger of collision, and then – suddenly – losing interest and passing you by without another glance. There is her whole personality in a nutshell. I am quite different, of course. With my height, I have to stand on tip-toe to look anybody in the eyes. (*To the* HEAD WAITER.) Do you know what you must do now, my good man, to make a lasting impression on the child? You must give us a demonstration.

HEAD WAITER: A demonstration of what, Your Grace?

DUCHESS: Of Léocadia entering the Blue Danube, of course.

HEAD WAITER (*who is dying to*): I really don't know if I can, Your Grace. . . .

DUCHESS: It is an order.

HEAD WAITER: Very good, Your Grace. But Your Grace must understand that I mean no disrespect by anything I do . . . after all, I'm a man . . . it's not easy for a man to imitate a lady. . . .

DUCHESS: Don't worry about that. We are here simply and solely to build up an atmosphere for the girl.

HEAD WAITER: All right, then. When Mademoiselle Léocadia Gardi came in, the orchestra had just started to play, by special request, a number which was very popular that year – 'The First Bouquet'.

DUCHESS: One moment! I have an idea. Hector, you can be the orchestra. Go up on the stage – that's right. You know 'The First Bouquet' – two years ago you nearly drove us all mad whistling it. Hum it. It will help this good fellow.

HECTOR (*delighted*): May I mime the violinist as well?

DUCHESS (*uninterested*): If you wish.

HECTOR *hums a catchy waltz to himself and debates mimically upon the desirability or otherwise of accompanying himself upon an imaginary violin.*

HEAD WAITER: If you are agreeable, Your Grace, I will direct my entrance at you.

DUCHESS: An excellent idea.

HEAD WAITER: Right! Orchestra!

HECTOR *attacks 'The First Bouquet'. The* HEAD WAITER, *with great seriousness, begins to mime Léocadia's entry into the Blue Danube. At this moment, the* BUTLER *enters precipitately, much agitated.*

BUTLER: Your Grace!

He stops, rooted to the spot, as his rival passes him, oblivious and apparently performing the steps of some outlandish tango, with his eyes fixed hypnotically on those of the DUCHESS, *who exclaims as he reaches her:*

DUCHESS: That's it! That's it! That's absolutely right! This man is a mimic – a born mimic! Do it again, quickly, while you are in the mood. And you, child, walk behind him and copy everything he does.

HECTOR *starts the waltz again. The* HEAD WAITER *repeats his performance, with* AMANDA, *who is bursting with laughter, following behind and imitating him. The* HEAD WAITER *finishes his promenade and turns to watch his pupil. He cries ecstatically:*

HEAD WAITER: Bravo, mademoiselle! Just like that! Now, come right up to me – look me in the eye! Be arrogant! Be haughty! I'm only a Head Waiter! I'm lower than mud! You don't even see me any more!

But AMANDA *has suddenly stopped dead, covered in confusion. For the* PRINCE *has pushed aside the* BUTLER, *who since his entrance has stood as though petrified, and stands there in the doorway, pale with anger.* HECTOR *stops humming, and the* DUCHESS *and the* HEAD WAITER *turn round, dumbfounded.*

PRINCE: Aunt Melisande!
DUCHESS: Albert!
PRINCE: What is the meaning of this masquerade?
DUCHESS: Theophilus, what have you done?
BUTLER (*looking ten years older, as he bows his head*): I came to warn Your Grace, but I was so dumbfounded by what I saw that I fear I—
DUCHESS (*terrible, with an imperious gesture*): Theophilus, you are dismissed!

The BUTLER *creeps out, a hundred years older.*

PRINCE (*dry, to the others*): Perhaps the rest of you would be kind enough to leave us also. I must speak to this young lady alone.

HECTOR *and the* HEAD WAITER *beat a hasty retreat. The* DUCHESS *also prepares to go. The* PRINCE *looks at* AMANDA *for the first time, to her great embarrassment. Suddenly he sees the Venetian negro. He leaps to it.*

Who has dared to lay hands on this statue?

DUCHESS (*at the door*): I did, Albert. I wished to clear a space for—

PRINCE (*in a fury, as he puts the statue back in its original place*): I gave orders that nobody, under any pretext whatsoever, was to touch anything that she had touched!

The DUCHESS, *who is really not very intimidated by this display of temper, is making complicated signs to* AMANDA *behind the* PRINCE'S *back. He studies* AMANDA *silently. The* DUCHESS *goes.*

I am afraid that my aunt has placed you in an embarrassing position, mademoiselle.

AMANDA (*simple*): I'm afraid she has, sir.

PRINCE (*unkind*): I don't doubt that you were desperate to find employment of some sort—

AMANDA: No, sir. That is to say, yes, sir. You see, your aunt had taken the trouble to get me dismissed from the milliner's where I worked before she summoned me here.

PRINCE (*amused*): She's an amazing woman.

AMANDA (*a little bitter*): Amazing is right. (*Pause.*) But since yesterday I've got to the point where nothing amazes me any more.

PRINCE: You have been here since yesterday?

AMANDA: Yes. You even spoke to me last night, in the park, by that obelisk with the stone bench round it—

PRINCE: Was that you? I must beg your pardon for not recognizing you. It was very dark. Why did you ask me the way to the sea?

AMANDA (*soft*): Apparently that was the particular phrase of which you had to be . . . reminded. . . .

The PRINCE *stops as though thunderstruck, and murmurs:*

PRINCE: Excuse me, can you tell me the way to the sea?

He sits down in an arm-chair, saying nothing, as if in a trance. Endless pause. AMANDA *clears her throat. No effect. She starts to tiptoe out. He suddenly cries:*

Don't go! Come back, where I can see you! You are plain. You walk badly. You are not in the least like her. You never could be like her. You're just a common little milliner, with no mystery, no aura—

AMANDA: What's that?

PRINCE (*stops, surprised*): What?

AMANDA: An aura?

PRINCE (*exploding*): If you imagine that I'm going to give you lessons in your own language into the bargain—!

AMANDA (*looking him straight in the face. With dignity*): I only wanted to know if it's an insult.

PRINCE (*looking at her, he cannot repress a little smile. He says quietly*): No, it is not an insult.

AMANDA: I'm glad.

Pause. She looks him up and down and then walks towards the door with as much dignity as she can muster. The PRINCE *cannot help asking:*

PRINCE: What would you have done if it had been an insult?

AMANDA (*turning*): I would have told you just what I think of you.

PRINCE (*quiet and suddenly very weary*): I don't care what anybody thinks of me.

He retires into his huge old-fashioned arm-chair and relapses into silence.

AMANDA *watches him from the doorway with a suspicion of pity in her eyes. Suddenly he begins to mutter with closed eyes:*

Can you tell me—?

He stops, then tries again in a different tone.

Can you tell me the way—?

He tries another tone, but his voice is not flexible.

. . . the way to . . .

He stops, weary. His features relax in sheer exhaustion. Tears come into AMANDA'S *eyes as she sees that he is really distraught, and she murmurs softly, as she did in the park:*

AMANDA: Can you tell me the way to the sea?

Pause.

PRINCE (*soft, almost humble*): Who taught you to imitate that voice?

AMANDA: Nobody. It's my own voice.

PRINCE (*after a pause*): Would you mind very much repeating that sentence once more?

AMANDA: Excuse me, can you tell me the way to the sea?

PRINCE (*soft, eyes closed*): The second turning on the left, mademoiselle.

AMANDA: Thank you.

PRINCE (*eyes still closed – suddenly*): Mademoiselle—

AMANDA (*surprised*): Yes?

PRINCE: You have dropped your glove.

AMANDA *looks at her feet, surprised, and then realizes that he is reliving his conversation of two years ago. Timidly, hazarding a guess, she says:*

AMANDA: Thank you. That is very kind of you.

PRINCE (*opening his eyes*): No. She didn't answer me. She just smiled, a tantalizing half-smile, and disappeared into the dusk.

He stands up, not looking at her. Suddenly he puts a hand to his eye, as though to wipe away a tear.

Forgive me.

AMANDA: It's you who must forgive me for being here.

Pause. AMANDA *looks at him, then says gravely:*

What I don't understand is that last night I said the very same thing to you in the same tone of voice, and you answered me quite calmly, as though I – oh, I don't know – as though it was the most ordinary thing in the world for someone to stand there in the twilight and ask you the way to the sea.

PRINCE: That's strange, isn't it?

AMANDA: Yes. It is strange.

PRINCE (*with difficulty, not looking at her*): Mademoiselle, I wonder whether – in spite of what I have said to you – in spite of what you must think of me – you would consider accepting my aunt's proposition, and for a little while – say for three days – you would . . .

AMANDA *bows her head. With all the dignity she can manage, she says:*

AMANDA: Last night, I refused. This morning, I said 'yes'. Just now I was on the point of going out to say 'no' again. . . .

PRINCE (*turning to her, kindly, for the first time*): Please say 'yes' again. It will make the score even.

AMANDA: But it makes me look such a fool, always changing my mind.

PRINCE: And how will I look?

AMANDA: Oh, but – it doesn't matter for you. I can't afford the luxury of going nuts about anybody at the moment.

PRINCE: And what would happen to you if you did 'go nuts', as you say, about someone?

AMANDA: Oh, dreadful things! I'd ladder my stockings and lose my gloves and miss my train and lose my job—

She stops and sighs, laughing in spite of herself.

Anyway, all those things did happen to me yesterday.

PRINCE (*on the defensive*): You have doubtless heard my story. I agree that for someone who leads your sort of existence, in which your job and the small material considerations of everyday life loom so importantly, it must be somewhat galling to think of so much money, time and trouble on the worship of a memory.

AMANDA (*quiet and simple*): Oh, no, you're quite wrong. When we got the telegram saying that my father would never come back from the war, my mother, who was just an ordinary housewife, went and slept on a camp-bed in the kitchen. And in the room that they had shared, she laid out everything that had belonged to him – she put his best suit, the one he was married in – on the bed next to her white wedding dress, and every year, on the anniversary of his death, the flowers she used to buy cost her far more – comparatively – than you could ever spend even if you rebuilt a whole town in your park.

PRINCE: I beg your pardon.

AMANDA (*very kind*): Granted. But I don't want you to think—

PRINCE: I no longer think it, mademoiselle. And I am profoundly grateful to you for what you have just told me, because it makes it possible for me to confide in you – a terrible confidence which I have never before entrusted to any one. My aunt is a lunatic – a charming lunatic perhaps – but a lunatic all the same. I am saner than she is, I assure you. The only reason I have submitted to the caprices of her folly, and allowed her to rebuild in the privacy of the estate every house that I visited with Léocadia – the only reason was the hope that this very privacy and isolation would help me a little in my terrible struggle.

AMANDA (*bewildered*): Your struggle?

PRINCE (*with a smile*): Yes. It's extraordinarily difficult to tell you this. And now that I am on the point of making my confession, I can see that it is almost comic. But please don't laugh at me . . . I agreed to all this simply because I am on the verge of forgetting.

AMANDA: Forgetting what?

PRINCE: The woman I loved. I can't even remember the exact colour of her eyes. I had completely forgotten her voice until just now . . . last night I was in the clouds. . . .

He taps his forehead.

To think that you could have stood there, in the same twilight, and asked me in that very voice the way to the sea . . . and I didn't cry out . . . I wasn't even surprised . . . I simply didn't notice. It's terrible . . . it's laughable . . . Prince Albert Troubiscoi rebuilds a whole town in his park to preserve the memory of his love, and then he can't even remember the first words she said to him. . . .

He sits down, worn out.

AMANDA: How can I help you, sir?

PRINCE (*low after a pause*): Stay here for three days, and let me watch you moving through those memory-ridden haunts where I seek for her, in vain. Try – forgive me for saying this – but please try to be not yourself, but her – just for three days.

AMANDA (*who is standing with one hand caressing the Venetian negro*): I will try.

PRINCE (*a sudden cry*): Stay there! Don't move, I beg you. . . . (*Reminiscent.*) The next day she came to this house after luncheon to ask my aunt if she would lend the park for a charity fête. My aunt was out, and so the butler called me. . . . I found her in here . . . standing just like that . . . she told me she loved that statue . . . we spent the whole afternoon together, and that evening she allowed me to take her to the Blue Danube for the first time. That was the restaurant where, the following evening, we discovered that we loved each other. . . .

His eyes are closed.

The Blue Danube. The most pretentious and ridiculous place in the world. With that fantastic head waiter, and that ghastly mock-Viennese music, which everyone was raving about that year . . . she hummed it to herself all the evening. . . .

He makes a poor attempt to sing the opening bars of the waltz.

Tra-la-la . . . how does that waltz go?

He tries again.

Tra-la-la. . . .

AMANDA (*helping him*): Tra-la-la . . .

PRINCE (*bolder*): Tra-la-la . . . *la*!

AMANDA *finishes the phrase. Then they repeat the chorus together. The orchestra takes up the melody, which swells up into a joyous burst of music as the lights dim, and then come up again upon . . .*

Act Three

SCENE: *The clearing in the park where the* DUCHESS *has rebuilt the Blue Danube café, which is brilliantly lit, the sparkling radiance from its tinkling chandeliers illuminating the old-fashioned charm of its baroque red plush and gilt décor. Three* GIPSIES, *who vaguely resemble skating instructors, ply their violins assiduously. They remind one of ancient, dusty moths – once brilliant creatures of the night, now mouldering neglected in a glass case, transfixed by pins. Indeed, so do the* HEAD WAITER *and the* CLOAKROOM ATTENDANT *– the latter with her bun and frilly apron looking like a superannuated usherette.* AMANDA *and the* PRINCE *have just arrived, and the* CLOAKROOM ATTENDANT, *ravished with delight, is helping* AMANDA *off with her furs. The* HEAD WAITER *hovers expectantly. They sit down at their table.*

HEAD WAITER (*as if he didn't know*): And what may I bring you, sir?
PRINCE: The same as last night.
HEAD WAITER: Very good, sir.

He writes down on his pad.

Pommery, '47.
AMANDA (*without thinking*): Oh . . . first of all . . . I would awfully like . . . I mean, I'm terribly thirsty, I do love it . . . a gin and lime with lots of water.

There is a moment of utter dismay. The music stops.

HEAD WAITER: But . . . that is . . . Mademoiselle Gardi did not . . . I'm sorry, mademoiselle, but. . . .
AMANDA (*in confusion*): No, no, *I'm* sorry. I must be crazy. Champagne . . . of course. The same as last night. Champagne it is.

The music starts again, relieved.

PRINCE (*stiff, after a pause*): If you are really thirsty . . . and if if you're so very fond of it . . . bring a gin and lime for mademoiselle.

HEAD WAITER (*stunned*): A gin and lime. I'll go and see if we . . . yes, very good, sir. . . .

AMANDA (*calling after him*): With lots of water, please!

HEAD WAITER (*more and more shocked*): Water! I've never heard of such a thing. . . . I suppose we can melt some ice. . . .

AMANDA: Thank you – you're very kind. I'll drink it up quickly.

HEAD WAITER (*as he goes, sotto voce*): I should hope so, and when I've removed the glass we will never refer to the incident again.

AMANDA (*with an apologetic smile*): It's very difficult, you know, to have no will of one's own for two whole days.

PRINCE (*dry*): Please try to be patient. The day after tomorrow you will be free.

AMANDA: I don't need to be patient, you know that. It's thrilling being somebody else. . . .

She fingers her bracelets.

Somebody rich . . . somebody in love. . . .

Meanwhile, the gin and lime is being prepared – an elaborate and complicated ritual involving large numbers of people and much coming and going. The CLOAKROOM ATTENDANT *and one of the* GIPSIES *who has temporarily abandoned his violin join in the proceedings, which develop into a kind of furtive ballet, underlined by an impertinent musical score which twists the still-recognizable theme of the waltz into an ironic commentary. At last, the precious glass is ready, and the* HEAD WAITER *brings it to the table.*

PRINCE: You weren't at all bad yesterday.

HEAD WAITER: Your gin and lime, mademoiselle.

He adds, with malice, for this is what upset him most:

With lots of water.

AMANDA (*who really is thirsty*): Oh, thank you!

She takes a mouthful and then suddenly looks at the glass.

Ooh, it's lovely and strong!

She seems to be on the point of enjoying herself genuinely, revelling in the unaccustomed lights, music, perfume and jewels. But suddenly she notices that the PRINCE *and the* HEAD WAITER *are watching her with icy impatience. Hastily she empties the glass in a single gulp, and cannot hide a grimace at the unwonted strength of the drink.*

Pardon.

She gives the glass to the HEAD WAITER, *who takes it with a satisfied sigh.*

HEAD WAITER: Ah!
PRINCE (*also relieved that this interlude is over*): Ah!

The orchestra, which had suspended operations during the sacrilegious moment, breaks out again into the most sentimental version of the waltz theme, and the HEAD WAITER *brings on the champagne bucket and serves it with all the ceremony fitting to a serious occasion, in an atmosphere restored to serenity.*

Yesterday was not at all bad, for a first attempt, in spite of a few mistakes, and – how can I put it without wounding you? – a trace of the . . . plebeian in your manner, which, I must admit, is not without a certain charm of its own, but which, naturally, strikes the wrong note.

AMANDA: I haven't said a single word of slang all day.

PRINCE (*off-hand, to* AMANDA'S *horror*): That's true. Of course, Léocadia spoke nothing but slang – but it would be asking too much to expect you to reproduce her language as well . . . and in any case, we said very little to each other, that first evening. The important thing was to see you sitting there, on the other side of the table, nibbling your flowers.

AMANDA (*apologetically*): I'm afraid I'm not much good with the flowers. I'm getting a bit discouraged about it.

PRINCE: Discouraged?

AMANDA: Yes. Oh, I love to suck juicy blades of grass out in the fields, but these great big flowers . . . they're bitter and sweet all at the same time . . . and having bits of them in my mouth all the evening – it's . . . well . . .

PRINCE (*dreamy*): She used to say that they reminded her of opium-poppy and mandragora, and all the baleful draughts of the inscrutable Orient.

AMANDA (*trying to raise a smile from the* HEAD WAITER, *who is watching her icily*): I don't know anything about those things. I only know orchids give me a stomach ache. But I was better this afternoon, wasn't I?

PRINCE: Much better. Perhaps you feel that I was not over-lavish with my compliments to you, mademoiselle?

AMANDA: You certainly weren't.

PRINCE: Well, I can tell you now that this afternoon, when we took the boat and idled away the long sunlit hours exploring the upper reaches of the river, your evocation of the divine spirit of Léocadia was very nearly faultless.

AMANDA (*pleased, with a triumphant look at the* HEAD WAITER): Thank you.

PRINCE (*without malice*): Of course, I realize that on that afternoon two years ago she deliberately dimmed the radiance of her blazing intellect to harmonize with my mood.

AMANDA (*deflated*): Thank you all the same.

She avoids the eye of the HEAD WAITER, *who goes out with a mocking grin.*

PRINCE (*oblivious*): Yes, you were quite perfect. A touch livelier than she perhaps . . . a little too much flesh-and-blood.

AMANDA: It's very difficult to be anything else when one *is* alive. But I'll do better this evening! I feel so light, as if I'm hardly weighing on my chair at all . . . but that's no wonder, considering the meals we've been having.

PRINCE: Léocadia always laid her glove down on her plate.

AMANDA: I know . . . lucky I've got plenty of pairs of gloves. . . . (*Afterthought.*) One day, you know, I'll eat one of them.

PRINCE (*regarding her dreamily*): Léocadia, blessed spirit . . . (*To* AMANDA.) I beg of you, mademoiselle, out of respect to her sacred spectre . . . even if your natural appetite overcomes you – as it must, as it has every right to – even if you do order huge meals to be sent up to your room each night after we have parted, I pray you, do not tell me about them.

AMANDA (*her eyes downcast*): I may be only flesh and blood, but I am honest. I really am trying, however hard it may be, to be like her for these three days – even when I'm not with you. I promise you I've eaten nothing but orchids and champagne, and my plate has been absolutely empty except for embroidered gloves! I generally go to bed at eight, but last night I sat up as late as Mademoiselle Gardi used to. If you'd walked past my window, you'd have seen me there in the small hours lying on a gilt chaise-longue like she did, and trying – unsuccessfully, I'm afraid – to read the poems of Mallarmé by candlelight. It was terribly uncomfortable.

PRINCE (*very surprised*): But why? You knew there was not the remotest chance that I would pass your window after I had formally bidden you 'good night'. Did you do it for fun?

AMANDA: I should say not! I like books that make me laugh, and I like to sleep. . . . Oh, how I'm going to sleep the day after tomorrow!

PRINCE: Then – why?

AMANDA (*a little ill at ease*): Because . . . well, when I do a job, I like to do it properly, that's all.

Pause. They have moved closer together, unconsciously. The GIPSIES *feel obliged to strike up a gay Viennese number. When the* PRINCE *begins to speak again, they finish the music softly, and sit down again.*

PRINCE (*reverting to his original idea*): That second evening was the turning-point of our lives . . . that is, of all the life which was left to us. A precious morning together, and a last valedictory afternoon. . . .

AMANDA: That was the evening when you discovered you loved each other, wasn't it?

PRINCE (*brusque*): Who told you that?

AMANDA: I can't remember – you, I think.

PRINCE: No, not me.

AMANDA: Then it must have been your aunt – or perhaps I just sensed it when we arrived here tonight.

PRINCE: Yes, it was on the second evening. And as that strange night wore on – superficially like so many other nights, with soft lights and music, with wine and conversation, we—

AMANDA (*interrupting*): What did you talk about that night, before you began talking about yourselves?

PRINCE: We talked of nothing but ourselves . . . we may have mentioned the subtle colours of the river at sunset, our favourite poets, her hats, the people around us who made us laugh . . . but we were talking about ourselves all the time. . . .

AMANDA: Did you do the talking, or did she?

PRINCE: Well . . . both of us . . . perhaps she more than I . . . why did you ask me that?

AMANDA (*shrinking into her red plush chair, says shyly, after a pause*): No reason . . . just that it seemed to me . . . if I had fallen in love with you after that long sunny afternoon on the river, I'd have wanted to sit quite still, feeling the smooth satin of my dress against my sunburnt skin, and the cool touch of diamonds on my arm, and the icy stem of my glass between my fingers . . . and just looked at you without saying a word.

PRINCE (*calmly*): That is because you are a young savage, incapable of analysing your own emotions.

AMANDA: I suppose I am.

PRINCE: Of course you are. And your attempts at self-analysis would undoubtedly have been hopelessly inept. Which reminds me, I meant to thank you for the perfect tact and discretion with which you have played your part up till now. I presume that you are not talkative by nature?

AMANDA: Oh, but I am. The other girls in the workshop called me 'Chinwag'.

PRINCE (*adjusting his monocle*): Chinwag?

AMANDA: Yes, because I never stopped talking.

PRINCE: In that case, you must have great natural tact, which is even better.

AMANDA (*laughing*): Oh, goodness, no! In the shop where I was before, they used to call me Flatfoot.

PRINCE: Flatfoot?

AMANDA: Because I was always putting my foot in things.

PRINCE: You do not appear to me to deserve either of those nicknames.

AMANDA (*laughs*): Oh, I do . . . that's why I'd be so pleased if I made a success of these three days. And if I can't talk like Mademoiselle Léocadia, I do at least want to keep silent in the same way that she did. There are so many different ways of saying nothing to the man you love. How did she say nothing to you?

PRINCE: She spoke a little less loudly.

AMANDA (*stupefied*): But she went on speaking?

PRINCE: Oh, yes. She would always answer her own questions, or else finish your reply for you. At other times, she just murmured words at random – in Rumanian, as a rule – that was her mother-tongue. That uninterrupted monologue, revealing every facet of her agile personality, those continual conversational fireworks, were one of her greatest charms. She would punctuate her talk with deep, fascinating ripples of throaty laughter, thrown into the conversation at the moment when they were least expected, and dying away into what was almost a sob.

AMANDA: I must seem very dull beside her.

PRINCE: No, no. Naturally nobody could expect you to emulate her verbal genius. You have done very well, mademoiselle, to present me with such an accurate and precious picture of her rare moments of silence.

He has taken her hand quite naturally towards the end of this speech. Now he suddenly drops it.

I beg your pardon.

AMANDA (*looking at her hand*): For what?

PRINCE: I took your hand. She hated anybody to touch her.

AMANDA: Even you?

PRINCE: Especially me. She used to say that I had coarse peasant hands – hands made to hurt and destroy.

AMANDA (*taking his hand quickly and looking at it*): Peasant hands?

PRINCE (*a little embarrassed*): The skin is hard, I know. But what with yachting and tennis . . . and then, I don't know if you agree with me, but I simply cannot play golf in gloves. . . .

AMANDA (*still looking at his hand*): How funny. You're a gentleman of leisure, and yet your hand does look like a peasant's. Hold our your arm so I can see it properly.

He holds out his arm, a little surprised. She shuts her eyes and after a pause, murmurs:

No. They are hard, but they would never do anybody any harm.

The PRINCE *takes away his hand. Pause. The* GIPSIES, *terrified of being caught red-handed in idleness, leap to their violins. The Leader comes to the table, playing his seductive melody. The* PRINCE *says nothing, but stares at his hand. After a moment,* AMANDA *ventures timidly:*

Penny for your thoughts?

PRINCE: I was thinking . . . if she had said – that evening – what you have just said – about my hands – I would have been wild with happiness.

AMANDA (*soft*): But if she talked so much, she must have told you, amongst other things, that she loved you.

PRINCE (*suddenly hanging his head like an embarrassed boy*): Oh, yes. But she was so adept at self-analysis, at pinning down the most fleeting and fugitive nuance of her vagabond spirit under the microscope of her intelligence, that I find it extremely difficult to remember the exact words she used to declare her love—

AMANDA: Not the exact words, perhaps – but you surely remember the moment when she said them.

PRINCE: Even that is difficult. She was crazy that evening – she started a thousand topics – tossed them into the air and caught them as they fell in cascades of coloured stars. She played at being every great lover in mythology – she compared me to a bull – to a swan. She even made me light an enormous cigar – a thing I detest – because she swore that some goddess was raped by Jupiter disguised as a puff of smoke! And all this intermingled with reminiscences of the ballets she had danced. That night I was Daphnis and Prince Siegfried, Jupiter and Mars. . . .

The violinist has rejoined his fellows, and the music dies softly into silence. AMANDA *asks in a small voice:*

AMANDA: But you are sure that she didn't once say, simply, 'I love you'?

PRINCE (*amused*): Léocadia was incapable of saying simply 'I love you' – even to her favourite greyhound or the little tame serpent which followed her everywhere.

AMANDA: I'm not talking about a little serpent, tame or not! I'm talking about you! I can't bear to think that she never said 'I love you, Albert'.

PRINCE (*sarcastic*): 'I love you, Albert'! Really, mademoiselle, you are ludicrous. Please get it into your head once and for all that this was not a flirtation between a shop girl and a butcher's boy on a park bench.

AMANDA: That's quite obvious. (*Trying to console him, gently.*) I expect she did say 'I love you' among all the other things, and you just didn't hear it.

PRINCE: I don't think so.

AMANDA: But when you come here in the evenings, and try to imagine her sitting here opposite you, don't you imagine her talking?

PRINCE (*heavy*): Of course . . . not straight away . . . it takes me several hours before I can conjure up the picture of her sitting there motionless . . . she used to move about such a lot! And even then, there are details which evade me . . . the eyes. . . . I can never quite remember the eyes. . . .

AMANDA (*soft*): You can see them tonight.

PRINCE: When I have built up a complete picture of her in my mind, then, very cautiously, I imagine her talking . . .

AMANDA (*unable to refrain from a slightly malicious note*): You imagine the monologue, do you?

PRINCE (*ingenuous*): Oh, no, that would be far too difficult – almost impossible. And then – the sweet ghost I conjure up is so fragile – like thistledown – a puff of wind, a tiny incongruous sound – and she vanishes. . . . I have to imagine her saying the simplest things . . . 'Yes . . . no . . . perhaps . . . this evening.' I try to make her say my name . . . she decorated me with a galaxy of ridiculous nicknames, you see . . . Florizel, Endymion, Prince Charming . . . she never called me by my real name – she found it unaesthetic . . . which it is, of course – but still, it is my name. So now I take my gentle revenge – I make her say 'Albert'. Once I sat here for a whole night, making her repeat over and over again 'My darling Albert'. But I am hoist with my own petard, for the only time she ever said that to me, she was making fun of me, and it is always that moment which I recapture when I visualize her lips forming my name.

AMANDA: And do you never make her say 'I love you'? That would be the moment when you had her in your power.

PRINCE (*lowering his eyes, embarrassed*): No. I dare not. And I cannot really imagine that she ever did say it . . . I have no recollection of her lips forming those words.

AMANDA (*almost tenderly*): Look at me.

He raises his head, surprised, and looks at her. Looking him straight in the eyes, she murmurs softly:

I love you, Albert.

He looks at her, pale, his face working.

I love you, Albert. Watch my lips, and remember how they look. I love you, Albert.

PRINCE (*a little hard, from a dry throat*): Thank you.

He tries to pour out some champagne but his hand is shaking, and he does not tip the bottle far enough. The HEAD WAITER, *who is hovering like a hawk, misinterprets this, and arrives at the canter.*

HEAD WAITER: Another bottle of champagne, sir?

PRINCE: Yes, please.

The HEAD WAITER *takes the ice-bucket. At once the orchestra, who seem to regard this as a signal, attack a composition of great brio and gaiety. The* PRINCE *turns to them, suddenly angry, and cries:*

No! Stop that music!

The players stop, amazed.

HEAD WAITER (*coming forward*): Forgive me, sir, but surely you have not forgotten that this particular piece of music was played at the exact moment when the second bottle of champagne was served? It was always the custom of this restaurant to start a new number when a fresh bottle of champagne was served. And that is what happened on that particular evening, I can assure you, sir.

PRINCE (*exasperated*): I tell you I don't want to hear that music! I don't care what happened that evening!

There is a shocked silence at these blasphemous words. The HEAD WAITER, *who is holding the ice-pail, trembles like a leaf. In the ghastly pause, the only sound is the rattling of the bottle in the metal bucket. The* PRINCE *and* AMANDA *look at each other, hostile. The* HEAD WAITER *trembles so violently that the champagne, thoroughly shaken up, suddenly expels its cork with a tremendous explosion. The* CLOAKROOM ATTENDANT, *watching from the doorway of her lair, lets out a squeak of alarm. The champagne falls in a deluge of bubbles. The* HEAD WAITER *mops it up, in an agony of mortification.*

HEAD WAITER: Please forgive me, sir. . . . It's the first time in thirty-seven years that that has happened . . . it must have been a bad bottle. I will bring another immediately.

AMANDA (*calmly to the retreating* HEAD WAITER) : And another gin and lime for me – with lots of water.

HEAD WAITER (*horrified*): Another gin and lime!

PRINCE (*between clenched teeth, never taking his eyes off her*): What is the meaning of this gratuitous insolence?

AMANDA (*calm*): It's not insolence. It's simply that I don't intend to put up with your stupid bad temper. So I'm going back to being 'me' for a bit. And 'me', I'm thirsty. And 'me', I don't like champagne.

PRINCE : Me! Me! Me! How you love saying that, don't you? Well, let me tell you that for the last two days you've never once stopped being 'you'. You've simply been making fun of something you are too ignorant to understand.

AMANDA : That's not true. I've tried as hard as I can to be her. I've done my level best, and I can't go on a moment longer. Please excuse me, and let me have my gin and lime.

PRINCE : Why did you hurt me by saying those words you knew she never said?

AMANDA : I hoped they would help you.

PRINCE : You're lying.

AMANDA : Yes, I'm lying.

She stands up.

(*Simply.*) Please forgive me what I'm going to say. But it seems to me that a love affair is too precious and beautiful a thing to play about with like this. I know you'll be furious with me, and probably drive me away – but I'll go back to Paris happier if I've told you what I think. She never loved you. But that isn't really important, because you can give all your heart to someone and get nothing in return – and anyway, I'm certain you know already, deep down, that she didn't love you. But there's worse to come, and I must say it before I go. You're young and rich and handsome and charming and your hands aren't really hard . . . just strong and useful . . . you ought to try to live, and be happy and forget the past – because I'm absolutely positive that you didn't love her either.

Silence. Nobody breathes. Then the PRINCE *says calmly:*

PRINCE: I'm afraid you are very stupid, mademoiselle, and unspeakably impudent into the bargain. Ferdinand, please bring mademoiselle's wrap. The path back to the house is rather dark, so someone will walk with you. My aunt's secretary will settle up with you in the morning.

AMANDA: You're not hurting anybody but yourself by bringing money into this.

PRINCE (*a bitter smile*): I had quite forgotten the admirably disinterested attitude of the proletariat towards filthy lucre. If you would prefer it, we will pay you nothing.

AMANDA: Oh, yes, you will. You'll give me the price of my return ticket, and three days' pay as a milliner at trade-union rates, with overtime. I can tell you the exact amount.

PRINCE (*icy*): You may go now.

The HEAD WAITER *creeps up, followed by the* CLOAKROOM ATTENDANT, *who carries* AMANDA'S *wrap. He stammers with emotion.*

HEAD WAITER: M-M-Mademoiselle's . . . wr-wrap. . . .

AMANDA: You can take it back to the house yourself. *I* don't wear furs in the summer. *I'm* quite warm enough, thank you.

She moves towards the door with dignity.

PRINCE (*calling her back*): Mademoiselle!

She stops.

Mademoiselle. I belong to a class which is invariably represented in humorous fiction as consisting entirely of effete young half-wits and dithering dotards. . . . I know I had a strange upbringing at the hands of old ladies and priests. I suppose it's only to be expected that you should think me an imbecile.

AMANDA: I never said that!

PRINCE: But you would have liked to. No, don't deny it; it is quite understandable. I have just accused you of being stupid

– we always brand people as imbeciles if their views differ from our own. No. You cannot dispute that people are prejudiced against a man like me, who lives in a sixteenth-century mausoleum, and rejoices in twenty-two Christian names and a procession of titles, all of which lost their significance centuries ago. It may surprise you when I tell you that it is just as difficult for a man in my position to convince people that he is not a blockhead as it would be for the scion of a long line of village idiots. And even then, once the village idiot's son has proved his intelligence, he is laden with scholarships and encouraged to become Prime Minister. But I am not.

AMANDA: I don't see at all what you're driving at.

PRINCE: Just this. You and I are neither of us idiots. Are we agreed on that? Nevertheless, my love story seems absolutely grotesque to you. You simply cannot imagine how I could have fallen in love with such a weird creature as Léocadia.

AMANDA: I never said 'weird'.

PRINCE: Only because you have been brought up never to speak ill of the dead. But if she had been here this evening, dressed like you, as like you in features as an identical twin, you would have been bursting with hysterical giggles all the evening at her behaviour. Isn't that so? Admit it.

AMANDA (*head bowed*): Yes, I would.

PRINCE: But since we have agreed that neither of us is an imbecile, we are going to explain ourselves to each other, once and for all. Sit down.

AMANDA: Why?

PRINCE: Because I am about to embark on an extremely long speech.

And indeed he is.

Right. Life is a wonderful thing to talk about, or to read about in history books – but it is terrible when one has to live it. It is almost impossible to sleep for more than twelve hours a day, and the remaining twelve hours have to be filled in somehow. There are, of course, the classic diversions –

drink and drugs. But personally I have no taste for happiness induced by chemical compounds. There is, too, the determined brightness of the Boy Scout breed, who fill every second with some useless but efficiently performed task – but that sort of behaviour requires a special talent which, mercifully, is distributed by providence as parsimoniously as any other. As for the method which consists of leaping out of the right side of the bed every morning in the chilly dawn, and doing Swedish exercises in front of an open window, repeating incessantly that every day and in every way things are getting better and . . . (*He shudders.*) No. That's nothing but a spiritual laxative, and not for me. Consequently – I was bored. 'But you have everything in the world', they used to say to me. 'It's downright ungrateful to be bored when there's so much poverty about.' What gloriously muddled thinking! One might just as well tell a man who can't afford the price of a loaf of bread that he has no right to complain, but on the contrary, is extremely lucky, for he has good digestion and so many millionaires are dyspeptic. He'd throw you downstairs, and quite right too. It's just the same with me. Comfort can be taken for granted just as easily as a good digestion, you know. And only a fool could find happiness in comfort alone. I was bored. 'Ah,' they said, 'if you had to work eight hours a day for your living, young man—' I don't doubt it. If I had been poor and confronted daily with a factory bench or a pile of ledgers, I would have had the precious opportunity of keeping my mind occupied all the week, and only being bored on Sundays, like everybody else. But it was my fate to be condemned to endure seven Sundays every week. I really did try to fill them. But somehow I didn't seem cut out for sitting on the committees of charity balls, or presiding over the meetings of societies for the encouragement of those breeds of horses which run faster than their competitors. As for the idea of working to amass a still larger fortune, I'm sure you'll agree that would be positively immoral. What more can I say? I have no artistic talent. I have no great gift of scholarship. I have a fairly good memory, it's true, but I find it ridiculous to press it into the service of recording knowledge which would never be of the slightest use to me. No, the only thing that remains for people like me is an organized and unremitting round of amusements. We all get caught up eventually in the terrible roundabout of the fashionable seasons, and, believe me, it's a dog's life. If the professional classes put half the energy, imagination and tenacity into their businesses that the idle rich do into being bored to tears in exactly the right place on exactly the right date all over Europe, they would soon make their fortunes. I haven't even any vices. Vices are wonderfully strong, simple things. But I haven't even one.

Pause, as the awful truth of what he has said penetrates his mind.

AMANDA (*soft*): Have you finished?

PRINCE: Almost. Through the clammy mists of boredom from which I had practically abandoned hope of escaping, there flashed suddenly, like a will-o'-the-wisp, a brilliant creature, whose light and warmth dispersed the fog for three short days. A preposterous character, I grant you, followed by her retinue of greyhounds and tame serpents, a creature who awoke at dusk and went to bed at dawn, and spent the night between in meaningless chatter. An orchid-eater who lived on champagne and passion, and who died for the sake of an extravagant gesture – strangled by her own scarf. And yet, this madwoman, with all her ridiculous affectations and frivolities, was intelligent. . . .

Pause. He looks at her, insolent.

Intelligence. Another goddess of whom you may have heard. Remembering her, what do I care if the guttersnipes run after me in the street, teasing me with their cruel mimicry? They used to run after her, too. In those three days, before the mists closed in again, leaving me groping for a memory I can never quite recapture, this lovely lunatic taught me the value of so many things . . . of two beautiful lips which only say 'I love you' among a thousand other things; of a cool skin which is a benison of delight to touch. (*Hard.*) And also the value of your silence, and of your simple love, so happy just to bask in the sun among the carnival litter of a picnic; and the value of our bitter joys, the joys of the rest of us, who can never share your uncomplicated happiness.

Pause.

(*A cry.*) I do not love you, mademoiselle! You are beautiful – even more beautiful than she – you are desirable, you are gay and tender and compact of all manner of delights – youth, nature, life . . . and even common sense into the bargain. But I do not love you!

AMANDA (*after a tiny pause*): Have you quite finished now?
PRINCE: Yes, I have finished.
AMANDA: Well, personally, you leave me cold.

She gets up with dignity, crosses the restaurant and goes out. The PRINCE, *having got his tirade off his chest, is very proud of himself. He looks round, and finds that he is alone. Automatically, he goes to his table and as the* HEAD WAITER *approaches, he says, pathetically* . . .

PRINCE: *You* never doubted that I loved her more than all the world, did you, Ferdinand?
HEAD WAITER (*pouring champagne, obsequious*): Oh, sir! How can you ask such a thing! You worshipped her. We all remarked on it, amongst ourselves. Such great love was unforgettable, sir – even to us, who only stand and wait.

As the PRINCE, *who had fallen into a reverie, puts his head in his hands, the* HEAD WAITER *turns to the orchestra, and says with an ignoble wink:*

Music!

The musicians, sniggering, strike up the waltz theme. The PRINCE *sits with his head in his hands, then wearily lays his head on the table and sleeps. The* HEAD WAITER *stops the music with a gesture. The* GIPSIES, *with audible sighs of relief, set about packing up their instruments, while the* WAITERS *clear away the tables and chairs. The* CLOAKROOM ATTENDANT *emerges from her lair carrying a selection of extremely mundane mackintoshes and caps, which the* GIPSIES *put on over their gay costumes. The* CLOAKROOM ATTENDANT *herself exchanges her perilously tottering high-heeled shoes for a pair of homely felt slippers; the* HEAD WAITER *dons a dignified overcoat and homburg hat. The glasses and bottles are stacked away. The Blue Danube has closed for the evening. Before they go, the* GIPSIES *complete the transformation scene by swinging back the hinged flats which represent the walls of the night-club – to reveal the façade of the Chime of Bells. A table is moved here, a chair there – and before our eyes a new scene is set, representing the terrace outside the little country inn. The* GIPSIES, *their work done, pick up their instruments and depart. The* HEAD WAITER, *after a last, proprietary look round, follows them. At his table in the shadows the* PRINCE *sleeps on, his head on his arms.* AMANDA *enters from the other side of the stage. Worn out with grief and exhaustion, she sinks on to the ground, at first in tears, then in uneasy sleep. Slowly, dawn creeps into the sky – a dawn of rose-pink and grey.*

There is the sound of a shot far away. Then another, closer. The DUCHESS *and* HECTOR *appear in antiquated hunting costume, armed with shot-guns. They are followed by a* GHILLY, *who carries spare guns and empty game bags.*

GHILLY: Your shot, Lord Hector.

HECTOR *fires.*

HECTOR (*annoyed*): Missed!
GHILLY: Your shot, Your Grace.

The DUCHESS *fires.*

DUCHESS (*delighted*): Missed! I am always delighted when I miss a bird. I love to see them in flight – they are so graceful, so carefree, so confident. I can never understand why, on certain arbitrary dates, we have to start pumping lead into the poor things.

Suddenly she sees something white lying on the ground, and screams.

Heavens! What's that white thing? Did you hit something, Hector?

HECTOR: I . . . I don't think so . . .

GHILLY (*inspecting* AMANDA): It's the young lady who is visiting Your Grace.

DUCHESS: Oh, my God. Is she hurt?

GHILLY: No. She's asleep, Your Grace.

DUCHESS (*going to* AMANDA): Asleep, and hurt, too. Her face is still covered with tears.

AMANDA *wakes, and gives a little cry when she sees the* DUCHESS.

AMANDA: Oh! Oh, it's you, madame! No, please don't speak to me. . . . I don't want to see anybody . . . I just want to get away from here as fast as I can.

DUCHESS (*motioning the others to go*): Get away, child? Why?

AMANDA: She's too strong for me, madame. . . . I laugh at her, and I think I'm stronger than she is . . . but I'm not. She's too strong for me. . . .

DUCHESS: She is very strong, child, but she is no stronger than you. Remember that she has one enormous disadvantage for any young woman. She is dead.

AMANDA: She wouldn't even let him hold her hand. But his hands aren't really hard . . . they are simple, strong hands, made for loving . . . if only he would listen to what his hands tell him . . . but he won't. So you see, I must go away, because she's stronger than I am.

DUCHESS: You are twenty years old, you are alive and in love. There is nobody in the whole world stronger than you are this morning. Look around you, instead of brooding over last night's miseries . . . look. It's morning now.

And sure enough the light has brightened and the scene is transformed as the DUCHESS *speaks.*

The sun is already trembling on the brink of dawn. Everything living stirs and opens at his touch, the crocuses, the young reluctant beech leaves, and the shutters of honest folk. Oh, and the smells! The first early-morning smells! The smell of the earth, the smell of wet grass, and the smell of new-made coffee, which is the incense we offer at Aurora's shrine.

And indeed the LANDLORD *of the inn has opened his shutters and is already brewing coffee. Later he brings out the little trees in tubs and the tables on to the terrace.*

And look . . . you can see the first colours of the day . . . vibrant green and tender pink. Soon you will hear the buzzing of the first bee, and feel the first tingle of warmth from the sun. Léocadia may have had the witchery of the night on her side . . . but you are twenty, and alive, and in love. Look up at the sun, and laugh! All the strength of the morning is yours.

The DUCHESS *disappears, discreetly. The sun suddenly comes out with a triumphant burst of music.* AMANDA *stretches her arms and laughs up into the sunshine. The music ends with her happy laughter. She goes over to the inn, where the* LANDLORD *has just finished arranging the terrace.*

AMANDA: Landlord!

The LANDLORD *takes no notice.*

(*Louder.*) Landlord!

Still no response. AMANDA *picks up a stone and beats a tattoo on a table-top. He looks at her, and then goes to see whether she has damaged the polished surface of his table, which he dusts angrily.*

Is this the Chime of Bells?

The LANDLORD *silently points to the inn sign.*

Thank you. Are you dumb?

LANDLORD: Yes.

AMANDA (*not batting an eyelid, she smiles*): Don't you find it an awful nuisance, being dumb?

LANDLORD (*half conquered by her smile, answers, still sulkily*): Oh, I manage.

AMANDA: Have you been dumb for a long time?

LANDLORD: Thirty-seven years.

AMANDA: Don't you do anything for it?

LANDLORD: I gargle.

AMANDA: Gargle? Do you really?

LANDLORD: No, not really. But then I'm not really dumb. My gargles are a Green Devil and a Skyrocket with every meal. Four a day. No more. I have to watch myself. My grandfather died of drink.

AMANDA: Why wouldn't you talk to me before?

LANDLORD: Can't be too careful. I didn't know you – never spoken to you before.

AMANDA: And now?

LANDLORD: Well, I've spoken to you now, haven't I? I know you.

Pause.

I sometimes take one in the morning, mind, if I'm pressed, in spite of my grandfather. Not often, but sometimes.

AMANDA: One what?

LANDLORD: Green Devil.

AMANDA: What's a Green Devil?

LANDLORD: It's a Skyrocket with a touch of bitters.

AMANDA: And what's a Skyrocket?

LANDLORD: Exactly the same as a Green Devil, but without the bitters. Shall I bring two Green Devils?

AMANDA: All right – two Green Devils. But d'you think the memory of your grandfather would prevent you from drinking mine as well? I'm not a bit thirsty this morning.

LANDLORD: Normally it would. But when a lady asks me – well, I'm prepared to stretch a point.

He goes into the inn, and returns with two glasses and a selection of bottles.

You from Dinard?

AMANDA: Yes.

LANDLORD: I suppose you wandered into the park by mistake?

AMANDA: Yes.

LANDLORD: I always get stray people in the summer who think this is a real hotel. It gives me quite a nice little bit of business on the side.

AMANDA: Isn't this a real hotel, then?

LANDLORD: Dear me, no. It's quite a story . . . the owner of this estate is a prince – a real one, mind. And he's rebuilt in his park all the places he used to visit with his girl friend years ago. How's that for an eccentric, eh? They say he does it to remind himself of her . . . personally I think it's all part of the council's crazy building scheme . . . full of Freemasons it is . . . rigged elections . . . bribery, you mark my words. Still, that's none of my business. I look the other way.

AMANDA: And used they to meet each other there?

LANDLORD: Who?

AMANDA: The Prince and his girl friend?

LANDLORD: So they tell me.

AMANDA (*amazed*): What d'you mean? Can't you remember?

LANDLORD (*embarking on the second drink*): No, I can't, and I'll tell you why. When they told the proprietors of this inn they wanted to knock it down and rebuild it here, brick by brick – well, they'd been there seventeen years, see? They were planning to retire – got a little cottage by the sea. So they put me in to run the place.

AMANDA: But what happens when the Prince comes? Suppose he asks you questions?

LANDLORD: Oh, they briefed me good and proper, don't you worry. I've got it all pat – how they arrived in a taxi, the pair of them, how they ordered lemonade . . . every detail, see? I couldn't tell it better if I'd been there and seen them for myself – and if ever I'm stuck, I make it up. But he never notices. Sometimes I wonder if he was there himself!

He goes back into the inn, delighted by the sensation he has caused.

AMANDA (*calling him back*): Landlord! Landlord!

LANDLORD (*reappearing in the doorway*): What is it now?

AMANDA: I like you.

LANDLORD (*suspicious*): Why?

AMANDA: You'll never know how much you've done for me.

LANDLORD: I have? (*He looks at her, on his guard.*) It was you ordered the Green Devils, you know. Three hundred francs.

AMANDA (*giving him the money*): There. And thank you very much.

At that moment the PRINCE, *who has woken up, comes over to the inn, his collar turned up, shivering in the fresh morning air. Suddenly he sees* AMANDA.

PRINCE: Are you still here?

AMANDA: Yes, I'm still here.

PRINCE: You must forgive me for my rudeness last night.

AMANDA: Don't let's talk about it.

PRINCE (*an echo*): . . . No . . . don't let's talk about it. . . .

He shivers.

AMANDA: You're shivering.

PRINCE: I always feel a little cold first thing in the morning.

AMANDA: Why don't you sit in the sun for a bit? It's quite warm already.

The PRINCE *moves forward, and looks at the inn.*

PRINCE: That's the inn where we went together . . . we sat inside near that little window with the red curtains. It was very cold that day.

AMANDA: We'll sit on the terrace, shall we? It's so warm this morning.

PRINCE (*coming back to earth as he bumps into a chair on the terrace*): Yes . . . forgive me . . . yes, if you like. . . . I . . . I tripped over a chair . . . clumsy of me . . . I'm afraid I'm only half awake. . . .

AMANDA: Don't you ever get up early?

PRINCE: I generally go to bed at dawn. But I'm afraid I dozed off in the nightclub . . . and now I hardly know whether I'm late to bed or early to rise.

He shivers.

How terribly cold it is.

AMANDA: Honestly, it's quite warm . . . listen to the bees . . . they wouldn't be buzzing like that if it was cold, now would they?

PRINCE (*ironic*): I suppose it's impossible for the bees to make a mistake.

He sees that AMANDA *is smiling.*

Why do you smile?

AMANDA: I thought you looked terrible last night. But you're even worse this morning.

PRINCE (*still shivering*): I do not look terrible.

The LANDLORD *comes out, surprised. He approaches the* PRINCE.

LANDLORD: Good morning, sir. Am I to serve the lemonade out here instead of indoors?

AMANDA: We don't want lemonade. Bring two cups of white coffee, good and hot. The gentleman is very cold.

LANDLORD (*thunderstruck*): White coffee! Oh, well. I only suggested lemonade because it always has been lemonade, every day for two years. If you'd rather have coffee, you shall have coffee. It's none of my business.

AMANDA (*calling after him*): Big cups, with bread and butter!

LANDLORD (*past surprise*): Big cups . . . with bread and butter.

He goes, muttering.

Wouldn't have believed it. She's a one, she is.

AMANDA: You don't mind if we have breakfast together?

PRINCE: No, I don't mind.

He shoos away an inquisitive bee.

Another of the brutes. . . .

AMANDA: Oh, don't hurt it!

PRINCE: I suppose it would amuse you to see me eaten alive?

AMANDA: It won't eat you!

PRINCE: Are you sure?

AMANDA: Positive!

PRINCE: You seem very much at home in the morning.

AMANDA: And it's very nice to have you with me . . . allow me to introduce you, Prince Albert . . . the trees . . . the sun . . . the bees. . . .

PRINCE (*looks at her, murmuring*): You are quite terrifying.

AMANDA: Really?

PRINCE: You are like a tiny pink and white ogre.

The LANDLORD *brings out coffee in big blue cups and a plate of bread and butter.*

LANDLORD: Two white coffees. Bread and butter.

He puts them on the table.

Are you sure you wouldn't like me to bring the lemonade as well, sir?

AMANDA: No!

LANDLORD: No, she says. I don't know what the place is coming to. . . .

He goes in again, grumbling. The PRINCE *watches* AMANDA, *who is buttering a piece of bread.*

PRINCE: Do you really propose to eat all that?

AMANDA: I certainly do. And it's no good looking at me like that. I'm not ashamed of myself. I'm hungry.

PRINCE: A tiny pink and white ogre, serene and sure of herself, without a trace of tears or shame. You frighten me. Who are you?

AMANDA: Just a girl in a white dress buttering a piece of bread in the sunshine.

PRINCE: Didn't I meet you the other evening in the park beside the obelisk?

AMANDA: Yes, and I asked you the way to the sea.

PRINCE: Was that three days ago?

AMANDA: It was. The next day we met again in your aunt's house, and then we hired a boat and rowed up the river almost as far as Dinard. Then yesterday evening, after that long lazy afternoon in the sunshine, we went to the Blue Danube. You remember – the café where those ridiculous gipsies churn out mock-Viennese music. . . .

She sings the refrain of the waltz. The PRINCE *joins in softly. The orchestra takes up the theme in the background. Then* AMANDA *stops singing and the music dies.*

And now it's morning. And we are having breakfast at the Chime of Bells – the little inn you wanted to show me. Oh, it's a nice place in the morning sun!

PRINCE (*a cry*): But this is the last day!

AMANDA (*calm*): The last? What do you mean? It's the third day – and it's only just beginning.

PRINCE: But – this evening?

AMANDA: This evening? We'll go wherever you like.

PRINCE: And tomorrow morning?

AMANDA: We'll have breakfast together, just like this morning, and it will be the beginning of our fourth day.

Pause. The PRINCE *shivers –* AMANDA *takes his arm.*

You're still cold. Let's go inside.

The PRINCE *enters the inn and goes straight to a little table near the window.*

(*Stopping him quite naturally.*) No, not there. That's out of the sun. This one is better.

PRINCE: No!

AMANDA: Why not? You've known me for three days, just as you knew her – and you are in love with me, just as you were with her.

PRINCE (*a cry*): I don't love you!

AMANDA (*soft*): If you didn't love me you wouldn't deny it so vehemently . . . oh, please, wake up from your horrible dream! It's morning now . . . look, the world is full of ordinary, solid, real things. Flowers you can smell and grass you can pull up and crush in your hands.

She is very close to him. Suddenly she says:

Put your two hands on my shoulders . . . you'll find everything will suddenly be so simple. . . .

PRINCE: I am afraid.

AMANDA: Touch me . . . please touch me!

PRINCE: If I touched you, Amanda, I think I would love you – but I don't want to touch you!

AMANDA (*with a little tender smile*): I'm not a bit frightened of you. Even yesterday, you seemed a very grand person, miles above me, but now you only seem like a little fish battering his tiny fins against the whole force of the mighty river. . . .

PRINCE (*sighing, in spite of himself*): Léocadia. . . .

AMANDA (*softly*): Yes, my love. Put your hands on my shoulders. . . .

Pause. Suddenly the PRINCE *puts his hands on* AMANDA'S *shoulders, and stands quite still. She closes her eyes.*

(*Whispering.*) Why don't you say anything? Now *I* am afraid. . . .

PRINCE (*a strange, wondering voice*): But it is so simple . . . and so real . . . and so safe. . . .

Suddenly he embraces her passionately. The shutters of the little inn close tactfully on them. The DUCHESS *and* HECTOR *come in, guns at the trail. The* GHILLY *walks behind them, carrying a bulging game bag.*

DUCHESS: It was you. I know it was you.

HECTOR: It couldn't have been me!

DUCHESS: You're such a clumsy oaf, I knew you'd have to go and kill a bird sooner or later.

HECTOR: I distinctly saw you taking aim! I'm prepared to swear it in a court of law!

DUCHESS: Really, Hector, you don't imagine I'd brief my lawyers just to make you admit you'd shot a heron.

GHILLY: It's not a heron, Your Grace – nor even a flamingo. It's an outlandish sort of bird you don't often see in these parts. Funny sort of creature. Its feathers are much too long, they get caught up in the branches when it tries to fly, and its feet are so arched it can't perch anywhere. You can see it miles away, with that tuft of bright-coloured feathers on its head . . . and as for the noise it makes . . . well, you heard that ridiculous squawk when Your Grace fired that shot – there's no other known species makes a noise like that.

HECTOR: You see? It was you. Germain corroborates me.

DUCHESS: Very well, it was me. Now are you satisfied? (*To the* GHILLY.) We don't need you any more, Germain. You can go – and take the bird with you.

GHILLY: What shall I do with it, Your Grace? It's not even any good for eating.

DUCHESS: Bury it.

GHILLY: Very good, Your Grace.

He touches his cap, and is about to go when the DUCHESS *stops him.*

DUCHESS: Germain. . . .

GHILLY: Your Grace?

DUCHESS (*very tender*): Bury it in my rose-garden.

The GHILLY *touches his cap, and goes. Pause.* HECTOR *and the* DUCHESS *sit on the bench side by side, pensive.*

(*Suddenly brusque.*) What are you thinking about, Hector?

HECTOR: It's funny. I was thinking about—

DUCHESS: So was I. It is funny. Poor Léocadia. She was reduced to strangling herself with her own scarf, and now we have killed her again – we have killed her memory. But Albert had to be saved. And if Amanda is the person who can save him, then good luck to her. But all the same . . . however useless, however frivolous and fundamentally unjust that poor, silly, orchidaceous scatterbrain may have been, surely nobody can blame us for pitying her now . . . and shedding a tear for her. . . .

HECTOR (*moved*): No . . . of course not. . . .

DUCHESS (*turning on him, severe*): I was not talking to you, Hector.

She looks up at the sky.

I was talking to Gaston.

She gets up briskly, and goes, followed by HECTOR, *at a jog trot as—*

THE CURTAIN FALLS

Point of Departure

Characters

FATHER

ORPHEUS

EURYDICE

MOTHER

WAITER

VINCENT

MATHIAS

GIRL

DULAC

ANOTHER GIRL

YOUNG MAN (MONSIEUR HENRI)

MANAGER

DRIVER

CASHIER

SECOND WAITER

SECOND YOUNG MAN

LOUDSPEAKER

VOICE

Original Title: Eurydice

Translator: Kitty Black

First produced in 1941

Act One

SCENE: *The refreshment-room of a provincial station. Over-decorated, worn and dirty. Marble-topped tables, mirrors, benches covered with threadbare red velvet. Seated at a too-high desk, like a Buddha on an altar, is the* CASHIER, *with a large bun and enormous breasts. Aged* WAITERS, *bald and dignified, spittoons, and sawdust.*

Before the rise of the curtain we hear a violin. It is ORPHEUS *playing quietly in the corner, beside his* FATHER, *absorbed in his miserable accounts in front of two empty glasses. In the background a single* CUSTOMER, *a young man with his hat pulled down over his eyes, wearing a macintosh, apparently lost in thought. Music for a moment, then the* FATHER *stops his additions and looks at* ORPHEUS.

FATHER: My boy?

ORPHEUS (*still playing*): Father?

FATHER: You don't expect your poor old father to go round with the hat in a station restaurant?

ORPHEUS: I'm playing for my own pleasure.

FATHER (*continuing*): A station restaurant with only one customer, who's pretending not to notice anyway. I know their little ways. They pretend not to be listening, and not to see the plate when you hold it out. But I pretend not to notice they're pretending. (*Pause, while* ORPHEUS *continues to play.*) D'you enjoy playing as much as that? I can't imagine how you, a musician, can still manage to like music. When I've been scratching away for a bunch of idiots playing cards in a café, there's only one thing I want to do . . .

ORPHEUS (*without stopping*): Go and play cards in another café.

FATHER (*surprised*): How did you know?

ORPHEUS: I guessed – over twenty years ago.

FATHER: Twenty years? Oh, come now! Twenty years ago I still had talent. . . . Twenty years ago, when I played in the orchestra, who could have believed your old father would come down to playing his harp in the street? Who'd have thought he'd be reduced to going round afterwards with a little saucer?

ORPHEUS: Mother would – every time you got yourself sacked from your current job . . .

FATHER: Your mother never loved me. Neither do you. You spend all your time trying to humiliate me. But don't think I'll put up with it always. You know I was offered a job as harpist at the casino at Palavas-les-Flots?

ORPHEUS: Yes, Father.

FATHER: And I refused because they had no vacancy for you?

ORPHEUS: Yes, Father. Or rather, no, Father.

FATHER: No, Father? Why, no, Father?

ORPHEUS: You refused because you know you play abominably and you'd be sacked the next morning.

FATHER (*turning away, hurt*): I shan't even answer you.

ORPHEUS *goes back to his playing.*

Must you?

ORPHEUS: Yes. Does it bother you?

FATHER: I can't concentrate. Eight times seven?

ORPHEUS: Fifty-six.

FATHER: Are you sure?

ORPHEUS: Quite sure.

FATHER: Isn't it odd? I hoped it might be sixty-three. Still, eight times nine are obviously seventy-two. . . . You know we've very little money left, my boy . . .

ORPHEUS: Yes, Father.

FATHER: Is that all you can say?

ORPHEUS: Yes, Father.

FATHER: You're thinking of my white hairs?

ORPHEUS: No, Father.

FATHER: I thought not. Oh, I'm used to it. (*He goes back to his additions.*) Eight times seven?

ORPHEUS: Fifty-six.

FATHER (*bitterly*): Fifty-six. . . . You didn't have to remind me. (*He closes his notebook and gives up his accounts.*) That wasn't such a bad meal for twelve francs seventy-five . . .

ORPHEUS: No, Father.

FATHER: You shouldn't have ordered a vegetable. If you know how to do things, you get your vegetable with the main course and they let you have a second sweet instead. When you're having the set meal, it's always better to choose the two sweets. The Neopolitan ice was a dream. . . . In one sense, we did better tonight for twelve francs seventy-five than yesterday for thirteen francs fifty *à la carte* at Montpellier. . . . You could say they had linen serviettes instead of paper ones. It was a place that gave itself airs, but fundamentally it was no better. And did you see they charged us three francs for the cheese? If they had at least brought the tray along like they do in proper restaurants! Once, my boy, I was taken to dine at Poccardi's, you know, in Paris. They brought the tray along . . .

ORPHEUS: You've told me about it before, Father.

FATHER (*hurt*): All right – I don't want to bore you.

ORPHEUS *goes back to his playing. After a moment the father is bored and decides to stop sulking.*

I say, my boy – that's horribly sad.

ORPHEUS: So is what I'm thinking.

FATHER: What are you thinking about?

ORPHEUS: About you, Father.

FATHER: About me? Well, what is it now?

ORPHEUS: Or rather, you and me.

FATHER: The outlook isn't very promising, of course, but we're doing our best, my boy.

ORPHEUS: I'm thinking that ever since Mother died I've followed you round the cafés with my violin. I've watched you struggling with your accounts at night. I've listened to you discussing the menus of the set meals and then I've gone to bed. In the morning I get up again.

FATHER: When you get to my age you'll see that that is life.

ORPHEUS: I'm thinking that if you were all alone, with your harp, you'd never be able to live.

FATHER (*worried suddenly*): You don't want to leave me?

ORPHEUS: No. Probably I'll never be able to leave you. I'm a better musician than you are, I am young and I'm sure life has better things to offer; but I couldn't live if I knew you were starving somewhere else.

FATHER: That's good of you my boy. Think of your old father.

ORPHEUS: Good, yes, but it's a big responsibility. Sometimes I dream something might come between us . . .

FATHER: Now, now, we understand each other so well . . .

ORPHEUS: There's the wonderful job where I earn enough to make you an allowance. But it's a dream. A musician never earns enough to pay for two rooms and four meals a day.

FATHER: Oh, my needs are very small, you know. A meal costing twelve francs seventy-five like today. A table at the café. A small glass of something, a fifteen-cent cigar and I'm as happy as a sandboy. (*Pause. He adds.*) If I had to, I could quite well do without the small something.

ORPHEUS (*going on with his dream*): Then there's the level crossing where one of us is knocked down by a train . . .

FATHER: Good heavens . . . which one?

ORPHEUS (*gently*): Oh, it doesn't really matter . . .

FATHER (*starting*): How strange you are. I don't want to die! You're full of gloom tonight, my boy. (*He burps genteelly.*) That rabbit was really excellent. Good heavens, you make me laugh! At your age I thought life was wonderful. (*He suddenly studies the* CASHIER.) And what about love? Had you thought you might fall in love?

ORPHEUS: What is love? Girls I might get to meet with you?

FATHER: My dear boy, can any of us guess where and how love will find us? (*He comes a little closer.*) Tell me, you don't think I look rather too bald? She's quite charming, that girl. A little provincial, perhaps. More my type than yours. What would you put her at? Forty? Forty-five?

ORPHEUS (*gives a pale little smile. He claps his father on the shoulder*): I'm going outside for a bit. . . . We've still got an hour before the train.

When he has gone, the FATHER *rises, walks all round the* CASHIER, *who blasts him with a look – the miserable customer. Suddenly, the* FATHER *feels he is old and ugly, poor and bald. He rubs his hand over his head and goes sadly back to pick up his instruments before going out.*

EURYDICE *enters abruptly.*

EURYDICE: Excuse me – that violin? Was someone playing it in here?

FATHER: Yes, mademoiselle. My son. My son Orpheus.

EURYDICE: It was beautiful!

The FATHER *bows, flattered, and goes out with the instruments.* EURYDICE'S MOTHER *enters in triumph. Boa, feather hat. Ever since 1920 she has grown younger every day.*

MOTHER: There you are, Eurydice. . . . This heat. . . . How I hate waiting at stations. The whole tour has been a disgrace – as usual. The manager ought to arrange that the leading actors don't spend all their time waiting for connexions. When you've spent the whole day on a platform, how can you give your best in the evening?

EURYDICE: There's only one train for the whole company and it's an hour late because of the storm yesterday. The manager can't help it.

MOTHER: You always find excuses for these incompetents!

WAITER (*who has come up*): May I take your orders, ladies?

MOTHER: Do you feel like something?

EURYDICE: After that star entrance of yours, it's the least we can do.

MOTHER: Have you any really good peppermint? I'll have a peppermint. In the Argentine, or in Brazil, where the heat was really exhausting, I always used to take a peppermint just before making my first entrance. Sarah gave me the tip. A peppermint.

WAITER: And for mademoiselle?

EURYDICE: Coffee, please.

MOTHER: Why aren't you with Mathias? He's wandering about like a soul in torment.

EURYDICE: Don't worry about him.

MOTHER: It was very wrong of you to upset that boy. He adores you. It was your fault in the first place. You shouldn't have let him be your lover. I told you so at the time, but it's too late to worry about that now. Besides, we all begin and end with actors. When I was your age I was much prettier than you. I could have been taken up by anyone I pleased. All I could do was waste my time with your father. . . . You see the charming results yourself.

WAITER (*who has brought the drinks*): A little ice, madame?

MOTHER: Never – think of my voice! This peppermint is disgusting. I hate the provinces, I hate these second-rate tours. But in Paris nowadays they only go mad over little idiots with chests as flat as their voices, who can't say three words without fluffing. . . . What has the boy done to upset you? You didn't even get into the same compartment at Montelimar? My dear child, a mother is a girl's natural confidante, particularly when they're the same age. . . . I mean, particularly when she's a very young mother. Come along, tell me. What has he done? . . .

EURYDICE: Nothing, Mother.

MOTHER: Nothing, Mother. That doesn't make sense. Only one thing is sure – he adores you madly. Maybe that's why you don't love him. We women are all the same. Nothing can make us change. How's your coffee?

EURYDICE: You have it – I don't want it.

MOTHER: Thank you, darling. I like plenty of sugar. Waiter! Bring some more sugar for mademoiselle. Don't you love him any more?

EURYDICE: Who?

MOTHER: Mathias.

EURYDICE: You're wasting your time, Mother.

The WAITER, *sulking, has brought the sugar.*

MOTHER: Thank you. It's covered with fly-blows! Charming. I – who have been round the world and stayed at all the best hotels – this is what I've come to. Oh well, I suppose it will melt . . . (*She drinks the coffee.*) I think you're absolutely right. You should always follow your instincts. I've always followed mine, like a thorough-going old pro. But then, you're not really an actress by vocation. Do sit up! Ah, here's Vincent. Darling boy! He looks quite put out. Now, do be nice to him. You know how fond of the boy I am.

VINCENT *enters, silver-haired, handsome and soft beneath a very energetic exterior. His gestures are ample, his smile full of bitterness. His eye a roving one. He kisses the mother's hand.*

VINCENT: Ah, there you are! I've been looking for you everywhere.

MOTHER: I've been here, with Eurydice.

VINCENT: This new little manager is absolutely useless! Apparently we've not got to wait here for more than an hour. We shan't have time for dinner again before the performance. I call it really annoying. We may all have the patience of angels, but you must admit it's really annoying!

EURYDICE: It's not the manager's fault we had such a storm yesterday.

MOTHER: I wish I knew why you always stand up for the little idiot.

VINCENT: He's an incompetent – a real incompetent! I can't think why Dulac keeps such a man in the job. The last thing I heard was that he's lost the basket with all the wigs. And tomorrow we've a matinée of *The Burgomaster*. Can you imagine what it will be like?

EURYDICE: I'm sure he'll find it again. It probably got left behind at Montelimar . . .

VINCENT: If it was, it'll probably arrive in time for tomorrow, but tonight, for *Guinevere's Disgrace* – what are we to do? He says it couldn't matter less because it's a modern play, but

I've given Dulac my last word. I cannot play the doctor without my goatee.

WAITER (*who has come up*): Can I take your order, sir?

VINCENT (*superb*): Nothing, thank you. A glass of water.

The WAITER *retreats, beaten.*

The first and second acts, perhaps, but I'm sure you'll agree with me, dear friend. With the best will in the world, how can I play the big scene in the last act without my goatee? What on earth should I look like?

EURYDICE *goes away bad-temperedly.*

MOTHER: Where are you going, darling?

EURYDICE: Just for a walk, Mother. (*She goes out abruptly.*)

VINCENT (*surveys her departure, Olympian. When she has gone*): Dear friend, you know I'm not in the habit of getting on my high horse, but your daughter's attitude towards me is nothing short of scandalous.

MOTHER (*simpering and trying to take his hand*): My big bear.

VINCENT: Our relationship towards each other is perhaps a little delicate, I agree – although you're perfectly free to do as you please, you're separated from her father – but really, anyone would say she delights in aggravating it.

MOTHER: She's a silly girl. You know how she protects that boy, as she protects all the lame things in the world, God knows why – old cats, lost dogs, helpless drunkards. The thought that you might persuade Dulac to send him away was too much for her, that's all.

VINCENT: It may have been too much for her, but there are ways of doing these things.

MOTHER: You know quite well that's what's wrong with her. . . . She's a good child, but she has no manners.

MATHIAS *enters abruptly. He is badly shaven, sombre, on edge.*

Oh, hullo, Mathias.

MATHIAS: Where's Eurydice?

MOTHER: She's just gone out.

MATHIAS *exits. The* MOTHER *watches him go.*

Poor boy. He's mad about her. She's always been good to him until just lately and now I don't know what's come over her. These last two or three days it's as though she were looking for something, or someone. . . . What? I don't know. . . . (*Far away the music of* ORPHEUS.) Why must that man keep scraping away like that? It's maddening.

VINCENT: He's waiting for his train.

MOTHER: That's no reason. That music and the flies. . . . It's so appallingly hot! (*The music has come nearer. They listen. During the next scene* EURYDICE *walks across the back as though looking for the music.*)
(*Abruptly, in a different voice.*) Remember the casino at Ostend? . . .

VINCENT: The year they launched the Mexican tango . . .

MOTHER: How handsome you were!

VINCENT: I still had my figure in those days . . .

MOTHER: And such an air about you. . . . Remember the first day? 'Madame, will you give me the pleasure of this dance?'

VINCENT: 'But, sir, I don't know how to dance the tango.'

MOTHER: 'Nothing simpler, madame. I hold you in my arms. You've only to let yourself go.' The way you said that! . . . Then you put your arms round me and everything swam together . . . the face of the old fool who was keeping me and was watching furiously . . . the barman – he was making love to me, too, at the time; he was a Corsican, and he said he'd like to kill me – the waxed moustaches of the gipsies, the big mauve irises and pale green ranunculas decorating the walls. . . . Ah! it was delicious. It was the year everyone wore broderie anglaise . . . I had an exquisite white dress . . .

VINCENT: I wore a yellow carnation in my buttonhole, and a bird's-eye check in green and brown . . .

MOTHER: When we danced you held me so tightly the pattern of my dress was driven right into my flesh. . . . The old fool noticed it and made a scene. I slapped his face and found myself in the street without a farthing. You hired a carriage with pink pompons and we drove all round the bay alone till it was dark . . .

VINCENT: Ah, the uncertainty, the delicious disturbance of that first day of days. The searching, the awareness, the groping towards the unknown. One does not yet know one's love and yet one knows it will last for the rest of one's life . . .

MOTHER (*suddenly with a change of voice*): Why on earth did we quarrel a fortnight later?

VINCENT: I don't know. I can't remember.

ORPHEUS *has stopped playing.* EURYDICE *is standing in front of him and they look at each other.*

EURYDICE: Was it you playing just now, too?

ORPHEUS: Yes.

EURYDICE: How beautifully you play!

ORPHEUS: Thank you.

EURYDICE: What was it called – what you were playing?

ORPHEUS: I don't know. I was improvising . . .

EURYDICE (*in spite of herself*): I'm sorry . . .

ORPHEUS: Why?

EURYDICE: I don't know. I would have liked it to have had a name.

A GIRL *passes along the platform, sees* EURYDICE *and calls.*

GIRL: Eurydice! Is that you?

EURYDICE (*without taking her eyes off* ORPHEUS): Yes.

GIRL: I've just seen Mathias. He's looking for you, darling . . . (*She disappears.*)

EURYDICE: Yes. (*She looks at* ORPHEUS.) Your eyes are light blue.

ORPHEUS: Yes. I don't know how to describe yours.

EURYDICE: They say it depends on what I'm thinking.

ORPHEUS: Just now they're dark green, like deep water beside the stone steps of a harbour.

EURYDICE: They say that's when I'm happy.

ORPHEUS: Who's 'they'?

EURYDICE: The others.

GIRL (*coming back, calling from the platform*): Eurydice!

EURYDICE (*without turning round*): Yes?

GIRL: Don't forget Mathias.

EURYDICE: Yes. (*Suddenly she asks:*) D'you think you'll make me very unhappy?

ORPHEUS (*smiling gently*): I don't think so.

EURYDICE: I don't mean unhappy as I am at this moment. It's a sort of pain, but a sort of joy as well. What frightens me is being unhappy and lonely when you leave me.

ORPHEUS: I'll never leave you.

EURYDICE: Will you swear that?

ORPHEUS: Yes.

EURYDICE: On my head?

ORPHEUS (*smiling*): Yes. (*They look at each other. Suddenly she says gently:*)

EURYDICE: I like it when you smile.

ORPHEUS: Don't you ever smile?

EURYDICE: Never when I'm happy.

ORPHEUS: I thought you said you were unhappy.

EURYDICE: Don't you understand? Are you a real man after all? How strange it is! Here we are, the two of us, standing face to face, with everything that's going to happen drawn up ready and waiting behind us . . .

ORPHEUS: D'you think much is going to happen?

EURYDICE (*gravely*): Everything. All the things that happen to a man and woman on earth, one by one . . .

ORPHEUS: Gay things, sweet things, terrible things?

EURYDICE (*gently*): Shameful things and filthy things. . . . We're going to be so unhappy.

ORPHEUS (*taking her in his arms*): How wonderful! . . .

VINCENT *and the* MOTHER, *dreaming cheek to cheek, continue softly.*

VINCENT: Ah, l'amour, l'amour! You see, my darling one, on this earth, where all our hopes are shattered, where all is deception and pain and disappointment, it's a marvellous consolation to remember we still have our love . . .

MOTHER: My big bear . . .

VINCENT: . . . All men are liars, Lucienne, faithless, false, hypocritical, vainglorious or cowards; all women are perfidious, artificial, vain, capricious or depraved; the world is nothing but a bottomless sink where the most monstrous beasts disport and distort themselves through oceans of slime. But there is one holy and sublime hope left in the world – the union of these two imperfect and horrible beings!

MOTHER: Yes, my darling. Perdican's big speech.

VINCENT (*stops, surprised*): Is it? I've played it so often!

MOTHER: Remember? You played it that first evening at Ostend. I was in *The Foolish Virgin* at the Kursaal, but I was only in the first act. I waited for you in your dressing-room. You came off stage still thrilling with the wonderful love-scene you'd been playing and you took me there and then, in doublet and hose . . .

VINCENT: Ah, those nights, those nights! The fusion of body and heart! The moment, the unique moment when you no longer know if it's the flesh or the spirit fluttering . . .

MOTHER: You're a wonderful lover, dear boy!

VINCENT: And you, the most adorable of mistresses!

MOTHER: What am I saying? You weren't a lover. You were the lover. The faithless and faithful, the strong and tender, the madman. You were love itself. How you made me suffer . . .

VINCENT: Ah, how often is one deceived in love, how often wounded and unhappy, Lucienne, but you love. When one is at the edge of the grave one turns back to survey the past and says: 'I have suffered much, sometimes been deceived, but I have loved. It is I who have lived and not a false creation brought into being by my vanity and my pride!'

MOTHER (*applauding*): Bravo, bravo!

VINCENT: De Musset again?

MOTHER: Yes, my darling.

EURYDICE *and* ORPHEUS *have listened to them, pressed together as if afraid.*

EURYDICE: Make them stop. Please, please, make them stop.

ORPHEUS (*going to the couple while* EURYDICE *hides*): Monsieur, madame, you certainly won't understand my attitude. It will seem strange to you. Even very strange. But I'm afraid you must both get out of here.

VINCENT: Out of here?

ORPHEUS: Yes, monsieur.

VINCENT: Is it closing time?

ORPHEUS: Yes, monsieur. Closing time for you.

VINCENT (*rising*): Really, I . . .

MOTHER (*also rising*): But you don't belong here. I know you – you're the one who was playing the fiddle . . .

ORPHEUS: You must both go away at once. I promise if I could explain, I would, but I can't explain anything. You wouldn't understand. Something very important is happening here.

MOTHER: The boy's mad . . .

VINCENT: But good gracious, I mean to say, it doesn't make sense! This place is open to everyone!

ORPHEUS: Not any more.

MOTHER: Well, really! This is too much! (*She calls:*) Madame, please! Waiter!

ORPHEUS (*pushing them towards the door*): No, don't call them; it's no use. Go away. I'll settle your bill myself.

MOTHER: But you can't be allowed to treat us like this!

ORPHEUS: I'm a peaceful soul, madame, very kind, very shy even. I promise you I'm very shy, madame, and until this minute I'd never have dared to do what I'm doing . . .

MOTHER: I've never seen such a thing!

ORPHEUS: No, madame, you've never seen such a thing. Anyway, I've never seen such a thing.

MOTHER (*to* VINCENT): Can't you say something?

VINCENT: Come away. You can see he's not in a normal condition.

MOTHER (*disappears, calling*): I shall report you to the station master.

EURYDICE (*coming out of hiding*): Ah! How horrible they were, weren't they? Horrible and stupid!

ORPHEUS (*turning to her, smiling*): Sh! Don't talk about them. How everything falls into place now that we are alone. How clear and simple everything has become. It's as though I were seeing the chandeliers and the plants . . . and the spittoons and the chairs for the first time. . . . Isn't a chair charming? You'd think it was an insect listening for the sound of our steps, ready to spring away on its four thin little legs. Careful! We mustn't move, or if we do, we must be very quick. . . . (*He makes a spring, dragging* EURYDICE.) Got it! Isn't a chair a clever invention? You can even sit on it. . . . (*He hands her to the chair with comical ceremony, then looks at her sadly.*) What I don't understand is why they invented the second chair . . .

EURYDICE (*pulling him down and making room for him on her chair*): It was for people who didn't know each other . . .

ORPHEUS (*taking her in his arms and crying out*): But I know you! Just now I was playing and you came along the platform and I didn't know you. . . . Now everything's changed, and it's wonderful! Everything round us has suddenly become extraordinary. Look . . . how beautiful the cashier is with her big bosom resting delicately on her counter. And the waiter! Look at the waiter! His long flat feet in his button-boots, his distinguished moustache and his noble, noble air. . . . This is an extraordinary evening: we were fated to meet each other, and to meet the noblest waiter in France. A waiter who might have been a governor, a colonel, a member of the Comédie Française. Waiter . . .

WAITER (*approaching*): Monsieur.

ORPHEUS: You are quite charming.

WAITER: But, monsieur . . .

ORPHEUS: Yes, yes, don't protest. I'm very sincere, you know, and I'm not used to paying compliments. You're quite charming. And we shall always remember you and the cashier, mademoiselle and I. You'll tell her so, won't you?

WAITER: Yes, monsieur.

ORPHEUS: Isn't it wonderful to be alive! I didn't know it was so exciting to breathe, to have blood rushing through your veins, muscles that can move . . .

EURYDICE: Am I heavy?

ORPHEUS: Oh no! Just the right weight to keep me down to earth. Until now I was too light. I floated. I bumped into furniture and people. My arms were stretched too wide, my fingers were losing their grip. . . . How funny it is, and how lightly the experts make their calculations of weight! I've just realized I was short of exactly your weight to make me part of the atmosphere . . .

EURYDICE: Oh, my darling, you're frightening me! You really are part of it now? You'll never fly away again?

ORPHEUS: Never again.

EURYDICE: What should I do, all alone on the earth, if you were to leave me? Swear you'll never leave me?

ORPHEUS: I swear.

EURYDICE: That's so easy to say. I hope you don't really mean to leave me. If you really want to make me happy, swear you'll never even want to leave me, even for a minute, even if the prettiest girl in the world looked at you.

ORPHEUS: I swear that, too.

EURYDICE (*rising abruptly*): You see how false you are! You swear that even if the prettiest girl in the world looked at you, you wouldn't want to leave me. But to know that she looked at you, you'd have to look at her. Oh, dear God, how unhappy I am! You've only just begun to love me, and already you're thinking of other women. Swear you wouldn't even see the idiot, my darling . . .

ORPHEUS: I should be blind.

EURYDICE: Even if you don't see her, people are so wicked, they'd tell you about her as quickly as they could, just so as they could hurt me. Swear you won't listen to them!

ORPHEUS: I should be deaf.

EURYDICE: I know – there's something much simpler. Swear

to me straight away, sincerely, of your own free will and not just to please me, that you won't ever think another woman pretty. . . . Even the ones supposed to be beautiful. . . . It doesn't mean a thing, you know.

ORPHEUS: I swear it.

EURYDICE (*suspiciously*): Not even one who looked like me?

ORPHEUS: Even that one. I'll watch out for her.

EURYDICE: You swear it of your own free will?

ORPHEUS: Of my own free will.

EURYDICE: Good. And you know you've sworn it by my head?

ORPHEUS: By your head.

EURYDICE: You know, don't you, that when you swear by someone's head, it means that person dies if you don't keep your word?

ORPHEUS: Yes, I know.

EURYDICE (*thinking*): Good. It's not because – in spite of looking like an angel, I'm sure you're capable of anything – it's not because you're thinking: 'Of course I can swear by her head. What do I risk? If she should die the moment I want to leave her, after all, it would be the best thing that could happen. It's so easy to leave the dead – no tears, no reproaches. . . .' Oh, I know you . . .

ORPHEUS (*smiling*): It's an ingenious idea, but that's not what I was thinking.

EURYDICE: Really and truly? It would be so much better if you told me straight away.

ORPHEUS: Really and truly.

EURYDICE: Swear it.

ORPHEUS (*raising his hand*): There.

EURYDICE (*going to him*): Good. Now I'll tell you. I only wanted to test you. We haven't really sworn anything. To swear properly, it's not enough to lift your hand, a vague little gesture you can interpret how you like. You must stretch out your arm like this, spit on the ground. . . . Don't laugh. This is very serious. We must do it properly. Some people say that not only does the person die suddenly if you break your word, but that she suffers horribly as well.

ORPHEUS (*gravely*): I've made a note of it.

EURYDICE: Good. Now you know what you'll make me risk if you lie, even a very little; you'll swear to me now, please, darling, stretching out your hand and spitting on the ground, that everything you've sworn was true.

ORPHEUS: I spit, I stretch out my hand, and I swear.

EURYDICE (*with a great sigh*): Good. I believe you. Besides, it's so easy to deceive me; I'm very trusting. You're smiling. Are you laughing at me?

ORPHEUS: I'm looking at you. I've just realized I haven't had time to look at you before.

EURYDICE: Am I ugly? Sometimes, when I've been crying, or laughing too much, I get a tiny red spot on the side of my nose. I'd rather tell you straight away, so you don't get a shock later on.

ORPHEUS: I'll remember.

EURYDICE: And I'm very thin. Not so thin as I look; when I'm in the bath, I don't think I'm too bad, but what I mean is, I'm not one of those women you can rest against comfortably.

ORPHEUS: I didn't expect to be very comfortable.

EURYDICE: I can only give you what I've got, can't I? So you mustn't imagine things . . . I'm very stupid, too – I never know what to say and you mustn't rely on me too much to make conversation.

ORPHEUS (*smiling*): You never stop talking!

EURYDICE: I never stop talking, but I wouldn't know how to answer you. That's why I talk all the time, to prevent people asking me questions. It's my way of keeping quiet. You'll see you won't like anything about me.

ORPHEUS: You're quite wrong. I like it when you talk too much. It makes a little noise and it's very restful.

EURYDICE: Really! I'm sure you like mysterious women. The Garbo type. Six feet high, huge eyes, big mouths, big feet, who spend the whole day smoking in the woods. I'm not like that at all. You must say good-bye to that idea straight away.

ORPHEUS: I have.

EURYDICE: Yes, you say that, but I can see in your eyes . . . (*She throws herself into his arms.*) Oh, darling, darling, it's too awful not to be the one you love! What can I do? Do you want me to grow? I'll try. I'll go in for exercises. Do you want me to look haggard? I'll put mascara on my eyelids, use much more make-up. I'll try and be sombre, to smoke . . .

ORPHEUS: Of course not!

EURYDICE: Yes, yes, I'll even try to be mysterious. It's not so very complicated. All you have to do is think of nothing. Any woman can do it.

ORPHEUS: What a little lunatic you are.

EURYDICE: I'll manage, you'll see! I'll be wise and extravagant and thrifty – sometimes – and obedient as a little odalisque, or terribly unjust the days you'd like to feel unhappy because of me. Oh, only those days, don't worry. . . . And then I'll make it up to you the days I'll be maternal – so maternal I'll be a little annoying – the days you'll have boils or toothache. Then on rainy days I can still be bourgeois, badly brought up, prudish, ambitious, highly strung, or just plain boring.

ORPHEUS: D'you think you can play all those parts?

EURYDICE: Of course, my darling, if I'm to keep you, I must be all the other women in one . . .

ORPHEUS: And when will you be yourself?

EURYDICE: In between. Whenever I've got the time – I'll manage.

ORPHEUS: It'll be a dog's life!

EURYDICE: That's what love is! . . . Anyway, it's easy for the lady-dogs. All they have to do is let the other dogs sniff them a little, then trot along with a dreamy air, pretending they haven't noticed anything. Men are much more complicated!

ORPHEUS (*pulling her to him, laughing*): I'm going to make you very unhappy!

EURYDICE (*pressing herself to him*): Oh yes! I shall make myself so small I shan't make any demands on you. All you'll need to do is let me sleep at night against your shoulder, hold my hand all day . . .

ORPHEUS: I like sleeping on my back, diagonally across the bed. I like taking long walks by myself . . .

EURYDICE: We could both try and sleep across the bed, and when we go for walks I'll walk a little behind you, if you like. Only a very little. Almost beside you all the same. But I shall love you so much, and I shall always be so true, so true. . . . Only you must always talk to me, so I won't have time to think of stupid things . . .

ORPHEUS (*dreams for a moment in silence with her in his arms; murmurs*): Who are you? I feel I've known you always.

EURYDICE: Why ask me who I am? It means so little . . .

ORPHEUS: Who are you? It's too late. I know quite well I could never leave you now. You appeared quite suddenly in this station. I stopped playing my violin, and now you're in my arms. Who are you?

EURYDICE: I don't know who you are, either. And yet I don't want you to explain. I'm happy. That's enough.

ORPHEUS: I don't know why I'm suddenly afraid of being hurt.

GIRL (*passing on the platform*): What? Still there? Mathias is expecting you in the third-class waiting-room. If you don't want a whole new series of rows, darling, you'd better go to him straight way . . .

She has gone.

ORPHEUS (*who has let* EURYDICE *go*): Who is this Mathias?

EURYDICE (*quickly*): No one, darling.

ORPHEUS: This is the third time someone's said he's looking for you.

EURYDICE: He's one of the boys in the company. No one at all. He's looking for me. All right. He's probably got something to say.

ORPHEUS: Who is this Mathias?

EURYDICE (*crying out*): I don't love him, darling, I've never loved him!

ORPHEUS: Is he your lover?

EURYDICE: These things are so quickly said, it's so easy to call everything by the same name. I'd rather tell you the truth at once, and tell you myself. Everything must be clear between us. Yes. He is my lover. (ORPHEUS *falls back a step.*) No, don't leave me. I so much wanted to be able to say, I'm only a girl. I've been waiting for you. Yours will be the first hand to touch me. I so much wanted to be able to tell you that – isn't it stupid? – it seemed to me it was true.

ORPHEUS: Has he been your lover long?

EURYDICE: I don't know. Six months perhaps. I've never loved him.

ORPHEUS: Then why?

EURYDICE: Why? Oh, don't keep asking me questions. When we don't know each other very well, when we don't know everything about each other, questions can become the most terrible weapons . . .

ORPHEUS: Why? I want to know.

EURYDICE: Why? Because he was unhappy, I suppose, and I was tired. And lonely. He was in love with me.

ORPHEUS: And before?

EURYDICE: Before, my darling?

ORPHEUS: Before him?

EURYDICE: Before him?

ORPHEUS: You've never had another lover?

EURYDICE (*after an imperceptible hesitation*): No. Never.

ORPHEUS: Then he taught you how to make love? Answer me. Why don't you say something? You said you only wanted the truth to be between us.

EURYDICE (*crying out in despair*): Yes, but, my darling, I'm trying to decide what will hurt you least! If it was him, who you'll probably see, or someone else, a long time ago, who you'll never see . . .

ORPHEUS: It's not a question of what hurts me least, but the truth!

EURYDICE: Well, when I was very small, a man, a stranger, took me, almost by force. . . . It lasted for a few weeks, and then he went away.

ORPHEUS: Did you love him?

EURYDICE: He hurt me, I was afraid. I was ashamed.

ORPHEUS (*after a pause*): Is that all?

EURYDICE: Yes, my darling. You see, it was very stupid, very sad, but very simple.

ORPHEUS (*in a low voice*): I'll try never to think of them.

EURYDICE: Yes, darling.

ORPHEUS: I'll try never to think of their faces close to yours, their eyes upon you, their hands touching you.

EURYDICE: Yes, darling.

ORPHEUS: I'll try not to think they've already held you close. (*Takes her in his arms again.*) There, now it's all begun again. I'm the one who's holding you close.

EURYDICE (*very gently*): It's wonderful in your arms. Like a tiny house, snug and secure, in the middle of the world. A tiny house where no one can ever come. (*He bends over her.*) Here? In this café?

ORPHEUS: In this café. I, who always feel embarrassed when people look at me, I wish it could be full of people . . . it will be a beautiful wedding! For witnesses we shall have had the cashier, the noblest waiter in France, and a shy little man, in a macintosh who pretends not to see us, though I'm sure he can . . .

He kisses her. The YOUNG MAN *in the macintosh, who has been sitting silently in the background from the beginning of the act, looks at them, then gets up noiselessly and comes to lean against a column nearer to them. They haven't seen him.*

EURYDICE (*freeing herself suddenly*): Now, you must leave me. There's something I must do. No, don't ask me. Go out for a moment. I'll call you back.

She goes with him to the door, then goes back to the door which opens on to the platform; she stops and stands motionless for a moment on the threshold. We feel she is looking at someone invisible who is also staring at her. Suddenly she says in a hard voice.

Come in.

MATHIAS *enters slowly without taking his eys off her. He stops on the threshold.*

You saw? I kissed him. I love him. What do you want?

MATHIAS: Who is he?

EURYDICE: I don't know.

MATHIAS: You're mad.

EURYDICE: Yes.

MATHIAS: For a week now you've been avoiding me.

EURYDICE: For a week, yes, but it wasn't because of him. I've only known him for an hour.

MATHIAS (*looks at her in sudden fear*): What did you say? (*He draws back.*)

EURYDICE: You know, Mathias.

MATHIAS: Eurydice, you know I cannot live without you.

EURYDICE: Yes, Mathias. I love him.

MATHIAS: You know I'd rather die at once than go on living alone, now that I've had you with me. I don't ask anything of you, Eurydice, nothing except not to be left alone . . .

EURYDICE: I love him, Mathias.

MATHIAS: Is that the only thing you can say?

EURYDICE (*softly, pitilessly*): I love him.

MATHIAS (*going out suddenly*): Very well. If that's the way you want it.

EURYDICE (*running after him*): Listen, Mathias, try to understand. I like you very much, only – I love him . . .

They have gone. The YOUNG MAN *in the macintosh watches them go. He goes out slowly after them. The stage is empty for a moment. We hear a bell ringing, then the whistle of a train in the distance.* ORPHEUS *comes in slowly, watching* EURYDICE *and* MATHIAS *disappear. Behind him his* FATHER *bursts in with his harp, while the train whistles and the bell becomes more insistent.*

FATHER: The train's coming, my boy. Platform two . . . Are you ready? (*Takes a step, suddenly becomes absentminded.*) Er . . . have you paid? I think you said it was your turn?

ORPHEUS (*gently, without looking at him*): I'm not going, Father.

FATHER: Why always wait until the last minute? The train will be in in two minutes and we've got to take the subway. With the harp, we've only just got time.

ORPHEUS: I'm not taking this train.

FATHER: What? You aren't taking this train? Why aren't you taking this train? We want to get to Palavas tonight; it's the only one.

ORPHEUS: Then take it. I'm not going.

FATHER: This is something new! What's the matter with you?

ORPHEUS: Listen, Father. I'm very fond of you. I know you need me, that it'll be terrible, but it had to happen one day. I'm going to leave you . . .

FATHER (*a man fallen from the clouds*): What are you saying?

ORPHEUS (*crying out suddenly*): You heard me quite well! Don't make me say it again to give you a lead into a pathetic scene! Don't hold your breath so that you can turn pale; don't pretend to tremble and tear your hair! I know all your tricks. It was all right when I was little. They don't impress me now. (*He repeats, in a low voice:*) I'm going to leave you, Father.

FATHER (*changing his tactics suddenly and wrapping himself in an exaggerated dignity*): I refuse to listen to you. You're not in your right mind. Come along.

ORPHEUS: Dignity doesn't work either. I told you I knew all your tricks.

FATHER (*hurt*): Forget my white hairs – forget my white hairs! I'm used to it. . . . But I repeat, I refuse to listen to you. That's clear enough, isn't it?

ORPHEUS: You must listen to me because you've only two minutes to understand. Your train's whistling already.

FATHER (*sneering nobly*): Ah! Ah!

ORPHEUS: Don't sneer nobly, I beg you! Listen to me. You've got to catch that train, and catch it alone. It's your only hope of arriving at Palavas-les-Flots in time to get the job as harpist.

FATHER (*babbling*): But I refused the job! I refused it on your account!

ORPHEUS: You can say you've thought it over, that you're deserting me, that you accept. Tortoni has probably not had time to find another harpist. He's your friend. He'll do his best for you.

FATHER (*bitterly*): Friends! Children! Everything that one has held sacred! They slam the door in your face one fine morning! I've paid dearly for the knowledge. Tortoni's friendship! Ah! Ah! (*He sneers nobly.*)

ORPHEUS: Don't you think he'll give you the job?

FATHER: He'll refuse it.

ORPHEUS: He offered it to you in the first place . . .

FATHER: He approached me, but I refused his offer. He's drunk his shame to the very dregs. You mustn't forget he's an Italian. Those people never forgive an insult.

ORPHEUS: Take the train, Father. As soon as you've gone I'll telephone to Palavas. I swear I'll make him forget you refused.

FATHER (*shouts in a voice the power of which is unsuspected in his frail body*): Never!

ORPHEUS: Don't shout! He's not such a bad chap. I'm sure he will listen to me.

FATHER: Never, do you hear? Your father will never abase himself.

ORPHEUS: But I'm the one who's going to be abased! I'll say it was all my fault.

FATHER (*a whistle from very much nearer; he falls nervously on his parcels*): The train, the train, my boy! Orpheus, don't carry on this painful scene which I find quite incomprehensible. Come with me. You can explain as we go along.

ORPHEUS: I'm not going with you, Father. I may join you again a little later.

FATHER: Why do you have to follow me? We've both got tickets.

The train whistles.

ORPHEUS: I'll telephone Tortoni straight away. (*Goes to desk.*) Madame, can I telephone from here?

FATHER (*catching him back*): Listen, my boy. Don't telephone that animal. I'd rather tell you straight away. The harpist's job . . .

ORPHEUS: Well?

FATHER: Well – he never offered it to me.

ORPHEUS: What?

FATHER: I said it to make you think better of me. I got wind of the job and begged him to have me. He refused.

ORPHEUS (*after a short pause*): I see . . . (*Says gently:*) I thought you could have that job. It's a pity. It would have settled so many things. (*Pause.*)

FATHER (*gently*): I am old, Orpheus . . .

The train whistles again.

ORPHEUS (*suddenly, in a sort of fever*): Take the train all the same, please, please, Father; go to Palavas-les-Flots; there are plenty of cafés there. It's the height of the season. I promise you you'll be able to earn your living!

FATHER: With nothing but the harp . . . you're joking!

ORPHEUS: But that's what people like – they always noticed the harp. You see so few about. Every beggar plays the violin in the street. But the harp – you've said it often enough yourself – that was what made us both look like artists.

FATHER: Yes, but you play the violin very well, and the women thought you were young and charming. They dug their elbows into their escorts and made them put two francs into the plate. When I'm alone, they'll keep their elbows to themselves.

ORPHEUS (*trying to laugh*): Of course they won't, Father – the more mature ones. You're an old Don Juan still!

FATHER (*throwing a glance at the cashier who humiliated him earlier and stroking his beard*): Between ourselves, an old Don Juan for chambermaids in cheap hotels . . . and only ugly chambermaids . . .

ORPHEUS: You're exaggerating, Father – you're still successful when you choose!

FATHER: So I tell you, but it doesn't always happen as I say. Besides, I've never told you this, my boy. I brought you up, I had my paternal pride – I don't know if you've noticed . . . I . . . I play the harp very badly. (*There is a terrible silence;* ORPHEUS *hangs his head; he cannot help smiling a little.*)

ORPHEUS: You couldn't help noticing, Father.

FATHER: You see, you say so yourself . . . (*Another pause.*)

The train whistles very close.

ORPHEUS (*shaking him suddenly*): Father, I can't do anything more for you. If I were rich, I'd give you some money. But I haven't any. Go and take your train. Keep everything we've got, and good luck.

FATHER: Just now you said you couldn't leave me!

ORPHEUS: Just now, yes. Now I can.

We hear the train coming into the station.

Here's your train. Hurry, pick up the harp.

FATHER (*still struggling*): You've met someone, haven't you?

ORPHEUS: Yes, Father.

FATHER: The girl who came and asked me who was playing the violin just now?

ORPHEUS (*kneeling in front of the suitcases*): Yes, Father. (*Takes some things from one case, puts them into the other.*)

FATHER: I talked a little with these people. She's an actress, you know, a tenth-rate company that plays in flea-pits. She's no better than she ought to be.

ORPHEUS: Yes, Father. We really must hurry . . .

FATHER (*kneeling, too, and rummaging in suitcases*): To think I'd found you an excellent girl, wonderful figure, gold medallist from the Marseilles Conservatoire – a Greek profile. A pianist! We could have given trios. I'd have taken up the cello . . . I'd never have believed this of you, Orpheus!

ORPHEUS: Neither would I, Father. Please hurry.

FATHER: I shall curse you! This will cost you dear!

ORPHEUS: Yes, Father.

FATHER (*rising*): Laugh away. I've still got a few hundred francs. I can earn my living from day to day; you'll have nothing.

ORPHEUS (*laughing, in spite of himself, and catching him by the shoulders*): My father, my dear old father, my terrible father. I'm very fond of you, but I can do nothing more for you.

LOUDSPEAKER (*outside*): Passengers for Béziers, Montpellier, Sete, Palavas-les-Flots.

ORPHEUS: Quick, you're going to miss it. You've got the harp, the big suitcase? I've got two hundred francs, keep the rest.

FATHER: Don't be so generous!

LOUDSPEAKER: Passengers for Béziers, Montpellier, Sete, Palavas-les-Flots!

FATHER (*suddenly*): Do you think I could get a rebate on your ticket?

ORPHEUS (*embracing him*): I don't know. I'm so happy, Father. I love her. I'll write to you. You ought to be a little pleased to see me happy. I so much want to live!

FATHER (*loading himself up*): I'll never be able to manage alone.

ORPHEUS: I'll help you. You must get a porter.

FATHER (*crying from the doorway like a ridiculous curse, and dropping some of his parcels in the process*): You're deserting your father for a woman! A woman who probably doesn't love you in return!

ORPHEUS (*crying out, too, following him*): I'm so happy, Father...

VOICE (*outside*): Mind the doors!

FATHER (*before going out*): You're sending me away to die!

ORPHEUS (*pushing him*): Hurry, Father, hurry!

Whistles, noise of the porters, steam. Suddenly, we hear the train starting up. EURYDICE *enters with a small suitcase and sits in a corner, making herself very inconspicuous.* ORPHEUS *comes back; he goes to her. She looks at him.*

It's all over.

EURYDICE (*comically*): It's all over with me, too.

ORPHEUS (*kissing her head*): Forgive me. He's rather ridiculous. He's my father.

EURYDICE: You mustn't ask me to forgive you. The woman talking about love just now, with all those noises, was my mother. I didn't dare tell you.

They are facing each other, smiling gently.

ORPHEUS: I'm glad you were ashamed. It's as if we were brothers.

EURYDICE (*smiling*): I can see you dragging along behind him, with your violin . . .

ORPHEUS: He used to play in an orchestra, but he always made me play on the terraces, between meals. One day a policeman picked us up. My father told him it would be too bad for him, that he had a cousin in the ministry. The policeman laughed at me. I was ten years old, and I cried. I was so ashamed. I thought we'd end up in the galleys . . .

EURYDICE (*crying, tears in her eyes*): Oh, my darling, and I wasn't even there! I'd have taken you by the hand, I'd have come with you when you were arrested. I'd have explained to you it wasn't so serious. When I was ten years old I knew everything.

ORPHEUS: In those days he played the trombone. He tried to play everything, poor dear, but he never succeeded. I used to say: 'I'm the son of the trombone', and they'd let me into the cinema. . . . How I loved *The Mysteries of New York* . . .

EURYDICE: And *The Mask of Death*! When you couldn't bear it any more, even after the fourth instalment. . . . Oh, how I wish I could have been beside you on the hard little seats. I wish I could have eaten oranges with you in the interval, asked if Pearl White's cousin really was a traitor, and what the Chinaman was thinking. . . . How I wish I could have been a child with you! What a pity it is . . .

ORPHEUS: It's all over now. We can't do anything about it. The oranges have been eaten, the cinemas repainted, and the heroine must be a very old lady.

EURYDICE (*gently*): It isn't fair . . .

A bell rings, then the whistle of an approaching train.

LOUDSPEAKER: Passengers for Toulouse, Béziers, Carcassonne, Platform Seven. The train arriving now.

ANOTHER LOUDSPEAKER (*farther away*): Passengers for Toulouse, Béziers, Carcassone, Platform Seven. The train arriving now.

Through the door opening on to the platform the members of the company pass with their baggage.

GIRL: Quickly, darling, or we'll have to stand all the way again. Naturally, the stars are travelling second. Who's paying the extra, I ask you? Who's paying the extra?

ANOTHER (*continuing a story*): Then, d'you know what she said to me? She said, I don't give a damn. I've my position to consider . . .

They have gone. The MOTHER *and* VINCENT *pass, overloaded with hat-boxes, enormous suitcases.*

MOTHER: Vincent, darling boy, the big case and the green box?

VINCENT: I've got them both. Off we go!

MOTHER: Be very careful. The handle's not very secure. It reminds me of one day at Buenos Aires. Sarah's hatbox burst open in the middle of the station. There were ostrich feathers all over the track . . .

They have gone. A fat man passes, puffing, behind them.

DULAC: Quickly, for God's sake, quickly! And check that the trunks have been loaded. Take your turn now. We mustn't lose our heads.

EURYDICE (*gently*): All the people in my life . . .

Running, and unable to run, comic, lamentable, absurd, the little MANAGER *comes last, tripping over too many suitcases, too many parcels slipping from his grasp. All in the midst of distant cries and the approaching whistles of the train.*

(*Gently, to* ORPHEUS.) Close the door.

ORPHEUS *closes the door. A sudden silence covers them.*

There. Now we're alone in the world.

LOUDSPEAKER (*farther away*): Passengers for Toulouse, Béziers, Carcassonne, Platform Seven. The train arriving now.

ORPHEUS *has gently come back to her. Noise of train reaching the station and a cry, a cry which becomes a noise that swells and stops suddenly, giving place to a terrible silence. The* CASHIER *has stood up and tried to see. The* WAITER *runs across the stage, calling to them as he passes:*

WAITER: Someone's thrown himself in front of the express – a young man!

People pass, running along the platform. ORPHEUS *and* EURYDICE *are facing each other, unable to look at one another. They say nothing. The* YOUNG MAN *in the macintosh appears on the platform. He comes in, then shuts the door and looks at them.*

EURYDICE (*gently*): I couldn't help it. I love you and I didn't love him.

There is a pause. They stare straight ahead. The YOUNG MAN *in the macintosh comes up to them.*

YOUNG MAN (*in an expressionless voice, without taking his eyes off them*): He threw himself in front of the engine. The shock itself must have killed him.

EURYDICE: How horrible!

YOUNG MAN: No. He chose a fairly good method. Poison is very slow, and causes so much suffering. One vomits, and twists about, and it is all disgusting. It's the same with sleeping-draughts. People think they'll go to sleep, but it's a death in the midst of hiccoughs and bad smells. (*He has come nearer, calm and smiling.*) Believe me . . . the easiest of all when you've very tired, when you've gone a long way with the same idea, is to slip into the water as if it were a bed. . . .

You stifle for a second, with a magnificent succession of visions . . . then you go to sleep. That's all!

EURYDICE: You don't think it hurt him to die?

YOUNG MAN (*gently*): It never hurts to die. Death never hurts anybody. Death is gentle. . . . What makes you suffer when you take certain poisons, or give yourself a clumsy wound, is life itself. The last remains of life. You must confide yourself more frankly to death as if to a dear friend. A friend with strong and delicate hands.

ORPHEUS *and* EURYDICE *are pressed against each other.*

EURYDICE (*gently, like an explanation*): We couldn't help ourselves. We love each other.

YOUNG MAN: Yes, I know. I've been listening to you. A fine young man, and a pretty girl. Ready to play the game without cheating, to the bitter end. Without any of those little concessions to comfort or ease which ageing and prosperous lovers allow themselves. Two courageous little animals, with supple limbs and sharp white teeth, ready to fight till dawn, as they should, and fall together, mortally wounded.

EURYDICE (*murmuring*): We don't even know you . . .

YOUNG MAN: But I know you. I'm very glad to have met you both. You're leaving here together? There's only one more train tonight. The train for Marseilles. Perhaps you'll be taking it?

ORPHEUS: Perhaps.

YOUNG MAN: I'm going there myself. I hope I'll have the pleasure of meeting you again?

He bows and exists. ORPHEUS *and* EURYDICE *turn to each other. They are standing, looking very small, in the middle of the empty hall.*

ORPHEUS (*gently*): My love.

EURYDICE: My dear love.

ORPHEUS: Our story is beginning . . .

EURYDICE: I'm a little afraid. . . . Are you good, or wicked? What's your name?

ORPHEUS: It's Orpheus. What's yours?

EURYDICE: Eurydice.

Curtain

Act Two

A room in a provincial hotel – huge, sombre and dirty. The ceilings are too high, lost in shadow, dusty double curtains, a big iron bed, a screen, a miserable light.

ORPHEUS *and* EURYDICE *are lying on the bed, fully dressed.*

ORPHEUS: To think everything might have gone wrong. . . . Supposing you'd turned to the right, I to the left. Not even that. Nothing more important than the flight of a bird, a child's cry, to make you turn your head for a second. I'd be busy scraping my fiddle on the terraces at Perpignan with father.

EURYDICE: And I'd be playing *The Orphans of the Storm* at the municipal theatre of Avignon. Mother and I play the two orphans.

ORPHEUS: Last night I thought of all the luck that brought us together. The little boy and the little girl, two strangers who one day began their journey, many years ago – a journey which took them both to that blessed railway station. . . . To think we might never have met; that we might have mistaken the day or the station.

EURYDICE: Or met while we were still too little, with parents who'd have taken us by the hand and dragged us away.

ORPHEUS: But we didn't mistake the day, or the minute. We never missed a step during the whole eventful journey. We're very clever.

EURYDICE: Yes, my darling.

ORPHEUS (*powerful and gay*): We're much stronger than the whole world, both of us.

EURYDICE (*looking at him with a little smile*): My hero! All the same, you were very frightened yesterday when we came into this room.

ORPHEUS: Yesterday we weren't stronger than all the people in the world. I didn't want our love to be at the mercy of this last little chance.

EURYDICE (*gently*): There are some things that one doesn't want to have in this world, and which are there, quiet and enormous, like the sea.

ORPHEUS: To think we might have been nothing, yesterday, when we came into this room. Not even a brother and sister as we are at this moment; nothing but two smiling enemies, polite and distant, talking of other things. Oh! How I hate love . . .

EURYDICE: Sh! You shouldn't say so . . .

ORPHEUS: Now, at least, we know each other. We know how heavy a sleeping head feels, the sound of our laughter. Now we have our memories to protect us.

EURYDICE: A whole evening, a whole night, a whole day – how rich we are!

ORPHEUS: Yesterday, we had nothing. We knew nothing, and we came into this room by chance, under the eye of that terrible waiter with the moustache who was sure we were going to make love. We began to undress, quickly, standing, face to face . . .

EURYDICE: You threw your clothes like a madman into the four corners of the room . . .

ORPHEUS: You were shaking all over. You couldn't undo the little buttons of your dress and I watched you pull them off without making a movement to help you. And then, when you were naked, suddenly you were ashamed.

EURYDICE (*hanging her head*): I thought I ought to be beautiful as well, and I wasn't sure . . .

ORPHEUS: We stood like that for a long time, face to face, without speaking, without daring to speak. . . . Oh, we were too poor, too naked, and it was too unjust to have to risk everything like that on a single throw. Then suddenly a wave of tenderness took me by the throat because I saw you had a tiny red spot on your shoulder.

EURYDICE: Then afterwards, it all became so simple . . .

ORPHEUS: You laid your head against me and fell asleep. And suddenly I felt myself becoming strong, filled with the strength of the weight of your head. It seemed to me we were lying naked on a shore and my tenderness was a rising sea that would little by little envelop our two bodies where we lay. . . . As if it needed our struggle and our nakedness on this tumbled bed to make us really two comrades.

EURYDICE: Oh, my darling – you thought all that and left me to sleep . . .

ORPHEUS: You said things in your dreams I couldn't answer . . .

EURYDICE: Did I? I often talk in my sleep. I hope you didn't listen.

ORPHEUS: Of course I did.

EURYDICE: I call that very mean of you! Instead of sleeping honestly, you spy on me. How do you think I can know what I say when I'm asleep?

ORPHEUS: I only understood three words. You sighed a terrible deep sigh. Your lips trembled a little, and then you said: 'It's so difficult.'

EURYDICE (*repeating*): It's so difficult.

ORPHEUS: What was so difficult?

EURYDICE (*stays for a moment without answering, then shakes her head and says in a little voice*): I don't know, my darling. I was dreaming.

Knock at the door. It is the WAITER, *who enters immediately. He has big grey moustaches, and a strange air.*

WAITER: Did you ring, sir?

ORPHEUS: No.

WAITER: Oh! I thought you did. (*Hesitates for moment, then goes out, saying:*) Excuse me, sir.

EURYDICE (*as soon as he has gone*): D'you think they're real?

ORPHEUS: What?

EURYDICE: His moustaches.

ORPHEUS: Of course. They don't look real. It's only false ones that look real – everyone knows that.

EURYDICE: He doesn't look as noble as the waiter at the station.

ORPHEUS: The one from the Comédie Française? He may have been noble, but he was very conventional. Under his imposing façade, I think he was a weakling. This one has more mystery about him.

EURYDICE: Yes. Too much. I don't like people with too much mystery. They frighten me a little. Don't they you?

ORPHEUS: A little, but I didn't like to tell you.

EURYDICE (*pressing herself to him*): Oh, my darling, hold me very tight. How lucky it is that there are two of us.

ORPHEUS: There are so many characters in our story already. . . . Two waiters, a noble weakling, a strange moustache, the lovely cashier and her enormous breasts . . .

EURYDICE: Such a pity she never said anything to us!

ORPHEUS: In all stories there are silent characters like her. She didn't say anything, but she watched us all the time. If she hadn't been silent all the time, what a lot of stories she could tell about us . . .

EURYDICE: And the porter?

ORPHEUS: The one who stammered?

EURYDICE: Yes, my darling. Wasn't he sweet? I'd have liked to put him in a box and keep him, with his fat watch-chain and brand-new cap.

ORPHEUS: Remember how he told us the names of all the stations where we didn't have to change, to make us remember, without any possible doubt, the name of the station where we really had to change!

EURYDICE: He was quite enchanting. I'm sure he brought us luck. But the other one, the brute, the conductor—

ORPHEUS: That fool! The one who couldn't understand we had a third-class ticket for Perpignan and another for Avignon, so what we wanted was to pay the difference on two second-class tickets to Marseilles?

EURYDICE: Yes, that one. Wasn't he ugly and stupid with his greasy uniform, his self-importance, and his oily fat cheeks?

ORPHEUS: He is our first ignoble character. There'll be others, you'll see. . . . All happy stories are full of despicable characters . . .

EURYDICE: Oh, but I refuse to keep him. I'll send him away. You must tell him I don't want him any more. I won't have such an idiot in my memories of you.

ORPHEUS: It's too late, my darling, we have no right to reject anyone.

EURYDICE: Then, all our lives, this dirty, self-satisfied man will be a part of our first day together?

ORPHEUS: All our lives.

EURYDICE: And the horrible old lady in black – the one I put out my tongue at because she was being unkind to her little maid. Will she be there, too, always?

ORPHEUS: Always – beside the little girl who never took her eyes off you, the big dog that insisted on following you, and all our charming characters.

EURYDICE: Don't you think we could just remember the first day with the big dog, the little girl, the gipsies who were dancing in the square and the little man with the stutter? . . . Are you sure we couldn't just forget the bad ones and only keep the good?

ORPHEUS: It would be too beautiful.

EURYDICE: Don't you think we could even try and remember them a little less ugly than they were – just for that very first day? Make the conductor a little less self-satisfied, the horrid lady a little less beastly, a little less hypocritical . . . or else make her maid a little fatter, so that the shopping-bag would seem less heavy?

ORPHEUS: Out of the question. They have happened now, the good with the evil. They've danced their little pirouettes, said their three words in your life . . . and there they are, inside you, as they are, for ever.

EURYDICE (*suddenly*): Then, you mean, if you've seen a lot of ugly things in your life, they stay inside you, too?

ORPHEUS: Yes.

EURYDICE: Carefully lying side by side, all the ugly pictures, all the people, even the ones we hate, even the ones we've run away from? All the sad words you've heard, do you think they still go on talking inside us? And everything you've ever done, does one's body remember that, too, d'you think?

ORPHEUS: Yes.

EURYDICE: You're sure that even the words we said without meaning them, the ones we can't recall, are still inside us when we talk?

ORPHEUS (*trying to kiss her*): Of course, darling fool . . .

EURYDICE (*freeing herself*): Wait, don't kiss me. Explain. Are you sure what you've just told me is true, or is it only what you think? Do other people say it, too?

ORPHEUS: Of course.

EURYDICE: Clever people? I mean, people who ought to know, people one ought to believe?

ORPHEUS: Of course.

EURYDICE: Then we can never really be alone, with all that around us. We can never be sincere, even when we mean what we say with all our strength. . . . If all the words are there, all the filthy bursts of laughter, if all the hands that have ever touched you are still sticking to your flesh, none of us can really change?

ORPHEUS: What are you talking about?

EURYDICE (*after a pause*): Do you think we'd do the same, if when we were little we knew that one day it would be vitally important to be clean and pure? And when we say these things – when we say: I made that movement, I said those words, I listened to that sentence, I deserted that man . . . (*She stops.*) . . . When one says those same things to someone else – to the man you love, for instance – do they think that kills all your memories around you?

ORPHEUS: Yes. They call that confessing yourself. Afterwards, they say that we are washed clean again, shining and pure . . .

EURYDICE: Oh! Are they very sure of that?

ORPHEUS: So they say.

EURYDICE (*after thinking for a little*): Yes, yes, but if ever they were wrong, or if they just said that for the effect; supposing they go on living twice as strong, twice as powerful, for having been repeated; if ever the other person began to remember, for always. . . . You can tell your clever people I don't trust them, and I think it's better not to say a word. . . . (ORPHEUS *looks at her; she sees this and adds quickly, pressing herself against him:*) Or else, my darling, when it's simple, as it was for us two yesterday, to tell everything, like me.

The WAITER *knocks and enters.*

WAITER: Did you ring, sir?

ORPHEUS: No.

WAITER: Oh! Sorry I disturbed you. (*Turns to go, then adds:*) I ought to tell you, sir, the bell is out of order. If you want me at any time, it's better if you call.

ORPHEUS: Thank you.

They think the WAITER *is going, but he changes his mind, crosses the room and goes to the double curtains; he opens and closes them again.*

WAITER: The curtains work.

ORPHEUS: So we see.

WAITER: In some rooms it's the opposite. The bell works and the curtains don't. (*Starts to go, then says again:*) Still, if monsieur tries to make them work later, and they don't, you've only to ring . . . (*Stops.*) I mean, call, because, as I said before, the bell . . . (*Makes a gesture and exits.*)

ORPHEUS: He's our first eccentric. We'll have lots of others. I should think he's really a very good man, entirely without malice.

EURYDICE: Oh, no. He looked at me all the time. Didn't you see how he kept looking at me?

ORPHEUS: You're dreaming.

EURYDICE: Oh, I liked the other much better – the nice one from the Comédie Française. . . . You could feel that even in a tragedy he wouldn't be very dangerous . . .

The WAITER *knocks and enters again. He gives very clearly the impression of having been behind the door.*

WAITER: Excuse me, sir. I forgot to tell you, madame asks if you'll be good enough to go downstairs. There's something missing on your form. Madame must send it in tonight and it isn't complete.

ORPHEUS: Does she want me right away?

WAITER: Yes, sir, if you'll be so kind.

ORPHEUS: All right, I'll come with you. (*To* EURYDICE.) Get dressed while I'm gone, then we'll go out for dinner.

The WAITER *opens the door for* ORPHEUS *and goes out after him. He comes back almost at once and goes to* EURYDICE, *who has raised herself on the bed.*

WAITER (*holding out an envelope*): Here's a letter for you. I was told to give it to you when you were alone. Madame isn't in her office. I was lying. There's only one floor to go. You have thirty seconds to read it.

He remains standing in front of her. EURYDICE *has taken the letter, trembling a little. She opens it, reads it, tears it into tiny pieces without moving a muscle of her face. Then she makes to throw away the bits.*

Never use the basket. (*He goes to the basket, kneels down and begins to pick up the pieces, which he stuffs into the pocket of his apron.*) Have you known each other long?

EURYDICE: One whole day.

WAITER: Then everything should still be fine.

EURYDICE (*gently*): Yes, it should be.

WAITER: The numbers I've seen passing through this room lying on the bed, just like you. And not only good-looking ones. Some were too fat, or too thin, or real monsters. All using their saliva to say 'our love'. Sometimes, when it's getting dark, as it is now, I seem to see them all over again – all together. The room is humming with them. Ah, love isn't very pretty.

EURYDICE (*hardly audible*): No.

ORPHEUS (*entering*): You still here?

WAITER: Just going, sir.

ORPHEUS: The manageress wasn't there.

WAITER: I must have taken too long coming up. I suppose she couldn't wait. It doesn't matter, sir; it will do this evening. (*Looks at them both again and goes out.*)

ORPHEUS: What was he doing here?

EURYDICE: Nothing. He was describing all the other lovers he's seen passing through this room.

ORPHEUS: Very amusing!

EURYDICE: He says sometimes he seems to see them all together. The whole room is humming with them.

ORPHEUS: And you listened to such stupidity?

EURYDICE: Perhaps it wasn't so stupid. You, who know everything, said that all the people one had ever met go on living in our memories. Perhaps a room remembers, too. . . . All the people who have been here are around us, coupled together, the fat ones, the thin ones, real monsters . . .

ORPHEUS: Little lunatic!

EURYDICE: The bed is full of them. How ugly love can be.

ORPHEUS (*dragging her away*): Let's go out to dinner. The streets are flushing with the first lamps of evening. We'll go and dine in a little restaurant smelling of garlic. You'll drink from a glass a thousand lips have touched, and the thousand fat behinds that have hollowed out the leather bench will make a tiny place for you where you'll be very comfortable. Come, let's go.

EURYDICE (*resisting*): You're laughing – you're always laughing. You're so strong.

ORPHEUS: Ever since yesterday! A hero! You said so yourself.

EURYDICE: Yes, yes, a hero who understands nothing, who feels nothing, who is so sure of himself he goes straight forward. Ah, you can take things lightly, you others – yes – now that you have made me so heavy. . . . You say things the moment you least expect them, you bring to life all the dirty lovers who have done things between these four walls, and then you don't give it another thought. You go out to dinner, saying, it's a fine day, the lamps are shining and the restaurant smells of garlic.

ORPHEUS: So will you, in a minute. Come, let's get out of here.

EURYDICE: It isn't nice here any more. It doesn't feel nice. How brief it was . . .

ORPHEUS: What's the matter? You're trembling.

EURYDICE: Yes.

ORPHEUS: You're quite pale.

EURYDICE: Yes.

ORPHEUS: How strange you look. I've never seen you look like this. (*He tries to make her follow him; she turns away.*)

EURYDICE: Don't look at me. When you look at me, I can feel it. It's as if you had put your two hands on my back, and entered, burning, into me. Don't look at me.

ORPHEUS: I've been looking at you ever since yesterday. (*He draws her away; she lets herself go.*)

EURYDICE (*murmuring, beaten*): You are strong, you know. . . . You look such a thin little boy and you are stronger than anyone. When you play your violin, like yesterday in the station, or when you talk, I turn into a little snake. . . . There's nothing I can do except crawl along slowly towards you.

ORPHEUS (*putting his arms round her, warming her*): Are you happy, little serpent?

EURYDICE: Sometimes you are quiet. Then I think I'm as free as I used to be. I pull on my thread with all my strength for a long minute. But you begin to talk again, the thread winds round the bobbin, and I come back towards my snare, content . . .

ORPHEUS: You ask such a terrible lot of things. Little snakes should warm themselves in the sun, drink milk and purr.

EURYDICE (*gently*): It's only cats that purr.

ORPHEUS (*stroking her hair*): It doesn't matter. Purr, I'm holding you close.

EURYDICE: You're a traitor. You scratch my head, I go to sleep in the sun of your being.

ORPHEUS: Then you say: 'It's so difficult.'

EURYDICE (*crying out suddenly and freeing herself*): Darling!

ORPHEUS: Yes.

EURYDICE: I'm so afraid it may be too difficult.

ORPHEUS: What?

EURYDICE: The first day, everything seems to easy. The first day all you have to do is to invent. You're sure we haven't invented everything?

ORPHEUS (*taking her head in his hands*): I'm sure I love you, and you love me. Sure as the stones, sure as the things made of wood and iron.

EURYDICE: Yes, but perhaps you thought I was someone else. And when you see me as I am . . .

ORPHEUS: Since yesterday I've been looking at you. I've heard you talking in your sleep.

EURYDICE: Yes, but I didn't say much. Supposing I go to sleep tonight and tell you everything?

ORPHEUS: Everything? What's everything?

EURYDICE: Stale and sticky words, ancient history. Or if someone, one of our characters, came and told you . . .

ORPHEUS: What could they come and tell me about you? I know you better than they do, now.

EURYDICE: Are you sure? (*She lifts her head and looks at him.*)

ORPHEUS (*continuing with joyous strength*): My little soldier, I've had you under my orders for a whole day, and I know you now. I've been rather horrid, haven't I, playing the captain ever since yesterday? 'Quick, here's the train. Get into the last carriage. Keep our places. I'm going to look for the man with the pillows. Wake up, this is Marseilles. We're getting out. Cheer up, the hotel's rather far, but we haven't enough money for a taxi. . . .' And the bewildered little soldier, her eyes still filled with sleep, picks up her suitcases with a little smile. One, two, one, two, and she follows her captain bravely into the night. . . . To think I could have brought a grand lady with me, wearing a hat with feathers and high-heeled shoes tap-tapping as she walked! I should have died of fear when I asked for a room. And in the carriage under the eyes of all those men pretending to be asleep so they could more easily strip you in imagination. . . . Who knows? Maybe she would have smiled, pulled up her skirt with a little movement, dropped her head on one side, pleased that the whole carriage wanted to take her and were only pretending to be asleep. . . . Oh, I should have died of shame . . . But my silent little brother turned into a wooden figure at my side. With crossed legs, a skirt grown suddenly mysteriously long, hidden hands, quite stiff. A little mummy blind to the glances of the false sleepers who, disappointed began to forget, snoring one after the other . . . I never thanked you for that.

EURYDICE (*gently, with lowered head*): You shouldn't thank me.

ORPHEUS: I haven't thanked you either for your courage . . .

EURYDICE (*faltering*): My courage?

ORPHEUS: For the days that will soon be here when we'll go without our dinner, smoking our last cigarette, one puff in turn. For the dresses you'll pretend not to see in the windows; for the sneering commercial travellers, the hostile hotel managers, the concierges . . . I haven't thanked you for the beds made up, the rooms swept out, the washing-up, your reddened hands, and the glove with a hole in it – the kitchen smell still caught up in your hair. Everything you gave when you agreed to follow me. (*Her head is still lowered; he looks at her in silence.*) I didn't think it would be possible to meet a comrade who would go with you, firm and lively, carrying her bag and not liking to smile either. The little silent companion who takes on all the jobs and at night is warm and beautiful beside you. A woman for you alone, more tender, more secret than the ones men are obliged to drag around all day, dressed in creations. My wild one, my savage, my little foreigner . . . I woke last night to ask myself if I wasn't as clumsy as all the others, full of stupid pride, and if I really did deserve to have you.

EURYDICE (*has raised her head and stares at him in the growing darkness*): You really think all that of me?

ORPHEUS: Yes, my love.

EURYDICE (*thinks a little, then says*): It's true. She'd be a very charming Eurydice.

ORPHEUS: It is you.

EURYDICE: Yes. You're right. She's the very wife for you. (*Short pause; she says gently in an odd little voice, stroking his hair:*) Mademoiselle Eurydice, your wife . . .

ORPHEUS (*springing up, strong and joyful*): I salute you! And now will you come and eat? The snake-charmer can't blow his flute any longer – he's dying of hunger.

EURYDICE (*in a different voice*): Put on the lights.

ORPHEUS: There's a sensible thing to say! Lights up everywhere. Floods of light. Drive away the phantoms.

ORPHEUS *turns on the switch. A hard light fills the room, making it ugly.* EURYDICE *has risen.*

EURYDICE: Darling, I don't want to go to a restaurant, with all those people. If you like, I'll go downstairs, I'll buy something, and we can eat it here.

ORPHEUS: In the room humming with noises?

EURYDICE: Yes. It doesn't matter any more.

ORPHEUS (*moving*): It'll be great fun. I'll come down with you.

EURYDICE (*quickly*): No, let me go alone. (*He stops.*) I'd like to do your shopping for you, just this once, like a respectable married woman.

ORPHEUS: All right. Buy all sorts of things.

EURYDICE: Yes.

ORPHEUS: We must have a party meal.

EURYDICE: Yes, darling.

ORPHEUS: Exactly as if we had plenty of money. It's a miracle the rich can never understand. . . . Buy a pineapple – a real one, just as the good Lord made it, not a sad American pineapple in a tin. We haven't got a knife. We'll never be able to eat it. But that's the way pineapples protect themselves.

EURYDICE (*with a little laugh, her eyes filled with tears*): Yes, my darling.

ORPHEUS: Buy some flowers – lots and lots of flowers . . .

EURYDICE (*faltering, with her poor little smile*): You can't eat flowers . . .

ORPHEUS: Nor you can. We'll put them on the table. (*Looks round.*) We haven't got a table. Never mind, buy lots of flowers all the same. And buy some fruit. Peaches, fat hot-house peaches, apricots, golden pears. A little bread to demonstrate the serious side of our nature, and a bottle of white wine we can drink out of the tooth-glass. Hurry, hurry! I'm dying of hunger.

EURYDICE *fetches her little hat and puts it on in front of the mirror.*

You're putting on your hat?

EURYDICE: Yes. (*Turns round suddenly and says in a strange hoarse voice:*) Adieu, my darling.

ORPHEUS (*cries to her, laughing*): You're saying good-bye, like at Marseilles?

EURYDICE (*from the doorway*): Yes.

She looks at him for a second longer, smiling and pityingly, and goes out abruptly. ORPHEUS *stays for a moment without moving, smiling at the absent* EURYDICE. *Suddenly his smile disappears, his face looks drawn, a vague fear seizes him, he runs to the door calling:*

ORPHEUS: Eurydice!

He opens the door, and recoils, stupefied. The YOUNG MAN *who spoke to them at the station is on the threshold, smiling.*

YOUNG MAN: She's just gone downstairs.

ORPHEUS *retreats, surprised, hesitating to recognize him.*

Don't you remember me? We met yesterday in the station restaurant, just after the accident. . . . You know, the young man who threw himself under the train. I've taken the liberty of coming to say good evening. I liked you both so much. We're neighbours. I'm in room eleven. (*Takes a step into the room, holding out a packet of cigarettes.*) Smoke? (ORPHEUS *takes a cigarette mechanically.*) I don't myself. (*Takes out a box of matches and lights one.*) Light?

ORPHEUS: Thanks. (*He closes the door again and asks mechanically:*) May I ask your name?

YOUNG MAN: When you meet people on journeys, half the charm is to know as little as possible about them. My name won't mean anything to you. Call me Monsieur Henri. (*He has come right into the room. He looks at* ORPHEUS *and smiles.* ORPHEUS *looks at him as if hypnotized.*) A fine town, Marseilles. This human ant-heap, this collection of riff-raff, this filth. There aren't as many suicides in the old port as they say, but all the same, it's a fine town. Do you expect to stay here long?

ORPHEUS: I don't know.

MONSIEUR HENRI: I didn't wait to be introduced before speaking to you yesterday. But you were so touching, the two of you, holding each other so closely in the middle of that huge hall. . . . A beautiful setting, wasn't it? Sombre and red, with the night falling and the station noises in the background . . . (*Looks at* ORPHEUS *for a long time, smiling.*) Little Orpheus and Mademoiselle Eurydice. . . . One doesn't get such a stroke of luck every day . . . I shouldn't have spoken to you. . . . Normally, I never speak to people. What's the good? But I couldn't resist the urge to know you better – I don't know why. You're a musician?

ORPHEUS: Yes.

MONSIEUR HENRI: I like music. I like everything that is sweet and happy. To tell the truth, I like happiness. But lets talk about you. It's of no interest to talk about me. But first let's have something to drink. It helps the conversation. (*Rises and rings the bell. He looks at* ORPHEUS *and smiles during the short wait.*) It gives me a great deal of pleasure to talk to you like this.

The WAITER *has entered.*

What'll you have? Whisky? Brandy?

ORPHEUS: If you like.

MONSIEUR HENRI: Some brandy, please.

WAITER: Just one?

MONSIEUR HENRI: Yes. (*To* ORPHEUS.) Forgive me, won't you. I never drink.

The WAITER *has gone out. He still watches* ORPHEUS, *smiling.*

I'm really delighted to have met you.

ORPHEUS (*embarrassed*): It's kind of you to say so.

MONSIEUR HENRI: You must be wondering why I take such an interest in you. (ORPHEUS *makes a movement.*) I was at the back of the restaurant yesterday when she came to you, as if called by your music. These moments when we catch a glimpse of Fate laying her snares are very exciting, aren't they?

The WAITER *has returned.*

Ah, your brandy.

WAITER: Here you are, sir. One brandy.

ORPHEUS: Thank you.

The WAITER *goes out.*

MONSIEUR HENRI (*who has watched him*): Did you notice how slowly and insolently the waiter went out of the room?

ORPHEUS: No.

MONSIEUR HENRI (*going to listen at the door*): He's certainly gone back to his post behind the door. (*Comes back to* ORPHEUS.) I'm sure he's been in here on several different occasions with different excuses; I'm sure he's tried to speak to you?

ORPHEUS: Yes.

MONSIEUR HENRI: You see, I'm not the only one to take an interest in you . . . I'll wager that the commercial travellers, the station attendants, the little girls in the streets have smiled at you since yesterday . . .

ORPHEUS: Everyone is kind to lovers.

MONSIEUR HENRI: It isn't only kindness. Don't you think they look at you a little too closely?

ORPHEUS: No. Why?

MONSIEUR HENRI (*smiling*): No reason. (*Dreams for a moment, then suddenly takes his arm.*) Listen, my friend, there are two races of beings. A race numerous, fertile, happy – common clay, that eat their sausages, give birth to children, count their pennies, year in, year out, in spite of epidemics and wars, until the end of time; people who can live, ordinary people, people you can't imagine dead. And then there are the others, the nobles, the heroes. The ones you can quite well imagine laid out, pale and triumphant, with a guard of honour, or between two gendarmes. Hasn't that ever attracted you?

ORPHEUS: Never; and this evening less than usual.

MONSIEUR HENRI (*going to him and laying his hand on his shoulder; looking at him, almost tenderly*): It's a pity. You shouldn't believe too blindly in happiness. Particularly not when you belong to the good race. You're only laying up disappointments for yourself.

The WAITER *knocks and enters.*

WAITER: There's a young lady here asking for Mademoiselle Eurydice. I told her she had gone out, but she doesn't seem to believe me. She insists on seeing you. May I ask her to come up?

GIRL (*entering and pushing the* WAITER *aside*): I've already come. Where's Eurydice?

ORPHEUS: She's gone out, mademoiselle. Who are you?

GIRL: One of her friends from the company. I must talk to her at once.

ORPHEUS: I tell you she's gone out. Besides, I don't think she has anything to say to you.

GIRL: You're wrong. She's got plenty to say. How long ago did she go out? Did she take her suitcase with her?

ORPHEUS: Her suitcase? Why should she take her suitcase? She's gone out to buy our dinner.

GIRL: She may have gone out to buy your dinner, but she had

very good reasons for taking her suitcase. She was supposed to meet us at the station to catch the eight-twelve train.

ORPHEUS (*crying out*): Meet who?

WAITER (*who has pulled out a fat copper watch*): It's ten minutes and forty seconds past eight now.

GIRL (*as if to herself*): She must be on the platform with him already. Thank you. (*She turns to go.*)

ORPHEUS (*catches her up in front of the door*): On the platform with who?

GIRL: Let me go. You're hurting me. You'll make me miss the train.

WAITER (*still looking at his watch*): Exactly eleven minutes past eight.

DULAC (*appearing in the doorway, to the* WAITER): It's eight-thirteen. Your watch is slow. The train has gone. (*To* ORPHEUS.) Let the girl go. I can answer you. On the platform with me.

ORPHEUS (*retreating*): Who are you?

DULAC: Alfredo Dulac. Eurydice's impresario. Where is she?

ORPHEUS: What do you want her for?

DULAC (*walking calmly into the room, chewing his cigar*): What do you want her for?

ORPHEUS: Eurydice is my mistress.

DULAC: Since when?

ORPHEUS: Since yesterday.

DULAC: She also happens to be mine. And has been, for a year.

ORPHEUS: You're lying!

DULAC (*smiling*): Because she forgot to tell you?

ORPHEUS: Eurydice told me everything before she came with me. For three months she'd been the mistress of the boy who threw himself under the train.

DULAC: Can you imagine anything so stupid! A young fool who was always playing such tricks. Everyone in the company was afraid of him. If the child said she was leaving him, he'd throw himself under the bus at Perpignan. What I don't understand is that she took the trouble to warn him. She slipped away without a sound, like a little bird . . .

ORPHEUS: Perhaps he was the only one she owed anything to.

DULAC: No. She forgot to come and tell me. Firstly because I'm the company manager. For two performances now I've had to fling on the understudy and that's never amusing. But also because the night before last – don't get excited – she spent the night with me.

ORPHEUS (*looking at him*): I don't know which you are – more detestable, or more ridiculous . . .

DULAC (*coming still farther forward*): Is that so?

ORPHEUS: In spite of all your airs, you're probably more ridiculous . . .

DULAC: Because the child was in this bed last night instead of mine? You're a child, too, my boy. A girl like Eurydice has to be humoured in her little caprices. She slept with the fool who killed himself yesterday, too. I can understand her liking you. You're good-looking, young . . .

ORPHEUS (*crying out*): I love Eurydice and she loves me!

DULAC: Did she tell you so?

ORPHEUS: Yes.

DULAC (*sitting calmly in the arm-chair*): She's an extraordinary girl. Luckily I know her so well.

ORPHEUS: Supposing I know her better than you?

DULAC: Since yesterday?

ORPHEUS: Yes, since yesterday.

DULAC: I don't pretend to be an expert. If it were a question of anything else – you look much more intelligent than I am – I'd probably say: 'Good', but there are two things I really understand. First my job . . .

ORPHEUS: And then, Eurydice?

DULAC: No, I don't make any such claim. I was going to use a much more modest expression: women. I've been an impresario for twenty years. I sell women, my boy, by the gross, to kick up their heels in provincial revues, or massacre the big arias from *Tosca* in a casino. I don't give a damn – besides, I love them. That makes at least one good reason out of two for pretending to understand them. Eurydice is perhaps an odd little girl – I'm the first to admit it – but considering the opportunities we've both had to see her, you'll agree with me that she is a woman . . .

ORPHEUS: No.

DULAC: How do you mean, no? She seemed to be an angel did she? Look at me squarely, my boy. Eurydice belonged to me for over a year. Do I look as though I could seduce an angel?

ORPHEUS: You're lying. Eurydice could never have belonged to you.

DULAC: You're her lover, so am I. Would you like me to describe her to you?

ORPHEUS (*recoiling*): No.

DULAC (*advancing, ignoble*): What's she like, your Eurydice? How do you get her out of bed in the morning? Can you drag her away from her thrillers and her cigarettes? Have you ever seen her for a moment without a scowl on her face like a little criminal? And her stockings? Could she find them when she once got up? Be frank with me. Admit her petticoat was hanging from the top of the cupboard, her shoes in the bathroom, her hat under the chair, and her bag completely lost. I've already bought her seven.

ORPHEUS: It isn't true.

DULAC: How do you mean, it isn't true! Is yours a tidy Eurydice? I don't believe in miracles. I hope, in any case, she's already made you start on the window-shopping. How many dresses has she asked you to buy since yesterday? How many hats? Between ourselves . . .

ORPHEUS: Eurydice came with me in the clothes she stood up in. With a single suitcase.

DULAC: I'm beginning to think we're not talking of the same person, or else she thought it wouldn't last for long. . . . She told you it would be for life? I'm sure she must have been sincere. She thought: 'It'll be for all my life, if he's strong enough to keep me, if papa Dulac doesn't find my tracks again, if he doesn't want to take me back.' And at the bottom of her heart, she must have known quite well that papa Dulac would find her. It's only what I would have expected of her.

ORPHEUS: No.

DULAC: Of course, my boy, of course. . . . Eurydice is a girl in a million, but her thought processes are exactly the same as any other girl's.

ORPHEUS: It isn't true!

DULAC: You won't admit anything's true! You're very odd. How long ago did she go downstairs?

ORPHEUS: Twenty minutes.

DULAC: Good. Is that true?

ORPHEUS: Yes.

DULAC: She insisted on going alone, didn't she?

ORPHEUS: Yes. She said it would be fun to buy our dinner alone.

DULAC: Is that true, too?

ORPHEUS: Yes.

DULAC: Very well, listen to me. Five minutes before I had a letter given to her, asking her to meet me on the platform.

ORPHEUS: No one brought her a letter. I haven't left her for for an instant since yesterday.

DULAC: Are you sure? (*He looks at the* WAITER; ORPHEUS *also looks at the* WAITER *without knowing why.*)

WAITER (*suddenly worried*): Excuse me, I think I'm being called. (*He disappears.*)

ORPHEUS: I did leave her for a moment, yes. That man came and told me I was wanted in the office.

DULAC: I told him to give my note to Eurydice when she was alone. He gave it to her while you were downstairs.

ORPHEUS (*going to him*): What did you say in your letter?

DULAC: I said I was expecting her on the eight-twelve train. I didn't have to say anything else . . . because Fate had knocked on her door and said: 'Eurydice, it's over.' I was sure she would obey me. It's only men who jump out of windows.

ORPHEUS: All the same, she didn't join you!

DULAC: That's true. She didn't come. But my Eurydice is

always late. I'm not very worried. Did you ask yours to buy a lot of things?

ORPHEUS: Some bread and fruit.

DULAC: And you say she went out twenty minutes ago? It seems a long time to me to buy bread and fruit. The street is full of shops. Maybe your Eurydice is unpunctual, too? (*To the* GIRL.) She must be at the station looking for us. Go and see.

ORPHEUS: I'm going with you!

DULAC: You're beginning to think she may have gone to meet us after all? I'm staying here.

ORPHEUS (*stops and cries to the* GIRL): If you see her, tell her . . .

DULAC: Quite useless. If she finds her at the station, then I'm right. Your faithful and tidy Eurydice was only a dream. And in that case, you have nothing more to say to her.

ORPHEUS (*calling to the* GIRL): Tell her I love her!

DULAC: She may perhaps shed a tear; she's very sentimental. That's all.

ORPHEUS (*still calling*): Tell her she isn't what the others think her. She is as I know her to be!

DULAC: Too complicated to explain at a railway station. Hurry along, and listen – I'm a sportsman – bring her here. In one minute she may be able to tell us herself what she is.

The GIRL *goes out, bumping into the* WAITER.

WAITER (*appearing in doorway*): Excuse me, sir . . .

ORPHEUS: What is it?

WAITER: There's an officer with a police van . . .

ORPHEUS: What does he want?

WAITER: He's asking if there's anyone here related to the young lady. She's had an accident, sir – in the bus for Toulon . . .

ORPHEUS (*crying like a madman*): Is she hurt? Is she downstairs?

He hurls himself out into the corridor. DULAC *follows him, throwing away his cigar with a stifled oath. The young* GIRL *disappears as well.*

DULAC (*as he goes out*): What the devil was she doing in the bus for Toulon?

The WAITER *is left facing* MONSIEUR HENRI, *who hasn't moved.*

WAITER: They'll never know what she was doing . . . she isn't hurt, she's dead. As they drove out of Marseilles the bus crashed into a petrol lorry. The other passengers were only cut by the glass. She's the only one . . . I saw her. They've laid her out in the police van. There's a tiny mark on her temple. You'd say she was asleep.

MONSIEUR HENRI (*does not seem to have heard; his hands driven into the pockets of his coat, he walks past the* WAITER; *in the doorway he turns round*): Make out my bill. I'm leaving. (*He goes out.*)

Curtain

Act Three

The station restaurant in shadow. It is night. A vague light comes from the platform, where only the signal lamps are lit. There is a strange humming noise coming from far away. The restaurant is empty. The chairs are piled on the tables. The stage is empty for a moment.

Then one of the doors from the platform opens slightly. MONSIEUR HENRI *enters, bringing* ORPHEUS *behind him, hatless, wearing a macintosh. He is haggard, exhausted.*

ORPHEUS (*looking round without understanding*): Where are we?

MONSIEUR HENRI: Don't you know?

ORPHEUS: I can't walk any farther.

MONSIEUR HENRI: You can rest now. (*Picks a chair off a table.*) Have a chair.

ORPHEUS (*sitting down*): Where are we? What did I have to drink? Everything's been turning round and round. What's been happening since yesterday?

MONSIEUR HENRI: It's still yesterday.

ORPHEUS (*realizing suddenly and crying out, trying to rise*): You promised . . .

MONSIEUR HENRI (*laying his hand on his shoulder*): Yes, I promised. Keep still. Relax. Have a cigarette? (*He holds out a cigarette, which* ORPHEUS *takes mechanically.*)

ORPHEUS (*still looking round while the match burns*): Where are we?

MONSIEUR HENRI: Guess.

ORPHEUS: I want to know where we are.

MONSIEUR HENRI: You told me you wouldn't be frightened.

ORPHEUS: I'm not frightened. All I want to know is if we've arrived at last.

MONSIEUR HENRI: Yes, we've arrived.

ORPHEUS: Where?

MONSIEUR HENRI: Just a little patience. (*He strikes another match, follows the wall round until he finds the electric light.*)

A tiny noise in the shadows, and a bracket lights up on the back wall, throwing out a meagre light.

D'you know now?

ORPHEUS: It's the station restaurant . . .

MONSIEUR HENRI: Yes.

ORPHEUS (*rising*): You were lying, weren't you?

MONSIEUR HENRI (*pushing him back in the chair*): No. I never lie. Keep still. Don't make a noise.

ORPHEUS: Why did you come into my room just now? I was lying on that tumbled bed. Utterly wretched. I was almost happy, shut up in my misery.

MONSIEUR HENRI (*in a low voice*): I couldn't bear to see you suffer.

ORPHEUS: What difference could it make to you if I were suffering?

MONSIEUR HENRI: I don't know. It's the first time it's happened. Something strange began to fail inside me. If you had gone on weeping, suffering, it would have begun to bleed like a wound . . . I was almost leaving the hotel. I put down my suitcase and came back again to comfort you. Then, as you wouldn't be comforted, I made you that promise to keep you quiet.

ORPHEUS: I am quiet now. I'm suffering in silence. If your nerves are sensitive, it should be enough for you.

MONSIEUR HENRI: You still don't believe me?

ORPHEUS (*taking his head in his hands*): I want to believe you with all my strength, but I don't believe you, no.

MONSIEUR HENRI (*laughs a little silently, then he pulls* ORPHEUS'S *hair*): Stubborn as a mule, aren't you? You're crying, and groaning and suffering, but you don't want to believe me. I like you very much. If I hadn't liked you so much, I'd have gone away yesterday as I always do. I wouldn't have gone into that room where you were sobbing.

I can't bear grief. (*He pulls his hair again with a strange sort of tenderness.*) Soon you won't be weeping any more – you won't have to ask yourself if you should or should not believe me.

ORPHEUS: Is she coming?

MONSIEUR HENRI: She is already here.

ORPHEUS: Here? (*Crying out suddenly.*) But she's dead. I saw them carry her away.

MONSIEUR HENRI: You want to understand, don't you? It's not enough that fate is making an enormous exception for you. You took my hand without a tremor, you followed me without even asking who I was, without slackening speed the whole night through, but on top of everything, you want to understand . . .

ORPHEUS: No. I want to see her again. That's all.

MONSIEUR HENRI: You aren't more curious than that? I bring you to the doors of death, and you think of nothing but your little friend. . . . You're perfectly right – death deserves nothing but your scorn. She throws out her huge nets, reaps haphazard, grotesque, enormous. An idiot capable of chopping off her own limbs with the rest. Those who have seen men getting on with the job, holding the trigger of a machine-gun, firing and bringing down their enemies with precision, know you are far more dangerous. Poor death . . . the fool. (*He has sat down near* ORPHEUS, *a little tired.*) I'm going to tell you a secret, just for yourself, because I'm fond of you. There's just one thing about death no one knows. She's very kind-hearted, horribly kind-hearted. She's afraid of tears and grief. Every time she can, whenever life allows her, she does it quickly . . . she unties, relaxes, while life persists, clutching blindly, even if the game is lost, even if the man cannot move, if he is disfigured, even if he might suffer always. Death alone is a friend. With the tip of her finger she can give the monster back his face, soothe the soul in torment she delivers.

ORPHEUS (*crying out suddenly*): I'd rather have had Eurydice disfigured, suffering, old!

MONSIEUR HENRI (*hanging his head, suddenly overcome*): Of course you would. You're all alike!

ORPHEUS: She has stolen Eurydice! This friend of yours! With her finger she has destroyed the young Eurydice, the gay Eurydice, the smiling Eurydice . . .

MONSIEUR HENRI (*rising suddenly as if he has had too much; then brusquely*): She's giving her back to you.

ORPHEUS: When?

MONSIEUR HENRI: At once. But listen carefully. Your happiness was over anyway. Those twenty-four hours, that pitiful little day, was all life had in store for you – your life – your cherished life. Today you wouldn't have been weeping because she was dead, but because she'd left you . . .

ORPHEUS: That's not true! She never went to meet that horrible man!

MONSIEUR HENRI: No. But she didn't come back to you either. She took the car for Toulon alone, without money, without baggage. Where was she flying to? What was she exactly, this little Eurydice you thought you could love?

ORPHEUS: Whatever she is, I love her still. I want to see her again. Ah, I beg of you, give her back to me, however imperfect. I want to suffer and be ashamed because of her. I want to lose her, and find her again. I want to hate her, and rock her gently afterwards, like a little child. I want to struggle, to suffer, to accept . . . I want to live.

MONSIEUR HENRI (*annoyed*): Of course you'll live . . .

ORPHEUS: With the mistakes, the failures, the despair, the fresh starts . . . the shame . . .

MONSIEUR HENRI (*looks at him, scornful and tender; murmurs*): Poor boy . . . (*He goes to him, and says in a different voice:*) Good-bye. She's being given back to you. She's out there, on the platform, standing on the same spot where you saw her yesterday for the first time – waiting for you, eternally. Do you remember the condition?

ORPHEUS (*already looking at the door*): Yes.

MONSIEUR HENRI: Say it out loud. If you forget, I can do nothing more for you.

ORPHEUS: I mustn't look at her.

MONSIEUR HENRI: It won't be easy.

ORPHEUS: If I look at her just once before the dawn, I lose her again for ever.

MONSIEUR HENRI (*stops, smiling*): You don't ask me why or how any more?

ORPHEUS (*still looking at the door*): No.

MONSIEUR HENRI (*still smiling*): Fine. Good-bye. You can start again from the beginning. Don't try to thank me. I'll see you later.

He goes out. ORPHEUS *stands for a moment without moving, then goes to the door and opens it on the deserted platform. First he says nothing, then in a low voice he asks without looking:*

ORPHEUS: Are you there?

EURYDICE: Yes, my darling. What a long time you've been.

ORPHEUS: I've been allowed to come back and fetch you. . . . Only I mustn't look at you before the morning.

EURYDICE (*appearing*): Yes, I know. They told me.

ORPHEUS (*taking her hand and pulling her along without looking at her; they cross the stage in silence until they reach a bench*): Come. We can wait for morning here. When the waiters arrive for the first train, at dawn, we shall be free. We'll ask them for some nice hot coffee and something to eat. You'll be alive. You haven't been too cold?

EURYDICE: Yes. That's the worst part. The terrible cold. But I've been forbidden to talk about anything. I can only tell you what happened up to the moment when the driver smiled into his little mirror and the petrol lorry fell on us like a mad beast.

ORPHEUS: The driver turned round to smile in the mirror?

EURYDICE: Yes. You know what the boys from the Midi are like. They think all the girls are looking at them. I didn't want to be looked at.

ORPHEUS: He was smiling at you.

EURYDICE: Yes. I'll explain it all later, my darling. He wrenched the steering-wheel round and everyone screamed.

I saw the lorry coming and the driver's smile twisting into a grimace. That's all. (*Pause. She adds in a little voice.*) After that I can't tell you anything.

ORPHEUS: Are you comfortable?

EURYDICE: Oh yes – here against you.

ORPHEUS: Put my coat round your shoulders. (*Puts his coat round her; pause; they are happy.*)

EURYDICE: Remember the waiter from the Comédie Française?

ORPHEUS: We'll see him again tomorrow.

EURYDICE: And the beautiful dumb cashier? Maybe we'll know what she thought of us at last? It's so convenient to be alive again. . . . As if we'd just met for the first time. (*She asks him as she did that first time:*) Are you good, or wicked? What's your name?

ORPHEUS (*entering into the game and smiling*): It's Orpheus. What's yours?

EURYDICE: Eurydice. . . . (*Then gently she adds:*) Only this time we've been warned. (*She hangs her head, then says after a tiny pause:*) Please forgive me. You must have been so afraid . . .

ORPHEUS: Yes. At first it's like a silent companion following you, staring at you from behind, listening to everything you say. Then suddenly, it leaps on you like a wild beast. At first it's a weight that becomes heavier and heavier on your shoulders, then it begins to move, to hammer on the back of your neck, to strangle you. You look at other people and they are calm, they have no beasts on their backs, they're not afraid, and they say: 'It's all right. She's just missed the tram. She's stopped to talk to someone . . .' But the beast is howling now and beating on your shoulder-blades. 'Does anyone miss trams in real life? No, you slip and fall under them when you get off. You bump into them when you try to cross the road. Does anyone in real life stop to talk? No!' You go mad suddenly, get carried off or run away. . . . Luckily, the waiter came in to deliver me with his real tragedy. When I saw you downstairs, lying in the van, it all stopped. I wasn't afraid any more.

EURYDICE: Did they put me in a van?

ORPHEUS: A police van. They laid you out on a bench at the back, with a policeman sitting beside you, like a little thief who had been arrested.

EURYDICE: Was I ugly?

ORPHEUS: There was a little blood on your temple. That's all. You seemed to be asleep.

EURYDICE: Asleep? If you knew how I was running. I was running as fast as I could go, like a mad thing. (*She stops; there is a tiny pause; she asks:*) You must have suffered horribly?

ORPHEUS: Yes.

EURYDICE: Please forgive me.

ORPHEUS (*in a low voice*): There's no need.

EURYDICE (*after another pause*): If they brought me back to the hotel it must have been because I was still holding my letter. I had written to you in the bus before we started. Did they give it to you?

ORPHEUS: No. They must have kept it at the police station.

EURYDICE: Ah! (*She asks, worried suddenly:*) Do you think they'll read it?

ORPHEUS: They may.

EURYDICE: D'you think we could stop them reading it? Couldn't we do something straight away? Send someone there, telephone them, tell them they have no right?

ORPHEUS: It's too late.

EURYDICE: But I wrote that letter to you! What I said was only for you. How could anyone else possibly read it? How could anyone else say those words? A fat man, with a dirty mind, perhaps, an ugly, self-satisfied, fat old man? He'll laugh, he'll surely laugh when he reads my agony. . . . Oh, stop him, stop him, please – please stop him reading it! It makes me feel as if I were naked in front of a stranger—

ORPHEUS: They may not even have opened the envelope.

EURYDICE: I hadn't time to close it! I was just going to when the lorry crashed into us. Probably that's why the driver looked at me in the glass. I put my tongue out, it made him smile, and I smiled, too . . .

ORPHEUS: You smiled. You could still smile?

EURYDICE: Of course not. I couldn't smile. You don't understand! I had just written you this letter where I told you I loved you, that I was suffering, but I had to go away . . . I put out my tongue to lick the envelope, he made a crack as all boys do, and everyone smiled . . . (*She stops, discouraged.*) Ah! It's not the same when you describe it. It's difficult. You see, it's too difficult . . .

ORPHEUS (*in a low voice*): What were you doing in the bus for Toulon?

EURYDICE: I was running away.

ORPHEUS: You had the letter from Dulac?

EURYDICE: Yes, that's why.

ORPHEUS: Why didn't you show me the letter when I came back?

EURYDICE: I couldn't.

ORPHEUS: What did he say in the letter?

EURYDICE: To meet him on the eight-twelve train, or else he'd come and fetch me.

ORPHEUS: Is that why you ran away?

EURYDICE: Yes. I didn't want you to see him.

ORPHEUS: You didn't think he might come and I'd see him just the same?

EURYDICE: Yes, but I was a coward. I didn't want to be there.

ORPHEUS: You've been his mistress?

EURYDICE (*crying out*): No! Is that what he told you? I knew he would, and you'd believe him! He's been chasing me for a long time; he hates me. I knew he'd tell you about me. I was afraid.

ORPHEUS: Why didn't you tell me yesterday, when I asked you to tell me everything? Why didn't you tell me you'd been his mistress?

EURYDICE: I wasn't.

ORPHEUS: Eurydice, now it would be better to tell me everything. No matter what happens, we are two poor wounded beings sitting on this bench, two poor souls talking without daring to look at each other—

EURYDICE: What must I say to make you believe me?

ORPHEUS: I don't know. That's what's so terrible . . . I don't know how I'm ever going to believe you . . . (*Pause; he asks, gently, humbly:*) Eurydice, so I won't have to worry afterwards, when you tell me the simplest things – tell me the truth now, even if it is terrible. Even if it will hurt me horribly. It can't hurt any more than the air I haven't been able to breathe since I've known you lied to me. . . . If it's too difficult to say, don't answer me, but please don't lie. Did that man tell the truth?

EURYDICE (*after an imperceptible pause*): No. He was lying.

ORPHEUS: You've never belonged to him?

EURYDICE: Never. (*There is a pause.*)

ORPHEUS (*in a low voice, staring straight in front of him*): If you're telling me the truth, it should be easy to see. Your eyes are as clear as a pool of water. If you're lying, or if you aren't sure of yourself, a dark green circle forms and shrinks around the pupil . . .

EURYDICE: The dawn will soon be here, my darling, and you can look at me . . .

ORPHEUS: Yes. (*Crying out suddenly.*) Into the depths of your eyes, in a single glance, like into water. To plunge head first into the depths of your eyes! Let me stay there! Let me drown there . . .

EURYDICE: Yes, my darling.

ORPHEUS: It's intolerable to be two! Two bodies, two envelopes, impenetrable around us. Each being complete with oxygen, with his blood, whatever we try to do, enclosed, alone, in this covering of flesh. We press ourselves one to the other, we rub each other to try to escape from this frightening solitude. A little pleasure, a little illusion, but we quickly find ourselves alone again, with our livers and our guts – our only friends.

EURYDICE: Be quiet!

ORPHEUS: So then we talk. We've discovered that. This sound of air in our throats and against our teeth. This human morse. Two prisoners tapping on the walls of their cells. Two prisoners who will never meet. Ah! We're all alone – don't you think we're too much alone?

EURYDICE: Come as close as you can to me.

ORPHEUS: Warmth, yes. Another warmth beside your own. That is something certain. A resistance, too, an obstacle. A warm obstacle. Then, someone must be there. I'm not altogether alone. I suppose we mustn't ask too much.

EURYDICE: Tomorrow, you can turn and look at me. Turn and kiss me.

ORPHEUS: Yes. For one moment I can enter into you. For one moment I can believe we are two twigs growing out of the same root. And then we must separate and become two again. Two mysteries. Two lies. Two people. (*He caresses her; dreams.*) There. One day you must breathe me with your breath, swallow me completely. It would be wonderful. I'd be quite small inside you, nice and warm – I'd be so comfortable.

EURYDICE (*gently*): Don't talk any more. Don't think. Let your hand wander over me. Let it be happy all alone. Everything will become so simple if you just let your hand love me alone. Without saying anything more.

ORPHEUS: D'you think that's what they call happiness?

EURYDICE: Yes. Your hand is happy at this moment. It doesn't ask anything more of me than to be there, obedient and warm beneath it. Don't ask anything more of me, either. We love each other, we are young; we're going to live. Agree to be happy, please . . .

ORPHEUS (*rising*): I can't.

EURYDICE: If you love me . . .

ORPHEUS: I can't.

EURYDICE: Be quiet, then, at least.

ORPHEUS: I can't do that either! All the words haven't yet been said. And we must say them all, one after the other. We must go now to the very end, word by word. And there are plenty of them!

EURYDICE: My darling, be quiet, I beg you!

ORPHEUS: Can't you hear? A swarm of them has been around

us ever since yesterday. Dulac's words, my words, your words, all the words that brought us here. And the words of all the people who looked at us as if we were two animals being led along. The ones that haven't been spoken yet, but which are there, attracted by the aroma of the rest; the most conventional, the most vulgar, the ones we hate the most. We're going to say them; we're surely going to say them. They must always be said.

EURYDICE (*rising, crying out*): My darling!

ORPHEUS: Ah, no! I want no more words – enough! We've choked ourselves with words since yesterday. Now I've got to look at you.

EURYDICE (*throwing herself against him, holding him close to her with her arms round his waist*): Wait, wait, please wait. What we must do is get through the night. It will soon be morning. Wait. Everything will be simple again. They'll bring us coffee, rolls and butter . . .

ORPHEUS: I can't wait till morning. It's too long to wait until we're old . . .

EURYDICE (*still holding him, her head pressed to his back, imploringly*): Oh, please, darling, please don't turn round, don't look at me. . . . What for? Let me live. . . . You are terrible, you know, terrible as an angel. You think the whole world can go forward, strong and clear as you are, driving away the shadows from each side of the road. . . . Some only have a little lantern which the wind blows about. And the shadows grow longer, jostling us, pulling us about, making us fall. . . . Oh, please, please, don't look at me, my darling, don't look at me just yet. . . . Maybe I'm not the person you wanted me to be. The one you invented in the happiness of the very first day. . . . But you can feel me, can't you, here against you? I'm here, I'm warm, I'm sweet, and I love you. I'll give you all the happiness that is in me. But don't ask more of me than I can give. Be content. . . . Don't look at me. Let me live. . . . Tell me, please . . . I so much want to live . . .

ORPHEUS: Live! Live! Like your mother and her lover, perhaps, with baby-talk, smiles and indulgences, and then a good meal, a little love-making, and everything's all right. Ah, no! I love you too much to live! (*He has turned round and looked at her. They are standing face to face, separated by an appalling silence; suddenly he asks, in a low voice:*) Did he hold you to him, that horrible man? Did he touch you with those hands all covered with rings?

EURYDICE: Yes.

ORPHEUS: How long have you been his mistress?

EURYDICE (*replying to him now with the same eagerness to lacerate herself*). For a year.

ORPHEUS: Is it true you were with him two days ago?

EURYDICE: Yes, the night before I met you; he called for me after the performance. He made a scene. He made a scene every time.

DULAC (*entering suddenly*): Admit that that time you came with me because you wanted to, little liar.

EURYDICE (*pulling herself away from* ORPHEUS, *runs to him*): Because I wanted to? I spat every time you kissed me.

DULAC (*calmly*): Yes, my dove.

EURYDICE: As soon as you left me I ran away. I undressed completely. I washed all over – changed all my clothes. You never knew that, did you?

DULAC (*to* ORPHEUS): Out of her mind, poor girl!

EURYDICE: I know you, my darling – you can laugh, but it's out of the wrong side of your face.

ORPHEUS: Why do you call him your darling?

EURYDICE (*crying out, sincerely*): I didn't!

DULAC (*sneeringly, to* ORPHEUS): You see? It all adds up with the rest, young man! I told you you would lose your way.

EURYDICE: Don't put on your olympian airs. Don't pretend to be so bloody clever . . . (*To* ORPHEUS:) Forgive me, darling, everyone in the theatre is 'darling'. Vincent, mother, everyone. That's why I said I didn't call him darling. I don't call him darling because I've been his mistress. I call him darling because everyone does. (*She stops, discouraged.*) Ah, it's so difficult, so difficult to have to explain everything always . . .

ORPHEUS: Now you've got to explain everything properly. You said he made a scene that night as he did every night. What scene?

EURYDICE: It was always the same.

DULAC: You aren't going to tell us you believed in it for a whole year?

EURYDICE: You see, you admit yourself you played it for a year.

DULAC: Don't pretend to be stupid, Eurydice; you aren't stupid at all. I ask if you, yourself, believed in that scene for a whole year.

EURYDICE: Why did you do it every time if you thought I didn't believe it?

DULAC: It had become a mere formality, that threat. I made it so that you could save your dirty pride, and pretend you had a reason which forced you to follow me without admitting you enjoyed it. Surely I couldn't be more gallant to a lady?

EURYDICE: What? When you came and threatened me, you didn't even believe it yourself? You deceived me every time? You dragged me away every time, and it wasn't true; you wouldn't really have sacked him?

DULAC: Of course not.

ORPHEUS: What did he threaten to do?

The little MANAGER *appears, in agony, awkward, clumsy. He raises his little hat before speaking.*

MANAGER: He threatened to send me away, monsieur. I'm his manager, and each time he threatened to dismiss me.

DULAC (*exploding, when he sees him*): He's a fool! He loses everything! I won't keep such an idiot in my company!

EURYDICE: You see, darling, this poor little man is all alone in the world. He has a little brother, ten years old. All they've got to live on is what he earns. . . . Besides, it's too unfair. Everyone dislikes him and tries to get him sent away.

MANAGER: You see, monsieur, I have to look after all the trunks, all the scenery, and I'm alone. (*He falls on to a bench, weeping.*) I'll never manage! I'll never manage!

EURYDICE: It's your fault – you're always shouting at him and frightening him out of his wits. I'm sure if you talked to him gently, he'd understand. Listen, Louis darling . . .

MANAGER: I'm listening, Eurydice . . .

EURYDICE (*to* ORPHEUS): You see, I call him darling, too. Everyone is always 'darling'. (*She goes back to the little man.*) Listen, darling Louis, it's really very simple. You get to the station where we have to change. You get out of the train very quickly. You run to the luggage van. You take care to get into the queue so that you're there as soon as they begin to unload. You count the trunks to make sure they haven't forgotten one . . .

MANAGER: Yes, but the others are in a hurry to get into town. They bring me their suitcases . . .

EURYDICE: You must tell them to wait. That you must first look after the trunks.

MANAGER: Yes, but they put their suitcases down beside me and tell me to look after them and go away. And the platform is full of people hurrying along . . .

EURYDICE: You mustn't let them go away! You must run after them!

MANAGER: I can't watch the trunks if I'm running after them! I'll never be able to manage. I'd much better go away . . .

DULAC (*roaring*): He's a fool! A fool, I tell you! This time it's settled. Signed, sealed and delivered. He leaves at Châtellerault!

EURYDICE: Don't shout at him all the time. If you do, how can you expect him to understand.

DULAC: He'll never understand. I tell you he's an incompetent. He leaves the company at Châtellerault, and that's my final word!

MANAGER: Monsieur Dulac, if you sack me, I don't know what I shall do. We'll both be stranded, my little brother and I . . . I promise you I'll be very careful, Monsieur Dulac!

DULAC: You're fired! You're fired, I tell you!

EURYDICE: I'll help you! I promise I'll manage so that he doesn't lose anything . . .

DULAC: I know what promises are worth! No, no, he's quite useless. Sacked, fired! I won't have him any more.

EURYDICE (*has fastened on to him, imploringly*): I swear to you he'll be careful. Dulac, I swear it . . .

DULAC (*looking at her*): Oh, you're always swearing, but you don't always keep your word.

EURYDICE (*in a lower voice*): Yes.

DULAC (*going to her, softly*): If I keep him just once more, you'll be good to me?

EURYDICE (*hanging her head*): Yes. (*She comes back to* ORPHEUS.) That's what happened every time. . . . Forgive me, darling! I was a coward, but I didn't love you yet. I didn't love anyone. And he only had me to look after him. (*Pause; she murmurs:*) I know you won't be able to look at me ever again.

ORPHEUS (*who has recoiled, in a low voice*): I shall always see you with that man's hands on you. I shall always see you as he described you in that room.

EURYDICE (*humbly*): Yes, my darling.

ORPHEUS: He wasn't even jealous when he came to fetch you. He said: 'A girl like Eurydice has to be humoured.'

EURYDICE (*retreating a little*): He said that?

ORPHEUS: What's your Eurydice like, he said. Can you get her out of bed in the morning, drag her away from her thrillers, her cigarettes? He even knew you were a coward. That if he came to fetch you, you wouldn't stay with me. Because you are a coward, aren't you? He knows you better than I do.

EURYDICE: Yes, my darling.

ORPHEUS: Explain, can't you? Why don't you try to explain?

EURYDICE (*retreating*): How can I explain? Do you want me to lie to you? I am untidy – it's true. I'm untidy, a coward . . .

MANAGER (*crying out suddenly*): It isn't true!

EURYDICE: What do you know about it?

MANAGER: You weren't a coward when you protected me against them all, I know. You weren't lazy when you got up at six o'clock to come and help me in secret while we waited for the others to come down . . .

DULAC (*falling from the clouds*): What? You got up in the morning to help that fool send off the trunks?

EURYDICE: Yes, Dulac.

MANAGER: She, who could never find anything, who muddles everything, she helped to file my papers, and stopped me making mistakes . . .

DULAC: Can you beat that?

ORPHEUS: But if what the little man says is true, tell me! Explain things better!

EURYDICE: It's true, but what Dulac says is true, too. It's too difficult.

All the characters of the play have come in while he has been speaking. They are grouped in the background behind EURYDICE.

ORPHEUS: It's true. It is too difficult. All these people who knew you are around you; all the hands that have touched you are there, crawling over you. All the words you have spoken are on your lips . . .

EURYDICE (*recoils still farther, with a poor little smile*): So you see, it's much better for me to die again.

DRIVER (*coming forward from the group*): Don't you see, she was too tired? Ashamed to try to explain herself? I do a little hunting, and I tell you, there are some animals like that. You catch them because they're tired, disgusted with life. They turn back on the dogs, and let them do as they please. It's the same with her, and the story of the bus I heard her getting muddled up just now . . .

ORPHEUS: Who are you?

EURYDICE: The driver of the bus, my darling. How nice of you to come.

DRIVER: He's got the idea you smiled at me. To begin with, have I got the sort of face you'd expect her to smile at? He thinks you started out with a smile, and it's only a step from that to believing you never loved him. Well, I was there. And I saw.

MANAGER: Oh, I'm so pleased. He's going to defend you. You'll tell him, won't you, monsieur?

DRIVER: Of course I'll tell him! That's what I'm here for.

ORPHEUS: What are you trying to tell me?

DRIVER: Why she smiled. I'd been watching her for a bit out of the corner of my eye . . . she was writing in a corner, with a little pencil, while she waited for us to start . . . she wrote and wrote and cried at the same time. When she'd finished writing she dried her eyes with a bit of a handkerchief rolled into a ball, and she stuck out her tongue to lick the envelope . . . then, just for the sake of saying something, I said: 'I hope your boy friend's worth the paper you've written on.'

EURYDICE: Then I smiled because I thought of you, my darling.

DRIVER: You see.

There is a pause. ORPHEUS *raises his head; looks at* EURYDICE, *who is standing humbly before him.*

ORPHEUS: If you loved me, why were you going away?

EURYDICE: I thought I'd never be able . . .

ORPHEUS: To what?

EURYDICE: To make you understand. (*They are facing each other, silent.*)

MOTHER (*exclaiming suddenly*): What I don't understand is why everything seems so terribly sad to those children! Tell me, big bear, we've been passionate lovers, but has it ever made us sad?

VINCENT: Not at all, not at all! Besides, I've always said: a little love, a little money, a little success and life is wonderful!

MOTHER: A little love? A great deal of love! That child thinks she's invented the whole thing with her little violinist. We've adored each other, too, haven't we? We've often wanted to kill ourselves for each other's sake. Remember Biarritz in 1913 when I tried to throw myself from the Virgin's Rock?

VINCENT: So fortunate I was able to hold you back by your cape, beloved!

MOTHER (*letting out a little cry at the memory; she begins to explain to* ORPHEUS): It was delightful. That year we all wore tiny capes lined with silk, in the same cloth as the jacket. Why did I want to kill myself that time?

VINCENT: Because the Princess Bosco kept me with her all night reading poetry . . .

MOTHER: No, no. The Princess Bosco was the time I tried to swallow vinegar. I took the wrong bottle. It was wine. I pulled such a horrible face!

VINCENT: Aren't we being stupid! It was the skating instructor!

MOTHER: No, no, of course not. The skating instructor was during the war, at Lausanne. No, no. The Virgin's Rock time you'd been unfaithful to me, I'm sure of it. Anyway, the details don't matter. What matters is that we've also loved each other passionately, enough to die for it. . . . Well, are we dead?

EURYDICE (*who has retreated*): No, Mother.

MOTHER: If you'd only listened to your mother! But you never will . . .

EURYDICE (*pushing her away*): Leave it now, Mother; we haven't time . . . (*To* ORPHEUS, *who has watched her going, motionless:*) You see, darling, we mustn't complain too much. . . . You were right. In trying to be happy, we might perhaps have become like them. . . . How horrible!

MOTHER: How horrible?

VINCENT: What do you mean?

ORPHEUS: Why didn't you confess everything the first day? The first day I might have been able to understand.

EURYDICE: D'you think it's because I was a coward? It wasn't . . .

ORPHEUS: Then why? Why?

EURYDICE: It's too difficult, my darling; I'll only get muddled again. Now, there's no more time. I must ask you to forgive me. . . . Don't move . . . (*She retreats again, stops in front of someone.*) Oh, you're the lovely dumb cashier. I've always felt you had something to say to us.

CASHIER: How beautiful you were when you came together

through the music. Beautiful, innocent and terrible, like love itself . . .

EURYDICE (*smiles at her and retreats still farther*): Thank you, madame. (*She stops in front of another person.*) The waiter from the Comédie Française! Our very first character. How are you?

WAITER (*with an overelaborate gesture*): Farewell, mademoiselle!

EURYDICE (*smiling in spite of herself*): You're very noble, very charming, you know. Good-bye, good-bye . . . (*She is still backing away; she stops in front of a* YOUNG MAN *in black, surprised.*) Who are you? I think you're mistaken; I don't remember you at all.

YOUNG MAN: I'm a clerk at the police station, mademoiselle. You have never seen me.

EURYDICE: Ah! Then you must be the one who has my letter. Give it back to me, please, monsieur. Give it back.

YOUNG MAN: I'm afraid that's impossible, mademoiselle.

EURYDICE: I don't want that big, fat, dirty man to read it!

YOUNG MAN: I can promise you the Inspector won't read it, mademoiselle. I realized at once it would be impossible for a man such as the Inspector to read that letter. I took it out of the file. The case is closed; no one will ever notice. I have it with me. I read it every day. . . . But it's different for me. (*He bows, noble and sad, takes the letter from his pocket and after walking up and down, in his somewhat flat voice.*) 'My darling, I'm in this bus and you're waiting for me in our room. I don't know what will happen to me. I try to think that you don't know yet what I'm doing, but I'm miserable, miserable on your account. I should have been allowed to keep all the suffering for myself. But how? You can be suffering with all your being, suffering so much you have to bite your lips to stop yourself screaming, so much that the tears fall by themselves – you can never take all the suffering on yourself; there will always be enough for two. The people in the bus are looking at me. They think it's sad because I'm crying. I hate tears. They're such stupid things. You cry when you bump yourself, or when you peel an onion. You cry when you're upset, or if you have another kind of sorrow. For the sorrow I feel now, I would have liked not to cry. I'm much too miserable to cry.'

He resettles his voice, turns the page and continues:

'I'm going away, my darling. Ever since yesterday I've been afraid, and when I was asleep you heard me say, "it's so difficult". You thought I was beautiful, my darling. I mean beautiful morally, because I know that physically you've never thought me very, very beautiful. You always thought of me as so strong, so pure, quite your little sister . . . I'd never have been able to be that. Particularly not now when this man is coming. He has had a letter given to me. Another man I've never talked to you about and who has been my lover, too. Don't believe I loved him – you'll see him, no one could love him. Don't think either that I gave in to him because I was afraid of him, as he'll probably tell you. You could never understand, I know that. But I felt so strong, and I thought so little of myself. I didn't love you properly, my darling; that's the whole secret. I didn't love you. I didn't know. The modesty of well-brought-up little girls made me laugh. The idea of keeping something out of pride, or for . . . for choice, was so ugly. . . . Ever since yesterday, my darling, I've become far more prudish than they. Ever since yesterday, I blush if someone looks at me. I tremble if I'm touched. I cry at the thought that anyone dared desire me. . . . That's the only reason I'm going away, my darling, all alone. . . . Not only because I'm afraid he'll tell you I belonged to him, not only because I'm afraid you may stop loving me . . . I don't know if you'll ever understand, but I'm going away because I'm red with shame. I'm going away, my captain, and I'm leaving you because you taught me how to be an honest little soldier . . .'

During the reading of the letter EURYDICE *has backed away slowly. She is right at the back of the stage by now.*

ORPHEUS: Forgive me, Eurydice.

EURYDICE (*tenderly from the back*): There's no need, my darling. It's I who ask you to forgive me. (*To the others:*) Please excuse me. I must go.

ORPHEUS (*crying out*): Eurydice!

He runs to the back like a madman. She has disappeared. All the other characters have faded away, too; ORPHEUS *is alone. He does not move. The morning breaks. A train whistles far away. A tremolo on the humming note we heard at the beginning of the scene. When the light of day is almost real the* WAITER *enters, looking very much alive.*

WAITER: Good morning, sir. Bitterly cold today. Can I get you something?

ORPHEUS (*sinking into a chair*): Yes. Anything. Some coffee.

WAITER: Certainly, sir.

He begins to take the chairs down from the tables. The CASHIER *enters and goes to her desk, humming a sentimental song from before the war. A* TRAVELLER *passes on the platform, hesitates, then enters timidly. He is overloaded with suitcases and musical instruments. It is* ORPHEUS'S FATHER.

FATHER: Oh, is that you, my boy? I didn't take the train to Palavas after all. Full. Full to bursting, my boy, and those swine wanted me to pay the difference to travel second. I got out. I'll complain to the management. A traveller is entitled to a seat in all classes. They should have let me travel second for nothing. Are you having some coffee?

ORPHEUS (*who seems not to see him*): Yes.

FATHER (*sitting down opposite him*): I could do with some myself. I spent the night in the waiting-room. It was anything but warm. (*He whispers in* ORPHEUS'S *ear.*) To tell you the truth, I slipped into the first class. An excellent leather sofa, my dear. I slept like a prince. (*He sees the* CASHIER, *gives her a stare, she turns away her eyes, so does he.*) She loses a lot by daylight, that woman. She's got a fine figure, but she looks extremely common. . . . Well, my boy, what are you going to do? Night brings good counsel. Are you coming with me after all?

ORPHEUS: Yes, Father.

FATHER: I knew you'd never desert your old father! We'll celebrate by having a good little dinner at Perpignan. I know of a wonderful place where for fifteen francs seventy-five you get four courses, including wine, coffee and liqueur. Oh, my dear boy, an excellent brandy! And if you pay an extra four francs, you get lobster instead of hors d'oeuvres. A good life, after all, my boy, a good life . . .

ORPHEUS: Yes, Father.

Curtain

Act Four

The hotel bedroom. ORPHEUS, *half lying on the bed,* MONSIEUR HENRI, *standing, leaning on the wall beside him. Ensconced in the only chair, the* FATHER. *He is smoking an enormous cigar.*

FATHER (*to* MONSIEUR HENRI): A Merveillitas, isn't it?

MONSIEUR HENRI: Yes.

FATHER: Must have cost a packet, a cigar like that.

MONSIEUR HENRI: Yes.

FATHER: Don't you smoke?

MONSIEUR HENRI: No.

FATHER: I don't understand why you carry such expensive cigars if you don't smoke yourself. Maybe you're a commercial traveller?

MONSIEUR HENRI: That's it.

FATHER: Big business, probably.

MONSIEUR HENRI: Yes.

FATHER: Then I understand. You've got to soften up the customers. At the right moment you pull out a Merveillitas. You ask him if he'll smoke? He accepts, of course. And bingo! It's in the bag. All you've got to do is subtract the cost of the cigar from the bill of sale, and it's been added anyway. You're all such jokers. I'd have adored to have been been in business. Wouldn't you, my boy? (ORPHEUS *doesn't answer; he looks at him.*) You must snap out of it, my boy. Look, give him a Merveillitas, too. If he doesn't finish it, I will. When I'm down in the mouth, a good cigar . . . (*Neither* ORPHEUS *nor* MONSIEUR HENRI *give any sign of having registered this remark; the* FATHER *sighs and adds more timidly:*) Well, we all have our tastes. (*Goes back to his smoking, with a glance now and then at the two silent men.*)

MONSIEUR HENRI (*gently, after a pause*): You must get up, Orpheus.

FATHER: Of course he must. I've been telling him so for hours . . .

ORPHEUS: No.

FATHER: He never listens to his father.

MONSIEUR HENRI: Go out and pick up your life where you dropped it, Orpheus.

FATHER: They're expecting us at Perpignan.

ORPHEUS (*half sits up and cries to him*): Be quiet!

FATHER (*cringing*): I only said they were expecting us at Perpignan. Nothing wrong in that, is there?

ORPHEUS: I'll never go back with you!

MONSIEUR HENRI (*gently*): All the same, your life is waiting for you, like an old coat you put on every morning.

ORPHEUS: Very well. I won't put it on.

MONSIEUR HENRI: Have you another? (ORPHEUS *doesn't reply. The* FATHER *smokes.*) Why won't you go back with him? I think your father's charming.

FATHER: How very kind of you . . .

MONSIEUR HENRI: Besides, you know him. That's important. You can tell him to be quiet, you can walk beside him in silence. Imagine what agony would be waiting for you without him. A stranger you meet at table, who tells you his life story; the old lady who questions you with amorous interest. The most worthless slut you meet in the street can insist that you speak to her. If you don't want to pay your way with stupid words, you'll be abominably alone.

ORPHEUS: I am alone. I'm used to it.

MONSIEUR HENRI: Let me put you on your guard against that phrase – alone. It invokes a shadow, a fragrance, a resting-place. What a stupid mistake! You will not be alone, no one's ever alone. We are with ourselves, which is something else, again, you know quite well. . . . Pick up your life with your father again. Every day he'll make his remarks on how hard times are, on the menus in the restaurants. It will occupy your mind. You'll be more alone with him than when you're by yourself.

FATHER (*lost in his cigar*): Talking of restaurants, I know a special one at Perpignan, the Restaurant Bouillon Jeanne-Hachette. Maybe you know it? It's used a great deal by your colleagues.

MONSIEUR HENRI: No.

FATHER: For fifteen francs seventy-five, you can have hors-d'oeuvres (including wine) – or lobster, if you pay an extra four francs – main dish (very generous), vegetables, cheese, sweet, fruit or pastries – wait, wait – coffee and liqueurs, brandy, or sweet liqueurs for the ladies. The little menu at the Jeanne-Hachette used to include a good cigar, like this one! I'm almost sorry I smoked it right away. (*His remark doesn't produce the expected result; he sighs.*) Oh, well! You're coming to Perpignan, my boy, aren't you? As my guest?

ORPHEUS: No, Father.

FATHER: You're making a mistake, my boy.

MONSIEUR HENRI: That's right, Orpheus. You're making a mistake. You ought to listen to your father. That little restaurant is the best place for forgetting Eurydice.

FATHER: Oh, I don't say they go in for orgies. You get a good meal, all the same.

MONSIEUR HENRI: The only place in the world where you won't find the ghost of Eurydice is that little restaurant at Perpignan. You should fly there as fast as you can, Orpheus.

ORPHEUS: Do you think I want to forget her?

MONSIEUR HENRI (*clapping him on the shoulder*): You must, my friend. As quickly as possible. You've been a hero for a whole day. In these few hours you've used up your share of emotion for the rest of your life. It's over. Now you can relax. Forget, Orpheus, forget the very name of Eurydice. Take your father's arm, go back and visit his restaurants. Life may take on its accustomed aspect; death become a question of reasonable odds again; despair will only be a word. Come along, get up, go off with your father. You've still got a fine career as a living man in front of you. (*He says this almost bitterly, leaning over* ORPHEUS, *who raises his head and looks at him.*)

FATHER (*after a pause, through his cigar*): You know, I've been in love, too, my boy.

MONSIEUR HENRI: You see, he's been in love as well. Look at him.

FATHER: It's true, look at me. I know how sad it is. I've suffered, too. I'm not speaking of your mother. When she died we'd already been out of love for a very long time. I lost a girl once I adored. A girl from Toulouse, a creature made of fire. Carried off in a week. Bronchitis. I sobbed like a child during the funeral. They had to take me into a café to recover. Look at me.

MONSIEUR HENRI: It's true. (*Gently.*) Look at him.

FATHER: I don't say that when I picked up my serviette and found myself sitting at the Grand Comptoir Toulousain, where we used to go together, I didn't feel a slight constriction of the heart. But what the hell! Life's like that. What can you expect? We've got to live it as it comes. (*He puffs dreamily at his cigar; sighs and murmurs:*) Oh, that Grand Comptoir Toulousain. . . . When I used to go there with her, before the war, to think we used to dine for one franc seventy-five!

MONSIEUR HENRI (*bending over* ORPHEUS): Life's like that. Life's like that, Orpheus. Listen to your father.

FATHER (*becoming more and more important through the words of* MONSIEUR HENRI): I'm even going to be very hard, my boy, and you'll be angry, but I'm much tougher than you, and when you come to my age, you'll see that I was right. It hurts at first. Naturally. But soon, you'll see, in spite of yourself, you feel a new softness. . . . One fine day – it took me like that – you have a bath, do up your tie, the sun is shining, you go into the street, and suddenly, bingo! you see the girls are pretty again. We're terrible, my boy, all the same; pitiless scoundrels.

MONSIEUR HENRI: Listen carefully, Orpheus . . .

FATHER: I don't say you take the first one who comes along.

No. We aren't animals, after all, and the first words sound a little odd. It's strange you can't help beginning to talk about the other. You say how lonely you are, how lost. And it's true, as well! You are sincere. Oh, you can imagine how much that sort of talk can influence a woman! It's obvious, you'll tell me I'm a brigand. I was still using the same technique ten years afterwards.

ORPHEUS: Be quiet, Father.

MONSIEUR HENRI: Why should you want him to be quiet? He's talking to you as life will talk to you through every mouth; he's saying what you'll see tomorrow in all the eyes if you get up and try to live again . . .

FATHER (*well in the groove by now*): Life! But life is wonderful, my boy . . .

MONSIEUR HENRI: Listen carefully.

FATHER: You mustn't forget you're still an inexperienced boy, and the man talking to you has lived – how he has lived! We were terrible at the Conservatoire of Niort! Real devils! Gilded youth! Always carrying a cane, with our pipes in our mouths, busy with some sort of scrape. In those days I hadn't thought about the harp. I was studying the bassoon and the cor anglais. Every night I walked five miles to play under the windows of a woman. Ah, we were gay gallants, bad hats, eccentrics. Afraid of nothing in this world. One day, the woodwind class challenged the brass. We bet we'd each drink thirty pints of beer. Ah! How sick we were! We were young and gay! We knew what life was like – we understood!

MONSIEUR HENRI: You see, Orpheus.

FATHER: When you have your health and strength, my boy, you've only got to go straight ahead. I don't understand you. First of all, good temper. Good temper is a question of balance. The whole secret – daily exercise. If I'm in the form I am at the moment, it's because I've never given up my exercises. Ten minutes every morning. You don't need more, but it's the ten minutes that matter. (*He gets up, and, the butt of the cigar in his teeth, begins to go through a ridiculous form of Swedish drill.*) One, two, three, four; one, two, three, four. Breathe deeply. One, two, three, four, five. One, two, three, four, five. One, two, three, four, five. One, two. One, two. One, two. One, two. One, two. If you do that you'll never have a sagging stomach, or varicose veins. Health through joy, joy through health and vice versa. One, two, three, four. Breathe deeply. One, two, three, four. That's the whole secret.

MONSIEUR HENRI: You see, Orpheus. It's very simple!

FATHER (*sitting down again, puffing like a grampus*): It's a question of will power. Everything in life is a question of will power. What's got me through the most difficult patches has been my will power. A will of iron! But, of course, there's a good and a bad way . . . I've been taken for an extremely pleasant man. Velvet, but steel underneath. I always went straight ahead. Never admitted any obstacles. Boundless ambition. But wait! I started with a tremendous technical equipment. First-class bassoon at the Conservatoire of Niort. Second-class cor anglais, second class in harmony. I was ready for anything – I was well equipped. But I like young men to be ambitious! Don't you want to be a millionaire?

MONSIEUR HENRI: Answer your father, Orpheus . . .

FATHER: Oh, money, money! But that's life, my boy! You're unhappy, but you're young. Think that you may become very rich. Think of the women, my boy, think of love! Blondes, brunettes, red-heads, peroxides! Such variety, such a choice! And all for you. You're the sultan, you take a walk, you lift your finger. That one! You're rich, you're young and handsome, she comes to you. And then it's a succession of enchanted nights. . . . Passion, cries, and bites, mad kisses, a warm shadow, something Spanish. Or else on the divans of secret boudoirs, from five to seven, wrapped in rich furs, the play of a wood fire on the nakedness of a blonde, capricious child, and more smiling, and bitter games. I've no need to tell you more, my boy! Sensations! Every possible sensation. A lifetime of sensations. Where's your grief? Gone up in smoke. (*He makes a gesture, and becomes serious.*) That's not the whole of life. There's respectability, a social life. You're strong, and powerful, a captain of industry. You've given up your music . . . a mask-like face, impenetrable. . . . Board meetings with brilliant minds. You juggle with the economic safety of Europe. You play with them all. Then the strike. The armed workmen. Violence. You appear alone before the factory. A shot is fired and misses you. You don't move. In a voice of thunder you speak to them. They expect promises, capitulation. They don't recognize you now. You are terrible. You castigate them. They hang their heads, go back to work. Beaten! It's magnificent. . . . Then, on the advice of your best friends, you go in for politics. Honoured, powerful, decorated, a senator. Always in the forefront. A great man and a great Frenchman. National funeral, flowers, a million flowers, muffled drums, long speeches. And I, modestly in a corner – they insisted on my attending the ceremony – a distinguished old man, ah, yes, my boy, I'll have grown old by then – but mastering my grief, erect and at attention. (*He declaims:*) 'Let us pay the homage due to a father's grief!' (*It is too beautiful; he breaks down.*) Ah, my boy, my boy, life is wonderful . . .

MONSIEUR HENRI: You see, Orpheus.

FATHER: The man talking to you has suffered. He has drunk his cup to the very dregs. Often he has been silent, biting his lip till the blood spurted, to keep from crying out. His gay companions never realized the tortures he was suffering, and yet. . . . Betrayal, scorn, injustice. . . . You wonder sometimes at my bent back, my premature white hairs, my child. If you knew how heavy is the weight of a life on the shoulders of a man . . .

He pulls in vain on the butt of his cigar; he looks at it, annoyed, then throws it away with a sigh. MONSIEUR HENRI *goes to him and holds out his case.*

MONSIEUR HENRI: Another cigar?

FATHER: Thank you. I'm embarrassed. Yes, yes, embarrassed. What an aroma! The band is a little jewel. Tell me, have you heard it said the girls who make them roll them on their thighs? (*He sighs.*) Their thighs . . . (*He stops.*) What was I saying?

MONSIEUR HENRI: The weight of a lifetime . . .

FATHER (*who has lost his lyrical fervour*): How do you mean, the weight of a lifetime?

MONSIEUR HENRI: If you knew how heavy the weight of a lifetime can be on a man's shoulders . . .

FATHER (*biting the end of his cigar*): Ah! That's right. If you know how heavy the weight of a lifetime can be . . . (*Stops, lights the cigar slowly and concludes simply:*) Well, it's heavy, my boy. Extremely heavy. (*Inhales a deep breath with delight.*) Marvellous. (*Winks at* MONSIEUR HENRI.) I feel as if I'm smoking the thigh itself! (*Starts to laugh and chokes in the smoke.*)

MONSIEUR HENRI (*to* ORPHEUS): You've listened to your father, Orpheus? One should always listen to one's father. Fathers are always right. (ORPHEUS *looks up at him;* MONSIEUR HENRI *smiles and adds softly:*) Even the fools, Orpheus. Life is made in such a way that foolish fathers know as much, sometimes more, than clever fathers. Life doesn't require intelligence. Sometimes it becomes the most embarrassing obstacle to her joyful progress.

ORPHEUS (*murmuring*): Life . . .

MONSIEUR HENRI: Don't say anything unkind about life. You were defending it yesterday.

ORPHEUS: It seems so long since yesterday.

MONSIEUR HENRI (*softly*): I told you life would take away Eurydice.

ORPHEUS: Don't blame life for that . . . 'Life' doesn't mean anything. It was I and I alone.

MONSIEUR HENRI (*smiling*): You alone. How proud you are.

ORPHEUS: Exactly . . . it's my pride.

MONSIEUR HENRI: Your pride? Really? You want pride to belong to you as well? Your love, your pride, now it's your despair. . . . Why should you have to put a possessive pronoun in front of each of your little threads! You're extraordinary. Why not say my oxygen, my ozone? You should say Pride, Love, Despair. They are the names of rivers. A little stream flows away from them and sprinkles you with a thousand others. That's all. The River Pride doesn't belong to you.

ORPHEUS: Nor the River Jealousy – I know. And the pain that is drowning me is probably coming from the River Pain which is drowning millions of others this very moment. It's the same icy water, the same nameless stream, and then? I'm not a man who can console himself by saying, 'That's life.' What difference does it make to me if life's like that? That a million grains of sand should be swept away at the same time as myself?

MONSIEUR HENRI: They're your brothers, or so they say.

ORPHEUS: I hate them – one by one. . . . So don't come and try to turn the crowd into a tender sister. We're alone. Quite, quite alone. That's the only certainty.

MONSIEUR HENRI (*bending over him*): You're alone because you've lost Eurydice. Supposing life held for you, your beloved life, a day when you would find yourself alone beside your living Eurydice.

ORPHEUS: No.

MONSIEUR HENRI: Yes. One day or the next, in a year, in five years, in ten if you like, without stopping loving her, perhaps, you might have realized you didn't want Eurydice any more, that Eurydice didn't want you either.

ORPHEUS: No.

MONSIEUR HENRI: Yes. It might have been as stupid as that. You'd have become the man who'd been unfaithful to Eurydice.

ORPHEUS (*crying out*): Never!

MONSIEUR HENRI: Why do you protest so loudly? For my sake or yours? Let's say, if you prefer it, you might have been the man who wanted to be unfaithful to Eurydice. It's no better.

ORPHEUS: I'd have been faithful to her always.

MONSIEUR HENRI: Maybe for a long time. Never daring to look at other women. With a slow and sure hatred that began to grow in you for all the girls you might have followed if it hadn't been for her . . .

ORPHEUS: That's not true.

MONSIEUR HENRI: Yes. Until the day when one of them walked past you, young and slender, without a shadow of grief, without a shadow of a thought; a bright new woman, Orpheus, confronted with your weariness. Then you would have been able to see that death, betrayal, lies, suddenly become the simplest things in the world, injustice takes on another name, faithfulness another aspect . . .

ORPHEUS: No. I'd have closed my eyes. I'd have run away.

MONSIEUR HENRI: For the first time, perhaps, and you'd have still walked beside your Eurydice with the eyes of a man who's trying to lose his dog in the street. But the fiftieth time, Orpheus! . . . (*He makes a gesture.*) In any case, Eurydice might have already abandoned you . . .

ORPHEUS (*plaintively this time*): No.

MONSIEUR HENRI: Why not? Because she loved you yesterday? A little bird capable of flying away without knowing why, ready to die for love.

ORPHEUS: We could never have stopped loving each other.

MONSIEUR HENRI: Maybe she wouldn't have stopped loving you. It's not so easy to stop loving someone. Tenderness is a stubborn emotion, you know. She might perhaps have had a way of giving herself to you before going to meet her lover, so humbly, so gently, that you might almost have been able to be happy again. It's true.

ORPHEUS: No, not us, not us!

MONSIEUR HENRI: You like the rest. You more than the rest. With your way of being tender, you'd have lacerated each other to the end.

ORPHEUS: No.

MONSIEUR HENRI: Yes. Or else one day, tired, smiling, venial, you might have decided tacitly to kill the pretence between you, and become happy and gentle to each other. And then we'd have seen a different Orpheus and Eurydice . . .

ORPHEUS: No! It would have lasted for ever, until she was white-haired and old beside me, and I was old beside her!

MONSIEUR HENRI: Life, your dear life, would never have allowed you to get to that point. The love of Orpheus and Eurydice would never have been allowed to escape her.

ORPHEUS: Yes, yes!

MONSIEUR HENRI: No, little man. You're all the same. You thirst for eternity and after the first kiss you're green with fear because you vaguely feel it can never last. Vows are quickly exhausted. Then you build houses, because stones at least will last; you have a child, as people in the olden days cut their throats, to stay beloved. You gaily risk the happiness of that tiny innocent recruit to this doubtful combat, wagering the most fragile thing in the world on your love of man and woman. . . . And it dissolves, and dissipates, and breaks exactly as if you'd sworn nothing.

FATHER (*half asleep*): When I tell you life is wonderful . . . (*He turns over in his chair, the hand holding the cigar falls; he murmurs, unconscious:*) On their thighs . . .

ORPHEUS *and* MONSIEUR HENRI *watch him in silence.*

MONSIEUR HENRI (*going to* ORPHEUS, *quickly, in a low voice*): Life would never have allowed you to keep Eurydice. But Eurydice can be given back to you for ever. The Eurydice of your first meeting, eternally pure and young, eternally herself . . .

ORPHEUS (*looks at him, after a pause, shaking his head*): No.

MONSIEUR HENRI (*smiling*): Why not?

ORPHEUS: I don't want to die. I hate death.

MONSIEUR HENRI (*gently*): You're unfair. Why should you hate death? She is beautiful. She alone can create the proper setting for love. You heard your father speaking of life just now. It was grotesque, wasn't it – absurd, horrible? Well, that's what it's like. . . . This ridiculous melodrama, this foolishness, this is life. This heaviness, these theatrical tricks, are life itself. Wander through life with your little Eurydice, and you'd meet her at the exit with her dress covered in finger marks, you'd find her strangely soiled. If you find her again, if you can find her again. I offer you a Eurydice intact, a Eurydice with the true aspect life would never have given you. Do you want her?

The FATHER *begins to snore horribly.*

Your father's snoring, Orpheus. Look at him. He's ugly. And pitiful. He has lived. Who knows? Maybe he hasn't been as stupid as he seemed just now. Maybe there's been one moment when he touched the heights of love and beauty. Look at him now, clutching to existence, with his poor carcass snoring and sprawling on the chair. Look at him well. People believe that the wear and tear on a face is the fear of death. What a mistake! The fear, on the contrary, is to find the staleness, the weakness of these fifteen-year-old faces, caricatured but intact under these beards, these spectacles, these dignified airs. It's the fear of life. These wrinkled adolescents, sneering, powerless, sarcastic, and more and more sure of themselves. These are men. . . . Look at your young father carefully, Orpheus, and remember Eurydice is waiting.

ORPHEUS (*suddenly, after a pause*): Where?

MONSIEUR HENRI (*going to him, smiling*): You always want to know everything, don't you? I'm very fond of you. I was sorry when you were unhappy. But it'll soon be over. You'll see how easy it becomes, pure, luminous, clear. . . . A world made for you, little Orpheus—

ORPHEUS: What must I do?

MONSIEUR HENRI: Put on your coat; it's cold tonight. Walk out of the town. Follow the main road. When the houses begin to spread out you'll reach a hill, near a little wood of olives. That's the place.

ORPHEUS: What place?

MONSIEUR HENRI: Your rendezvous with death. At nine o'clock. It's nearly that now. Don't keep her waiting.

ORPHEUS: I'll see Eurydice again?

MONSIEUR HENRI: Immediately.

ORPHEUS (*picking up his coat*): Very well. Good-bye.

MONSIEUR HENRI: Au revoir, my friend.

The snoring of the FATHER *increases until it becomes a sort of continuous drum roll which will not stop before the end of the scene. The light changes imperceptibly.* MONSIEUR HENRI *has stood quite still, his hands in his pockets; suddenly he says softly:*)

Come in.

The door opens slowly. EURYDICE *enters and stands at the back of the room.*

EURYDICE: He's agreed?
MONSIEUR HENRI: Yes, he's agreed.
EURYDICE (*clasping her hands*): My darling, my darling, come quickly, quickly.
MONSIEUR HENRI: He's coming.
EURYDICE: He won't feel any pain, will he?
MONSIEUR HENRI (*gently*): Did you feel anything?
WAITER (*knocking and entering*): Excuse me, please; I must turn down the bed. (*He closes the double curtains and turns down the bed. He walks past* EURYDICE *several times without seeing her. He looks at the* FATHER *and smiles.*) Monsieur is snoring. They say it's a sign of health. My mother used to say it's only people who do themselves well who snore. I heard Monsieur talking; I was afraid to disturb him.
MONSIEUR HENRI: I was talking to myself.
WAITER: I do that, too, sometimes. You can say extraordinary things to yourself other people would never think of. How's the young man, Monsieur?
MONSIEUR HENRI: Well.
WAITER: It must have been a terrible blow.
MONSIEUR HENRI: Yes.
WAITER: D'you think he'll ever get over it?
MONSIEUR HENRI: Yes. What time do you make it?
WAITER: Ten to nine, sir. (*He finishes the bed in silence.*)

Nothing is heard but the increasing sound of the FATHER'S *snoring.*

MONSIEUR HENRI (*suddenly*): Waiter?

WAITER: Yes, sir?

MONSIEUR HENRI: Have my bill ready. I'm leaving tonight.

WAITER: Monsieur said that yesterday . . .

MONSIEUR HENRI: I've made up my mind. This time I'm really going.

WAITER: Very good, sir. You've finished your business in Marseilles?

MONSIEUR HENRI: Yes. (*The* WAITER *starts to go.*) What time is it now?

WAITER: Nine o'clock exactly, sir. (*He goes out, leaving the door wide open.*)

MONSIEUR HENRI (*to* EURYDICE, *who hasn't moved*): Here he is.

EURYDICE (*softly*): Can he look at me?

MONSIEUR HENRI: Now he can – without ever being afraid of losing you.

ORPHEUS *enters, hesitates on the threshold, as if dazzled by the light.* EURYDICE *runs to him, throwing her arms round him.*

EURYDICE: Darling, what a time you've been!

Nine o'clock strikes in the distance. The FATHER *stops snoring suddenly, and wakes up with a lot of snorting.*

FATHER (*pulling at his cigar which has gone out*): I've been asleep! Where's Orpheus?

MONSIEUR HENRI *does not reply.*

(*Looks around him, worried.*) He's gone out? Answer me, can't you? Where is Orpheus?

MONSIEUR HENRI (*pointing to the two of them in each other's arms, though the* FATHER *cannot see them*): He's with Eurydice at last!

The FATHER *rises, aghast, dropping his cigar.*

Curtain

Antigone

Characters

CHORUS

ANTIGONE

NURSE

ISMENE

HAEMON

CREON

FIRST GUARD
(*Jonas*)

SECOND GUARD
(*a Corporal*)

THIRD GUARD

MESSENGER

PAGE

EURYDICE

Original Title: Antigone

Translator: Lewis Galantière

First produced in 1942

THE SETTING: *A grey cloth cyclorama, semicircular, hangs at the back of the set. At the bottom of the cyclorama a stair, of three steps, sweeps in a semicircle. Downstage, right and left, two archways. The curtains part in the centre for entrance and exit.*

A table stands left of centre-stage, with matching chairs set at either end. A small stool is placed right of the chair at the right of the table.

Antigone

ANTIGONE, *her hands clasped round her knees, sits on the top step. The* THREE GUARDS *sit on the steps, in a small group, playing cards.* CHORUS *stands on the top step.* EURYDICE *sits on the top step, just left of centre, knitting. The* NURSE *sits on the second step, left of* EURYDICE. ISMENE *stands in front of the arch, left, facing* HAEMON, *who stands left of her.* CREON *sits in the chair at the right end of the table, his arm over the shoulder of his* PAGE, *who sits on the stool beside his chair. The* MESSENGER *is leaning against the downstage portal of the right arch.*

The curtain rises slowly: then the CHORUS *turns and moves downstage.*

CHORUS: Well, here we are.
These people are about to act out for you the story of Antigone.
That thin little creature sitting by herself, staring straight ahead, seeing nothing, is Antigone. She is thinking. She is thinking that the instant I finish telling you who's who and what's what in this play, she will burst forth as the tense, sallow, wilful girl whose family would never take her seriously and who is about to rise up alone against Creon, her uncle, the King.
Another thing that she is thinking is this: she is going to die. Antigone is young. She would much rather live than die. But there is no help for it. When your name is Antigone, there is only one part you can play; and she will have to play hers through to the end.
From the moment the curtain went up, she began to feel that inhuman forces were whirling her out of this world, snatching her away from her sister, Ismene, whom you see smiling and chatting with that young man; from all of us who sit or

stand here, looking at her, not in the least upset ourselves – for we are not doomed to die tonight.

CHORUS *turns and indicates* HAEMON.

The young man talking to Ismene – to the gay and beautiful Ismene – is Haemon. He is the King's son, Creon's son. Antigone and he are engaged to be married. You wouldn't have thought she was his type. He likes dancing, sports, competition; he likes women, too. Now look at Ismene again. She is certainly more beautiful than Antigone. She is the girl you'd think he'd go for. Well. . . . There was a ball one night. Ismene wore a new evening frock. She was radiant. Haemon danced every dance with her. And yet, that same night, before the dance was over, suddenly he went in search of Antigone, found her sitting alone – like that, with her arms clasped round her knees – and asked her to marry him. We still don't know how it happened. It didn't seem to surprise Antigone in the least. She looked up at him out of those solemn eyes of hers, smiled sort of sadly and said 'Yes'. That was all. The band struck up another dance. Ismene, surrounded by a group of young men, laughed out loud. And . . . well, here is Haemon expecting to marry Antigone. He won't, of course. He didn't know, when he asked her, that the earth wasn't meant to hold a husband of Antigone, and that this princely distinction was to earn him no more than the right to die sooner than he might otherwise have done.

CHORUS *turns towards* CREON.

That grey-haired, powerfully built man sitting lost in thought, with his little page at his side, is Creon, the King. His face is lined. He is tired. He practises the difficult art of a leader of men. When he was younger, when Oedipus was King and Creon was no more than the King's brother-in-law, he was different. He loved music, bought rare manuscripts, was a kind of art patron. He would while away whole afternoons in the antique shops of this city of Thebes. But Oedipus died. Oedipus' sons died. Creon had to roll up

his sleeves and take over the kingdom. Now and then, when he goes to bed weary with the day's work, he wonders whether this business of being a leader of men is worth the trouble. But when he wakes up the problems are there to be solved; and like a conscientious workman, he does his job.
Creon has a wife, a Queen. Her name is Eurydice. There she sits, the old lady with the knitting, next to the Nurse who brought up the two girls. She will go on knitting all through the play, till the time comes for her to go to her room and die. She is a good woman, a worthy, loving soul. But she is no help to her husband. Creon has to face the music alone. Alone with his page, who is too young to be of any help.
The others? Well, let's see.

He points towards the MESSENGER.

That pale young man leaning against the wall is the Messenger. Later on, he will come running in to announce that Haemon is dead. He has a premonition of catastrophe. That's what he is brooding over. That's why he won't mingle with the others.
As for those three red-faced card players – they are the guards. One smells of garlic, another of beer; but they're not a bad lot. They have wives they are afraid of, kids who are afraid of them; they're bothered by the little day-to-day worries that beset us all. At the same time – they are policemen: eternally innocent, no matter what crimes are committed; eternally indifferent, for nothing that happens can matter to them. They are quite prepared to arrest anybody at all, including Creon himself, should the order be given by a new leader.
That's the lot. Now for the play.
Oedipus, who was the father of the two girls, Antigone and Ismene, had also two sons, Eteocles and Polynices. After Oedipus died, it was agreed that the two sons should share his throne, each to reign over Thebes in alternate years.

Gradually, the lights on the stage have been dimmed.

But when Eteocles, the elder son, had reigned a full year, and the time had come for him to step down, he refused to yield up the throne to his younger brother. There was civil war. Polynices brought up allies – seven foreign princes; and in the course of the war they were defeated, each in front of one of the seven gates of the city. The two brothers fought, and they killed one another in single combat just outside the city walls. Now Thebes is at peace and Creon is King.

CHORUS *is leaning, at this point, against the left proscenium arch. By now the stage is dark, with only the cyclorama bathed in dark blue. A single spot lights up the face of* CHORUS.

Creon has issued a solemn edict that Eteocles, with whom he had sided, is to be buried with pomp and honours, and that Polynices is to be left to rot. The vultures and the dogs are to bloat themselves on his carcass. Nobody is to go into mourning for him. No gravestone is to be set up in his memory. And above all, any person who attempts to give him religious burial will himself be put to death.

While CHORUS *has been speaking the characters have gone out one by one.* CHORUS *disappears through the left arch.*
It is dawn, grey and ashen, in a house asleep. ANTIGONE *steals in from out of doors, through the arch, right. She is carrying her sandals in her hand. She pauses, looking off through the arch, taut, listening, then turns and moves across downstage. As she reaches the table she sees the* NURSE *approaching through the arch, left. She runs quickly towards the exit. As she reaches the steps the* NURSE *enters through the arch and stands still when she sees* ANTIGONE.

NURSE: Where have you been?

ANTIGONE: Nowhere. It was beautiful. The whole world was grey when I went out. And now – you wouldn't recognize it. It's like a postcard: all pink, and green and yellow. You'll have to get up earlier, Nurse, if you want to see a world without colour.

NURSE: It was still pitch black when I got up. I went to your room, for I thought you might have flung off your blanket in the night. You weren't there.

ANTIGONE (*comes down the steps*): The garden was lovely. It was still asleep. Have you ever thought how lovely a garden is when it is not yet thinking of men?

NURSE: You hadn't slept in your bed. I couldn't find you. I went to the back door. You'd left it open.

ANTIGONE: The fields were wet. They were waiting for something to happen. The whole world was breathless, waiting. I can't tell you what a roaring noise I seemed to make alone on the road. It bothered me that whatever was waiting, wasn't waiting for me. I took off my sandals and slipped into a field. (*She moves down to the stool and sits.*)

NURSE (*kneels at* ANTIGONE'S *feet to chafe them and put on the sandals*): You'll do well to wash your feet before you go back to bed, miss.

ANTIGONE: I'm not going back to bed.

NURSE: Don't be a fool! You get some sleep! And me, getting up to see if she hasn't flung off her blanket; and I find her bed cold and nobody in it!

ANTIGONE: Do you think that if a person got up every morning like this, it would be just as thrilling every morning to be the first girl out of doors?

NURSE *puts* ANTIGONE'S *left foot down, lifts her other foot and chafes it.*

NURSE: Morning my grandmother! It was night. It still is. And now, my girl, you'll stop trying to squirm out of this and tell me what you were up to. Where've you been?

ANTIGONE: That's true. It was still night. There wasn't a soul out of doors but me who thought that it was morning. Don't you think it's marvellous – to be the first person who is aware that it is morning?

NURSE: Oh, my little flibbertigibbet! Just can't imagine what I'm talking about, can she? Go on with you! I know that game. Where have you been, wicked girl?

ANTIGONE (*soberly*): No. Not wicked.

NURSE: You went out to meet someone, didn't you? Deny it if you can.

ANTIGONE: Yes. I went out to meet someone.

NURSE: A lover?

ANTIGONE: Yes, Nurse. Yes, the poor dear. I have a lover.

NURSE (*stands up; bursting out*): Ah, that's very nice now, isn't it? Such goings-on! You, the daughter of a king, running out to meet lovers. And we work out fingers to the bone for you, we slave to bring you up like young ladies! (*She sits on a chair, to the right of the table.*) You're all alike, all of you. Even you – who never used to stop to primp in front of a looking-glass, or smear your mouth with rouge, or dindle and dandle to make the boys ogle you, and you ogle back. How many times I'd say to myself, 'Now that one, now: I wish she was a little more of a coquette – always wearing the same dress, her hair tumbling round her face. One thing's sure,' I'd say to myself, 'none of the boys will look at her while Ismene's about, all curled and cute and tidy and trim. I'll have this one on my hands for the rest of my life.' And now, you see? Just like your sister, after all. Only worse: a hypocrite. Who is the lad? Some little scamp, eh? Somebody you can't bring home and show to your family, and say, 'Well, this is him, and I mean to marry him and no other.' That's how it is, is it? Answer me!

ANTIGONE (*smiling faintly*): That's how it is. Yes, Nurse.

NURSE: Yes, says she! God save us! I took her when she wasn't that high. I promised her poor mother I'd make a lady of her. And look at her! But don't you go thinking this is the end of this, my young 'un. I'm only your nurse and you can play deaf and dumb with me; I don't count. But your Uncle Creon will hear of this! That, I promise you.

ANTIGONE (*a little weary*): Yes. Creon will hear of this.

NURSE: And we'll hear what he has to say when he finds out that you go wandering alone o' nights. Not to mention Haemon. For the girl's engaged! Going to be married! Going to be married, and she hops out of bed at four in the morning to meet somebody else in a field. Do you know what

I ought to do to you? Take you over my knee the way I used to do when you were little.

ANTIGONE: Please, Nurse, I want to be alone.

NURSE: And if you so much as speak of it, she says she wants to be alone!

ANTIGONE: Nanny, you shouldn't scold, dear. This isn't a day when you should be losing your temper.

NURSE: Not scold, indeed! Along with the rest of it, I'm to like it. Didn't I promise your mother? What would she say if she was here? 'Old Stupid!' That's what she'd call me. 'Old Stupid. Not to know how to keep my little girl pure! Spend your life making them behave, watching over them like a mother hen, running after them with mufflers and sweaters to keep them warm, and egg nogs to make them strong; and then at four o'clock in the morning, you who always complained you never could sleep a wink, snoring in your bed and letting them slip out into the bushes.' That's what she'd say, your mother. And I'd stand there, dying of shame if I wasn't dead already. And all I could do would be not to dare look her in the face; and 'That's true,' I'd say. 'That's all true what you say, Your Majesty.'

ANTIGONE: Nanny, dear. Dear Nanny. Don't cry. You'll be able to look Mamma in the face when it's your time to see her. And she'll say, 'Good morning, Nanny. Thank you for my little Antigone. You did look after her so well.' She knows why I went out this morning.

NURSE: Not to meet a lover?

ANTIGONE: No. Not to meet a lover.

NURSE: Well, you've a queer way of teasing me, I must say! Not to know when she's teasing me! (*She rises to stand behind* ANTIGONE.) I must be getting awfully old, that's what it is. But if you loved me, you'd tell me the truth. You'd tell me why your bed was empty when I went along to tuck you in. Wouldn't you?

ANTIGONE: Please, Nanny, don't cry any more. (ANTIGONE *turns partly towards the* NURSE, *puts an arm up to the* NURSE'S *shoulder. With her other hand* ANTIGONE *caresses the* NURSE'S *face.*) There now, my sweet red apple. Do you remember how I used to rub your cheeks to make them shine? My dear, wrinkled red apple! I didn't do anything tonight that was worth sending tears down the little gullies of your dear face. I am sure, and I swear that I have no other lover than Haemon. If you like, I'll swear that I shall never have any other lover than Haemon. Save your tears, Nanny, save them, Nanny dear; you may still need them. When you cry like that I become a little girl again; and I mustn't be a little girl today. (ANTIGONE *rises and moves upstage.*)

ISMENE *enters through the arch, at the left. She pauses in front of the arch.*

ISMENE: Antigone! What are you doing up at this hour? I've just been to your room.

NURSE: The two of you, now! You're both going mad, to be up before the kitchen fire has been started. Do you like running about without a mouthful of breakfast? Do you think it's decent for the daughters of a king? (*She turns to* ISMENE.) And look at you, with nothing on, and the sun not up! I'll have you both on my hands with colds before I know it.

ANTIGONE: Nanny dear, go away now. It's not chilly, really. Summer's here. Go and make us some coffee. Please, Nanny, I'd love some coffee. It would do me so much good.

NURSE: My poor baby! Her head's swimming, what with nothing on her stomach, and me standing here like an idiot when I could be getting her something hot to drink. (NURSE *exits.*)

A pause.

ISMENE: Aren't you well?

ANTIGONE: Of course I am. Just a little tired. I got up too early. (ANTIGONE *sits on a chair, suddenly tired.*)

ISMENE: I couldn't sleep, either.

ANTIGONE: Ismene, you ought not to go without your beauty sleep.

ISMENE: Don't make fun of me.

ANTIGONE: I'm not, Ismene, truly. This particular morning, seeing how beautiful you are makes everything easier for me. Wasn't I a miserable little beast when we were small? I used to fling mud at you, and put worms down your neck. I remember tying you to a tree and cutting off your hair. Your beautiful hair! How easy it must be never to be unreasonable with all that smooth silken hair so beautifully set round your head.

ISMENE (*abruptly*): Why do you insist upon talking about other things?

ANTIGONE (*gently*): I am not talking about other things.

ISMENE: Antigone, I've thought about it a lot.

ANTIGONE: Have you?

ISMENE: I thought about it all night long. Antigone, you're mad.

ANTIGONE: Am I?

ISMENE: We cannot do it.

ANTIGONE: Why not?

ISMENE: Creon will have us put to death.

ANTIGONE: Of course he will. That's what he's here for. He will do what he has to do, and we will do what we have to do. He is bound to put us to death. We are bound to go out and bury our brother. That's the way it is. What do you think we can do to change it?

ISMENE (*releases* ANTIGONE'S *hand and draws back a step*): I don't want to die.

ANTIGONE: I'd prefer not to die, myself.

ISMENE: Listen to me, Antigone. I thought about it all night. I'm older than you are. I always think things over, and you don't. You are impulsive. You get a notion in your head and you jump up and do the thing straight off. And if it's silly, well, so much the worse for you. Whereas, *I* think things out.

ANTIGONE: Sometimes it is better not to think too much.

ISMENE: I don't agree with you! (ANTIGONE *looks at* ISMENE, *then turns and moves to the chair behind the table.* ISMENE *leans on the end of the table top, towards* ANTIGONE.) Oh, I know it's horrible. And I pity Polynices just as much as you do. But all the same, I sort of see what Uncle Creon means.

ANTIGONE: I don't want to 'sort of see' anything.

ISMENE: Uncle Creon is the King. He has to set an example!

ANTIGONE: But I am not the King; and I don't have to set people examples. Little Antigone gets a notion in her head – the nasty brat, the wilful, wicked girl; and they put her in a corner all day, or they lock her up in the cellar. And she deserves it. She shouldn't have disobeyed!

ISMENE: There you go, frowning, glowering, wanting your own stubborn way in everything. Listen to me. I'm right oftener than you are.

ANTIGONE: I don't want to be right!

ISMENE: At least you can try to understand.

ANTIGONE: Understand! The first word I ever heard out of any of you was that word 'understand'. Why didn't I 'understand' that I must not play with water – cold, black, beautiful flowing water – because I'd spill it on the palace tiles. Or with earth, because earth dirties a little girl's frock. Why didn't I 'understand' that nice children don't eat out of every dish at once; or give everything in their pockets to beggars; or run in the wind so fast that they fall down; or ask for a drink when they're perspiring; or want to go swimming when it's either too early or too late, merely because they happen to feel like swimming. Understand! I don't want to understand. There'll be time enough to understand when I'm old. . . . If I ever *am* old. But not now.

ISMENE: He is stronger than we are, Antigone. He is the king. And the whole city is with him. Thousands and thousands of them, swarming through all the streets of Thebes.

ANTIGONE: I am not listening to you.

ISMENE: His mob will come running, howling as it runs. A thousand arms will seize our arms. A thousand breaths will breathe into our faces. Like one single pair of eyes, a thousand eyes will stare at us. We'll be driven in a tumbrel through their hatred, through the smell of them and their cruel, roaring laughter. We'll be dragged to the scaffold for torture, surrounded by guards with their idiot faces all bloated, their animal hands clean-washed for the sacrifice, their beefy eyes squinting as they stare at us. And we'll know that no shrieking and no begging will make them understand that we want to live, for they are like slaves who do exactly as they've been told, without caring about right or wrong. And we shall suffer, we shall feel pain rising in us until it becomes so unbearable that we *know* it must stop. But it won't stop; it will go on rising and rising, like a screaming voice. Oh, I can't, I can't, Antigone!

A pause.

ANTIGONE: How well you have thought it all out.
ISMENE: I thought of it all night long. Didn't you?
ANTIGONE: Oh, yes.
ISMENE: I'm an awful coward, Antigone.
ANTIGONE: So am I. But what has that to do with it?
ISMENE: But, Antigone! Don't you want to go on living?
ANTIGONE: Go on living! Who was it that was always the first out of bed because she loved the touch of the cold morning air on her bare skin? Who was always the last to bed because nothing less than infinite weariness could wean her from the lingering night? Who wept when she was little because there were too many grasses in the meadow, too many creatures in the field, for her to know and touch them all?
ISMENE (*clasps* ANTIGONE'S *hands, in a sudden rush of tenderness*): Darling little sister!
ANTIGONE (*repulsing her*): No! For heaven's sake! Don't paw me! And don't let us start snivelling! You say you've thought it all out. The howling mob – the torture – the fear of death. . . . They've made up your mind for you. Is that it?
ISMENE: Yes.
ANTIGONE: All right. They're as good excuses as any.
ISMENE: Antigone, be sensible. It's all very well for men to believe in ideas and die for them. But you are a girl!

ANTIGONE: Don't I know I'm a girl? Haven't I spent my life cursing the fact that I was a girl?

ISMENE (*with spirit*): Antigone! You have everything in the world to make you happy. All you have to do is reach out for it. You are going to be married; you are young; you are beautiful—

ANTIGONE: I am not beautiful.

ISMENE: Yes, you are! Not the way other girls are. But it's always you that the little boys turn to look back at when they pass us in the street. And when you go by the little girls stop talking. They stare and stare at you, until we've turned a corner.

ANTIGONE (*a faint smile*): 'Little boys – little girls.'

ISMENE (*challengingly*): And what about Haemon?

A pause.

ANTIGONE: I shall see Haemon this morning. I'll take care of Haemon. You always said I was mad; and it didn't matter how little I was or what I wanted to do. Go back to bed now, Ismene. The sun is coming up, and, as you see, there is nothing I can do today. Our brother Polynices is as well guarded as if he had won the war and were sitting on his throne. Go along. You are pale with weariness.

ISMENE: What are you going to do?

NURSE (*calls from offstage*): Come along, my dove. Come to breakfast.

ANTIGONE: I don't feel like going to bed. However, if you like, I'll promise not to leave the house till you wake up. Nurse is getting me breakfast. Go and get some sleep. The sun is just up. Look at you: you can't keep your eyes open. Go.

ISMENE: And you will listen to reason, won't you? You'll let me talk to you about this again? Promise?

ANTIGONE: I promise, I'll let you talk. I'll let all of you talk. Go to bed, now. (ISMENE *goes to the arch and exits.*) Poor Ismene!

NURSE (*enters through the arch, speaking as she enters*): Come along, my dove. I've made you some coffee and toast, with jam. (*She turns towards the arch as if to exit.*)

ANTIGONE: I'm not really hungry, Nurse.

The NURSE *stops, looks at* ANTIGONE, *then moves behind her.*

NURSE (*very tenderly*): Where is your pain?

ANTIGONE: Nowhere, Nanny dear. But you must keep me warm and safe, the way you used to do when I was little. Nanny! Stronger than all fever, stronger than any nightmare, stronger than the shadow of the cupboard that used to snarl at me and turn into a dragon on the bedroom wall. Stronger than the thousand insects gnawing and nibbling in the silence of the night. Stronger than the night itself, with the weird hooting of the nightbirds that frightened me even when I could hear them. Nanny, stronger than death, give me your hand, Nanny, as if I were ill in bed, and you sitting beside me.

NURSE: My sparrow, my lamb! What is it that's eating your heart out?

ANTIGONE: Oh, it's just that I'm a little young still for what I have to go through. But nobody but you must know that.

NURSE (*places her other arm round* ANTIGONE'S *shoulder*): A little young for what, my kitten?

ANTIGONE: Nothing in particular, Nanny. Just – just this. Oh, it's so good that you are here. I can hold your calloused hand, your hand that is so prompt to ward off evil. You are very powerful, Nanny.

NURSE: What is it you want me to do for you, my baby?

ANTIGONE: There isn't anything to do, except put your hand like this against my cheek. (*She places the* NURSE'S *hand against her cheek. A pause, then, as* ANTIGONE *leans back, her eyes shut.*) There! I'm not afraid any more. Not afraid of the wicked ogre, nor of the sandman, nor of the dwarf who steals little children. (*A pause.* ANTIGONE *resumes on another note.*) Nanny . . .

NURSE: Yes?

ANTIGONE: My dog, Puff . . .

NURSE (*straightens up, draws her hand away*): Well?

ANTIGONE: Promise me that you will never scold her again.

NURSE: Dogs that dirty up a house with their filthy paws deserve to be scolded.

ANTIGONE: I know. Just the same, promise me.

NURSE: You mean you want me to let her make a mess all over the place and not say a thing?

ANTIGONE: Yes, Nanny.

NURSE: You're asking a lot. The next time she wets my sitting-room carpet, I'll—

ANTIGONE: Please, Nanny, I beg of you.

NURSE: It isn't fair to take me on my weak side, just because you look a little peaked today. . . . Well, have it your own way. We'll mop up and keep our mouth shut. You're making a fool of me, though.

ANTIGONE: And promise me that you will talk to her. That you will talk to her often.

NURSE (*turns and looks at* ANTIGONE): Me, talk to a dog!

ANTIGONE: Yes. But mind you: you are not to talk to her the way people usually talk to dogs. You're to talk to her the way I talk to her.

NURSE: I don't see why both of us have to make fools of ourselves. So long as you're here, one ought to be enough.

ANTIGONE: But if there was a reason why I couldn't go on talking to her—

NURSE (*interrupting*): Couldn't go on talking to her! And why couldn't you go on talking to her? What kind of poppycock—

ANTIGONE: And if she got too unhappy, if she whined and whined, waiting for me with her nose under the door as she does when I'm out all day, then the best thing, Nanny, might be to have her mercifully put to sleep.

NURSE: Now what *has* got into you this morning? (HAEMON *enters through the arch.*) Running round in the darkness, won't sleep, won't eat – (ANTIGONE *sees* HAEMON) – and now it's her dog she wants killed. I never—

ANTIGONE (*interrupting*): Nanny! Haemon is here. Go inside please. And don't forget that you've promised me. (NURSE *goes to the arch and exits.* ANTIGONE *rises.*) Haemon, Haemon! Forgive me for quarrelling with you last night. (*She crosses quickly to* HAEMON *and they embrace.*) Forgive me for everything. It was all my fault. I beg you to forgive me.

HAEMON: You know that I've forgiven you. You had hardly slammed the door, your perfume still hung in the room, when I had already forgiven you. (*He holds her in his arms and smiles at her. Then draws slightly back.*) You stole that perfume. From whom?

ANTIGONE: Ismene.

HAEMON: And the rouge? and the face powder? and the frock? Whom did you steal them from?

ANTIGONE: Ismene.

HAEMON: And in whose honour did you get yourself up so elegantly?

ANTIGONE: I'll tell you everything. (*She draws him closer.*) Oh, darling, what a fool I was! To waste a whole evening! A whole, beautiful evening!

HAEMON: We'll have other evenings, my sweet.

ANTIGONE: Perhaps we won't.

HAEMON: And other quarrels, too. A happy love is full of quarrels, you know.

ANTIGONE: A happy love, yes. Haemon, listen to me.

HAEMON: Yes?

ANTIGONE: Don't laugh at me this morning. Be serious.

HAEMON: I am serious.

ANTIGONE: And hold me tight. Tighter than you have ever held me. I want all your strength to flow into me.

HAEMON: There! With all my strength.

A pause.

ANTIGONE (*breathless*): That's good. (*They stand for a moment, silent and motionless.*) Haemon! I wanted to tell you. You know – the little boy we were going to have when we were married?

HAEMON: Yes?

ANTIGONE: I'd have protected him against everything in the world.

HAEMON: Yes, dearest.

ANTIGONE: Oh, you don't know how I should have held him in my arms and given him my strength. He wouldn't have been afraid of anything, I swear he wouldn't. Not of the falling night, nor of the terrible noonday sun, nor of all the shadows on all the walls in the world. Our little boy, Haemon! His mother wouldn't have been very imposing: her hair wouldn't always have been brushed; but she would have been strong where he was concerned, so much stronger than all those real mothers with their real bosoms and their aprons round their middle. You believe that, don't you, Haemon?

HAEMON (*soothingly*): Yes, yes, my darling.

ANTIGONE: And you believe me when I say that you would have had a real wife?

HAEMON: Darling, you are my real wife.

ANTIGONE (*pressing against him and crying out*): Haemon, you loved me! You did love me that night, didn't you? You're sure of it!

HAEMON (*rocking her gently*): What night, my sweet?

ANTIGONE: And you are very sure, aren't you, that that night, at the dance, when you came to the corner where I was sitting, there was no mistake? It was me you were looking for? It wasn't another girl? And you're sure that never, not in your most secret heart of hearts, have you said to yourself that it was Ismene you ought to have asked to marry you?

HAEMON (*reproachfully*): Antigone, you are idiotic. You might give me credit for knowing my own mind. It's you I love, and no one else.

ANTIGONE: But you love me as a woman – as a woman wants to be loved, don't you? Your arms round me aren't lying, are they? Your hands, so warm against my back – they're not lying? This warmth that's in me; this confidence, this sense that I am safe, secure, that flows through me as I stand here with my cheek in the hollow of your shoulder: they are not lies, are they?

HAEMON: Antigone, darling, I love you exactly as you love me. With all of myself.

They kiss.

ANTIGONE: I'm sallow, and I'm scrawny. Ismene is pink and golden. She's like a fruit.

HAEMON: Look here, Antigone—

ANTIGONE: Ah, dearest, I am ashamed of myself. But this morning, this special morning, I must know. Tell me the truth! I beg you to tell me the truth! When you think about me, when it strikes you suddenly that I am going to belong to you – do you have the feeling that – that a great empty space is being hollowed out inside you, that there is something inside you that is just – dying?

HAEMON: Yes, I do, I do.

A pause.

ANTIGONE: That's the way I feel. And another thing. I wanted you to know that I should have been very proud to be your wife – the woman whose shoulder you would put your hand on as you sat down to table, absentmindedly, as upon a thing that belongs to you. (*After a moment, she draws away from him. Her tone changes.*) There! Now I have two things more to tell you. And when I have told them to you, you must go away instantly, without asking any questions. However strange they may seem to you. However much they may hurt you. Swear that you will!

HAEMON (*beginning to be troubled*): What are these things that you are going to tell me?

ANTIGONE: Swear, first, that you will go away without one word. Without so much as looking at me. (*She looks at him, wretchedness in her face.*) You hear me, Haemon. Swear it, please. This is the last mad wish that you will ever have to grant me.

A pause.

HAEMON: I swear it, since you insist. But I must tell you that I don't like this at all.

ANTIGONE: Please, Haemon. It's very serious. You must listen to me and do as I ask. First, about last night, when I came to your house. You asked me a moment ago why I wore Ismene's dress and rouge. It was because I was stupid. I wasn't very sure that you loved me as a woman; and I did it – because I wanted you to want me. I was trying to be more like other girls.

HAEMON: Was *that* the reason? My poor—

ANTIGONE: Yes. And you laughed at me. And we quarrelled; and my awful temper got the better of me and I flung out of the house. . . . The real reason was that I wanted you to take me; I wanted to be your wife before—

HAEMON: Oh, my darling—

ANTIGONE (*shuts him off*): You swore you wouldn't ask any questions. You swore, Haemon. (*She turns her face away and goes on in a hard voice:*) As a matter of fact, I'll tell you why. I wanted to be your wife last night because I love you that way very – very strongly. And also because— Oh, my darling, my darling, forgive me; I'm going to cause you quite a lot of pain. (*She draws away from him.*) I wanted it also because I shall never, never be able to marry you, never! (HAEMON *is stupefied and mute; then he moves a step towards her.*) Haemon! You took a solemn path! You swore! Leave me quickly! Tomorrow the whole thing will be clear to you. Even before tomorrow: this afternoon. If you please, Haemon, go now. It is the only thing left that you can do for me if you still love me. (*A pause as* HAEMON *stares at her. Then he turns and goes through the arch.* ANTIGONE *stands motionless, then moves to the chair at end of the table and lets herself down on it. In a mild voice, as of calm after storm:*) Well, it's over for Haemon, Antigone.

ISMENE *enters through the arch, pauses for a moment in front of it when she sees* ANTIGONE, *then crosses behind the table.*

ISMENE: I can't sleep. I'm terrified. I'm so afraid that even though it is daylight, you'll still try to bury Polynices. Antigone, little sister, we all want to make you happy – Haemon, and Nurse, and I, and Puff whom you love. We love you, we are alive, we need you. And you remember what Polynices was like. He was our brother, of course. But he's dead; and he never loved you. He was a bad brother. He was like an enemy in the house. He never thought of you. Why should you think of him? What if his soul does have to wander through endless time without rest or peace? Don't try something that is beyond your strength. You are always defying the world, but you're only a girl, after all. Stay at home tonight. Don't try to do it, I beg you. It's Creon's doing, not ours.

ANTIGONE: You are too late, Ismene. When you first saw me this morning, I had just come in from burying him.

ANTIGONE *exits through the arch.*

The lighting, which by this time has reached a point of early-morning sun, is quickly dimmed out, leaving the stage bathed in a light blue colour.

ISMENE *runs out after* ANTIGONE.

On ISMENE'S *exit the lights are brought up suddenly to suggest a later period of the day.*

CREON *and the* PAGE *enter through the curtain upstage.* CREON *stands on the top step; his* PAGE *stands at his right side.*

CREON: A private of the guards, you say? One of those standing watch over the body? Show him in.

The PAGE *crosses to the arch and exits.* CREON *moves down to the end of the table.*

PAGE *re-enters, preceded by the* FIRST GUARD, *livid with fear. The* PAGE *remains on the upstage side of the arch. The* GUARD *salutes.*

GUARD: Private Jonas, Second Battalion.

CREON: What are you doing here?

GUARD: It's like this, sir. Soon as it happened, we said: 'Got to tell the chief about this before anybody else spills it. He'll want to know right away.' So we tossed a coin to see which one would come up and tell you about it. You see, sir, we thought only one man had better come, because, after all, you don't want to leave the body without a guard. Right? I mean, there's three of us on duty, guarding the body.

CREON: What's wrong about the body?

GUARD: Sir, I've been seventeen years in the service. Volunteer. Wounded three times. Two mentions. My record's clean. I know my business and I know my place. I carry out orders. Sir, ask any officer in the battalion; they'll tell you. 'Leave it to Jonas. Give him an order: he'll carry it out.' That's what they'll tell you, sir. Jonas, that's me – that's my name.

CREON: What's the matter with you, man? What are you shaking for?

GUARD: By rights it's the corporal's job, sir, I've been recommended for a corporal but they haven't put it through yet. June, it was supposed to go through.

CREON (*interrupts*): Stop chattering and tell me why you are here. If anything has gone wrong, I'll break all three of you.

GUARD: Nobody can say we didn't keep our eye on that body. We had the two-o'clock watch – the tough one. You know how it is, sir. It's nearly the end of the night. Your eyes are like lead. You've got a crick in the back of your neck. There's shadows, and the fog is beginning to roll in. A fine watch they give us! And me, seventeen years in the service. But we was doing our duty all right. On our feet, all of us. Anybody says we were sleeping is a liar. First place, it was too cold. Second place— (CREON *makes a gesture of impatience.*) Yes, sir. Well, I turned round and looked at the body. We wasn't only ten feet away from it, but that's how I am. I was keeping my eye on it. (*Shouts.*) Listen, sir, I was the first man to see it! Me! They'll tell you. I was the one let out that yell!

CREON: What for? What was the matter?

GUARD: Sir, the body! Somebody had been there and buried it. (CREON *comes down a step on the stair. The* GUARD *becomes more frightened.*) It wasn't much, you understand. With us three there, it couldn't have been. Just covered over with a little dirt, that's all. But enough to hide it from the buzzards.

CREON: By God, I'll—! (*He looks intently at the* GUARD.) You are sure that it couldn't have been a dog, scratching up the earth?

GUARD: Not a chance, sir. That's kind of what we hoped it was. But the earth was scattered over the body just like the priests tell you you should do it. Whoever did that job knew what he was doing all right.

CREON: Who could have dared? (*He turns and looks at the* GUARD.) Was there anything to indicate who might have done it?

GUARD: Not a thing, sir. Maybe we heard a footstep – I can't swear to it. Of course, we started right in to search, and the corporal found a shovel, a kid's shovel no bigger than that, all rusty and everything. Corporal's got the shovel for you. We thought maybe a kid did it.

CREON (*to himself*): A kid! (*He looks away from the* GUARD.) I broke the back of the rebellion; but like a snake, it is coming together again. Polynices' friends, with their gold, blocked by my orders in the banks of Thebes. The leaders of the mob, stinking of garlic and allied to envious princes. And the temple priests, always ready for a bit of fishing in troubled waters. A kid! I can imagine what he is like, their kid: a baby-faced killer, creeping in the night with a toy shovel under his jacket. (*He looks at his* PAGE.) Though why shouldn't they have corrupted a real child? Very touching! Very useful to the party, an innocent child. A martyr. A real white-faced baby of fourteen who will spit with contempt at the guards who kill him. A free gift to their cause: the precious, innocent blood of a child on my hands. (*He turns to the* GUARD.) They must have accomplices in the Guard itself. Look here, you. Who knows about this?

GUARD: Only us three, sir. We flipped a coin, and I came right over.

CREON: Right. Listen, now. You will continue on duty. When the relief squad comes up, you will tell them to return to barracks. You will uncover the body. If another attempt is made to bury it, I shall expect you to make an arrest and bring the person straight to me. And you will keep your mouths shut. Not one word of this to a human soul. You are all guilty of neglect of duty, and you will be punished; but if the rumour spreads through Thebes that the body received burial, you will be shot – all three of you.

GUARD (*excitedly*): Sir, we never told nobody, I swear we didn't! Anyhow, I've been up here. Suppose my pals spilled it to the relief; I couldn't have been with them and here, too. That wouldn't be my fault if they talked. Sir, I've got two kids. You're my witness, sir, it couldn't have been me. I was here with you. I've got a witness! If anybody talked, it couldn't have been me! I was—

CREON (*interrupting*): Clear out! If the story doesn't get round, you won't be shot. (*The* GUARD *salutes, turns and exits, at the double.* CREON *turns and paces upstage, then comes down to the end of the table.*) A child! (*He looks at the* PAGE.) Come along, my lad. Since we can't hope to keep this to ourselves, we shall have to be the first to give out the news. And after that, we shall have to clean up the mess. (*The* PAGE *crosses to the side of* CREON. CREON *puts his hand on the* PAGE'S *shoulder.*) Would you be willing to die for me? Would you defy the Guard with your little shovel? (*The* PAGE *looks up at* CREON.) Of course you would. You would do it, too. (*A pause.* CREON *looks away from the* PAGE *and murmurs:*) A child!

(CREON *and the* PAGE *go slowly upstage centre to the top step. The* PAGE *draws aside the curtain, through which* CREON *exits with the* PAGE *behind him.*)

As soon as CREON *and the* PAGE *have disappeared,* CHORUS *enters and leans against the upstage portal of the arch, left. The lighting is brought up to its brightest point to suggest mid-afternoon.* CHORUS *allows a pause to indicate that a crucial moment has been reached in the play, then moves slowly downstage, centre. He stands for a moment silent, reflecting, and then smiles faintly.*

CHORUS: The spring is wound up tight. It will uncoil of itself. That is what is so convenient in tragedy. The least little turn of the wrist will do the job. Anything will set it going: a glance at a girl who happens to be lifting her arms to her hair as you go by; a feeling when you wake up on a fine morning that you'd like a little respect paid to you today, as if it were as easy to order as a second cup of coffee; one question too many, idly thrown out over a friendly drink – and the tragedy is on.

The rest is automatic. You don't need to lift a finger. The machine is in perfect order; it has been oiled since time began, and it runs without friction. Death, treason and sorrow are on the march; and they move in the wake of storm, of tears, of stillness. Every kind of stillness. The hush when the executioner's axe goes up at the end of the last act. The unbreathable silence when, at the beginning of the play, the two lovers, their hearts bared, their bodies naked, stand for the first time face to face in the darkened room, afraid to stir. The silence inside you when the roaring crowd acclaims the winner – so that you think of a film without a sound-track, mouths agape and no sound coming out of them, a clamour that is no more than a picture; and you, the victor, already vanquished, alone in the desert of your silence. That is tragedy.

Tragedy is clean, it is restful, it is flawless. It has nothing to do with melodrama – with wicked villains, persecuted maidens, avengers, sudden revelations and eleventh-hour repentances. Death, in a melodrama, is really horrible because it is never inevitable. The dear old father might so easily have been saved; the honest young man might so easily have brought in the police five minutes earlier.

In a tragedy, nothing is in doubt and everyone's destiny is

known. That makes for tranquillity. There is a sort of fellow-feeling among characters in a tragedy: he who kills is as innocent as he who gets killed: it's all a matter of what part you are playing. Tragedy is restful; and the reason is that hope, that foul, deceitful thing, has no part in it. There isn't any hope. You're trapped. The whole sky has fallen on you, and all you can do about it is to shout. Don't mistake me: I said 'shout': I did not say groan, whimper, complain. That, you cannot do. But you can shout aloud; you can get all those things said that you never dared say – or never even knew till then. And you don't say these things because it will do any good to say them: you know better than that. You say them for their own sake; you say them because you learn a lot from them.

In melodrama, you argue and struggle in the hope of escape. That is vulgar; it's practical. But in tragedy, where there is no temptation to try to escape, argument is gratuitous: it's kindly.

Voices of the GUARDS *and scuffling sounds heard through the archway.* CHORUS *looks in that direction, then, in a changed tone:*

The play is on. Antigone has been caught. For the first time in her life, little Antigone is going to be able to be herself.

CHORUS *exits through the arch.*

A pause, while the offstage voices rise in volume, then the FIRST GUARD *enters, followed by the* SECOND *and* THIRD GUARDS, *holding the arms of* ANTIGONE *and dragging her along. The* FIRST GUARD, *speaking as he enters, crosses swiftly to the end of the table. The* TWO GUARDS *and* ANTIGONE *stop downstage.*

FIRST GUARD (*recovered from his fright*): Come on, now, miss, give it a rest. The chief will be here in a minute and you can tell him about it. All I know is my orders. I don't want to know what you were doing there. People always have excuses; but I can't afford to listen to them, see. Why, if we had to listen to all the people who want to tell us what's the matter with this country, we'd never get our work done.

(*To the* GUARDS.) You keep hold of her and (*to* ANTIGONE) you keep quiet.

ANTIGONE: They are hurting me. Tell them to take their dirty hands off me.

FIRST GUARD: Dirty hands, eh? The least you can do is try to be polite, miss. Look at me: I'm polite.

ANTIGONE: Tell them to let me go. I shan't run away. My father was King Oedipus. I am Antigone.

FIRST GUARD: King Oedipus' little girl! Well, well, well! Listen, miss, the night watch never picks up a lady but they say, you better be careful: I'm sleeping with the police commissioner.

The GUARDS *laugh.*

ANTIGONE: I don't mind being killed, but I don't want them to touch me.

FIRST GUARD: And what about corpses, and dirt, and suchlike? You wasn't afraid to touch them, was you? 'Their dirty hands!' Take a look at your own hands. (ANTIGONE, *handcuffed, smiles despite herself as she looks down at her hands. They are grubby.*) You must have lost your shovel, didn't you? Had to go at it with your fingernails the second time. By God, I never saw such nerve! I turn my back for about five seconds; I ask a pal for a chew; I say 'thanks'; I get the tobacco stowed away in my cheek – the whole thing don't take ten seconds; and there she is, clawing away like a hyena. Right out in broad daylight! And did she scratch and kick when I grabbed her! Straight for my eyes with them nails she went. And yelling something fierce about, 'I haven't finished yet; let me finish!' The girl's mad!

SECOND GUARD: I pinched a nut like that the other day. Right on the main square she was, hoisting up her skirts and showing her behind to anybody that wanted to take a look.

FIRST GUARD: Listen, we're going to get a bonus out of this. What do you say we throw a party, the three of us?

SECOND GUARD: At the old woman's? Behind Market Street?

THIRD GUARD: Suits me. Sunday would be a good day. We're off duty Sunday. What do you say we bring our wives?

FIRST GUARD: No. Let's have some fun this time. Bring your wife, there's always something goes wrong. First place, what do you do with the kids? Bring them, they always want to go to the loo just when you're right in the middle of a game of cards or something. Listen, who would have thought an hour ago that us three would be talking about throwing a party now? The way I felt when the old man was interrogating me, we'd be lucky if we got off with being docked a month's pay. I want to tell you, I was scared.

SECOND GUARD: You sure we're going to get a bonus?

FIRST GUARD: Yes. Something tells me this is big stuff.

THIRD GUARD (*to* SECOND GUARD): What's-his-name, you know – in the Third Battalion? He got an extra month's pay. Caught a man setting fire to a house.

SECOND GUARD: If we get an extra month's pay, I vote we throw the party at the Arabian's.

FIRST GUARD: You're crazy! He charges twice as much for liquor as anybody else in town. Unless you want to go upstairs, of course. Can't do that at the old woman's.

THIRD GUARD: There's no way to keep this from our wives. You get an extra month's pay, and what happens? Everybody in the battalion knows it, and your wife knows it, too. They might even line up the battalion and give it to you in front of everybody, so how could you keep your wife from finding out?

FIRST GUARD: Well, we'll see about that. If they do the job out in the barrack-yard – of course that means women, kids, everything.

ANTIGONE: I should like to sit down, if you please.

A pause, as the FIRST GUARD *thinks it over.*

FIRST GUARD: Let her sit down. But keep hold of her. (*The*

two GUARDS *start to lead her towards the chair at the end of the table. The curtain upstage opens, and* CREON *enters, followed by his* PAGE. *The* FIRST GUARD *turns and moves upstage a few steps, sees* CREON.) 'Tenshun! (*The three* GUARDS *salute.* CREON, *seeing* ANTIGONE *handcuffed to* THIRD GUARD, *stops on the top step, astonished.*)

CREON: Antigone! (*To the* FIRST GUARD.) Take off those handcuffs! (*The* FIRST GUARD *crosses above the table to the left of* ANTIGONE.) What is this? (CREON *and his* PAGE *come down off the steps.*)

The FIRST GUARD *takes the key from his pocket and unlocks the cuff on* ANTIGONE'S *hand.* ANTIGONE *rubs her wrist as she crosses below the table towards the chair at the end of the table. The* SECOND *and* THIRD GUARDS *step back to the front of the arch. The* FIRST GUARD *turns upstage towards* CREON.

FIRST GUARD: The watch, sir. We all came this time.
CREON: Who is guarding the body?
FIRST GUARD: We sent for the relief.

CREON *comes down.*

CREON: But I gave orders that the relief was to go back to barracks and stay there! (ANTIGONE *sits on the chair at the left of the table.*) I told you not to open your mouth about this!
FIRST GUARD: Nobody's said anything, sir. We made this arrest, and brought the party in, the way you said we should.
CREON (*to* ANTIGONE): Where did these men find you?
FIRST GUARD: Right by the body.
CREON: What were you doing near your brother's body? You knew what my orders were.
FIRST GUARD: What was she doing? Sir, that's why we brought her in. She was digging up the dirt with her nails. She was trying to cover up the body all over again.
CREON: Do you realize what you are saying?
FIRST GUARD: Sir, ask these men here. After I reported to you, I went back, and first thing we did, we uncovered the body. The sun was coming up and it was beginning to smell,

so we moved it up on a little rise to get him in the wind. Of course, you wouldn't expect any trouble in broad daylight. But just the same, we decided one of us had better keep his eye peeled all the same. About noon, what with the sun and the smell, and as the wind dropped and I wasn't feeling none too good, I went over to my pal to get a chew. I just had time to say 'Thanks' and stick it in my mouth, when I turned round and there she was, clawing away at the dirt with both hands. Right out in broad daylight! Wouldn't you think when she saw me come running she'd stop and leg it out of there? Not her! She went right on digging as fast as she could, as if I wasn't there at all. And when I grabbed her, she scratched and bit and yelled to leave her alone, she hadn't finished yet, the body wasn't all covered yet, and the like of that.

CREON (*to* ANTIGONE): Is this true?

ANTIGONE: Yes, it is true.

FIRST GUARD: We scraped the dirt off as fast as we could, then we sent for the relief and we posted them. But we didn't tell them a thing, sir. And we brought in the party so's you could see her. And that's the truth, so help me God.

CREON (*to* ANTIGONE): And was it you who covered the body the first time? In the night?

ANTIGONE: Yes, it was. With a toy shovel we used to take to the seashore when we were children. It was Polynices' own shovel; he had cut his name in the handle. That was why I left it with him. But these men took it away; so the next time, I had to do it with my hands.

FIRST GUARD: Sir, she was clawing away like a wild animal. Matter of fact, first minute we saw her, what with the heat haze and everything, my pal says, 'That must be a dog,' he says. 'Dog!' I says. 'That's a girl, that is!' And it was.

CREON: Very well (*He turns to the* PAGE.) Show these men to the ante-room. (*The* PAGE *crosses to the arch, and stands there, waiting.* CREON *moves behind the table. To the* FIRST GUARD:) You three men will wait outside. I may want a report from you later.

FIRST GUARD: Do I put the cuffs back on her, sir?

CREON: No. (*The three* GUARDS *salute, do an about-turn and exit through the arch, right. The* PAGE *follows them out. A pause.*) Had you told anybody what you meant to do?

ANTIGONE: No.

CREON: Did you meet anyone on your way – coming or going?

ANTIGONE: No, nobody.

CREON: Sure of that, are you?

ANTIGONE: Perfectly sure.

CREON: Very well. Now listen to me. You will go straight to your room. When you get there, you will go to bed. You will say that you are not well and that you have not been out since yesterday. Your nurse will tell the same story. (*He looks towards the arch, through which the* GUARDS *have exited.*) And I'll get rid of those three men.

ANTIGONE: Uncle Creon, you are going to a lot of trouble for no good reason. You must know that I'll do it all over again tonight.

A pause. They look one another in the eye.

CREON: Why did you try to bury your brother?

ANTIGONE: I owed it to him.

CREON: I had forbidden it.

ANTIGONE: I owed it to him. Those who are not buried wander eternally and find no rest. If my brother were alive, and he came home weary after a long day's hunting, I should kneel down and unlace his boots, I should fetch him food and drink, I should see that his bed was ready for him. Polynices is home from the hunt. I owe it to him to unlock the house of the dead in which my father and my mother are waiting to welcome him. Polynices has earned his rest.

CREON: Polynices was a rebel and a traitor, and you know it.

ANTIGONE: He was my brother.

CREON: You heard my edict. It was proclaimed throughout Thebes. You read my edict. It was posted up on the city walls.

ANTIGONE: Of course I did.

CREON: You knew the punishment I decreed for any person who attempted to give him burial.

ANTIGONE: Yes, I knew the punishment.

CREON: Did you by any chance act on the assumption that a daughter of Oedipus, a daughter of Oedipus' stubborn pride, was above the law?

ANTIGONE: No, I did not act on that assumption.

CREON: Because if you had acted on that assumption, Antigone, you would have been deeply wrong. Nobody has a more sacred obligation to obey the law than those who make the law. You are a daughter of law-makers, a daughter of kings. Antigone. You must observe the law.

ANTIGONE: Had I been a scullery maid washing my dishes when that law was read aloud to me, I should have scrubbed the greasy water from my arms and gone out in my apron to bury my brother.

CREON: What nonsense! If you had been a scullery maid, there would have been no doubt in your mind about the seriousness of that edict. You would have known that it meant death; and you would have been satisfied to weep for your brother in your kitchen. But you! You thought that because you come of the royal line, because you were my niece and were going to marry my son, I shouldn't dare have you killed.

ANTIGONE: You are mistaken. Quite the contrary. I never doubted for an instant that you would have put me to death.

A pause, as CREON *stares fixedly at her.*

CREON: The pride of Oedipus! Oedipus and his headstrong pride all over again. I can see your father in you – and I believe you. Of course you thought that I should have you killed! Proud as you are, it seemed to you a natural climax to your existence. Your father was like that. For him as for you, human happiness was meaningless; and mere human misery was not enough to satisfy his passion for torment. (*He sits on a stool behind the table.*) You come of people for whom the human vestment is a kind of straitjacket: it cracks at the seams. You spend your lives wriggling to get out of it. Nothing less than a cosy tea party with death and destiny will quench your thirst. The happiest hour of your father's life came when he listened greedily to the story of how, unknown to himself, he had killed his own father and dishonoured the bed of his own mother. Drop by drop, word by word, he drank in the dark story that the gods had destined him, first to live and then to hear. How avidly men and women drink the brew of such a tale when their names are Oedipus – and Antigone! And it is so simple, afterwards, to do what your father did, to put out one's eyes and take one's daughters begging on the highways.

Let me tell you, Antigone: those days are over for Thebes. Thebes has a right to a King without a past. My name, thank God, is only Creon. I stand here with both feet firm on the ground; with both hands in my pockets; and I have decided that so long as I am King – being less ambitious than your father was – I shall merely devote myself to introducing a little order into this absurd kingdom; if that is possible.

Don't think that being a king seems to me romantic. It is my trade; a trade a man has to work at every day; and like every other trade, it isn't all beer and skittles. But since it is my trade, I take it seriously. And if, tomorrow, some wild and bearded messenger walks in from some wild and distant valley – which is what happened to your dad – and tells me that he's not quite sure who my parents were, but thinks that my wife Eurydice is actually my mother, I shall ask him to do me the kindness to go back where he came from; and I shan't let a little matter like that persuade me to order my wife to take a blood test and the police to let me know whether or not my birth certificate was forged. Kings, my girl, have other things to do than to surrender themselves to their private feelings. (*He looks at her and smiles.*) Hand *you* over to be killed! (*He rises, moves to the end of the table and sits on the top of the table.*) I have other plans for you. You're going to marry Haemon; and I want you to fatten up a bit so that you can give him a sturdy boy. Let me assure you that Thebes needs that boy a good deal more than it needs your death. You will go to your room, now, and do as you have been told; and you won't say a word about this to anybody. Don't fret about the guards: I'll see that their mouths are shut. And don't annihilate me with those eyes. I know that you think I am a brute, and I'm sure you must consider me very prosaic. But the fact is, I have always been fond of you, stubborn though you always were. Don't forget that the first doll you ever had came from me. (*A pause.* ANTIGONE *says nothing, rises and crosses slowly below the table towards the arch.* CREON *turns and watches her; then:*) Where are you going?

ANTIGONE (*stops downstage. Without any show of rebellion*): You know very well where I am going.

CREON (*after a pause*): What sort of game are you playing?

ANTIGONE: I am not playing games.

CREON: Antigone, do you realize that if, apart from those three guards, a single soul finds out what you have tried to do, it will be impossible for me to avoid putting you to death? There is still a chance that I can save you; but only if you keep this to yourself and give up your crazy purpose. Five minutes more, and it will be too late. You understand that?

ANTIGONE: I must go and bury my brother. Those men uncovered him.

CREON: What good will it do? You know that there are other men standing guard over Polynices. And even if you did cover him over with earth again, the earth would again be removed.

ANTIGONE: I know all that. I know it. But that much, at least, I can do. And what a person can do, a person ought to do.

Pause.

CREON: Tell me, Antigone, do you believe all that flummery about religious burial? Do you really believe that a so-called shade of your brother is condemned to wander for ever homeless if a little earth is not flung on his corpse to the accompaniment of some priestly abracadabra? Have you ever listened to the priests of Thebes when they were mumbling their formula? Have you ever watched those dreary bureaucrats while they were preparing the dead for burial – skipping half the gestures required by the ritual, swallowing half their words, hustling the dead into their graves out of fear that they might be late for lunch?

ANTIGONE: Yes, I have seen all that.

CREON: And did you never say to yourself as you watched them, that if someone you really loved lay dead under the ministrations of the priests, you would scream aloud and beg the priests to leave the dead in peace?

ANTIGONE: Yes, I've thought all that.

CREON: And you still insist upon being put to death – merely because I refuse to let your brother go out with that grotesque passport; because I refuse his body the wretched consolation of that mass-production jibber-jabber, which you would have been the first to be embarrassed by if I had allowed it. The whole thing is absurd!

ANTIGONE: Yes, it's absurd.

CREON: Then why, Antigone, why? For whose sake? For the sake of them that believe in it? To raise them against me?

ANTIGONE: No.

CREON: For whom, then, if not for them and not for Polynices either?

ANTIGONE: For nobody. For myself.

A pause as they stand looking at one another.

CREON: You must want very much to die. You look like a trapped animal.

ANTIGONE: Stop feeling sorry for me. Do as I do. Do your job. But if you are a human being, do it quickly. That is all I ask of you. I'm not going to be able to hold out for ever.

CREON (*takes a step towards her*): I want to save you, Antigone.

ANTIGONE: You are the King, and you are all-powerful. But that you cannot do.

CREON: You think not?
ANTIGONE: Neither save me nor stop me.
CREON: Prideful Antigone! Little Oedipus!
ANTIGONE: Only this can you do: have me put to death.
CREON: Have you tortured, perhaps?
ANTIGONE: Why would you do that? To see me cry? To hear me beg for mercy? Or swear whatever you wish, and then begin over again?

A pause.

CREON: You listen to me. You have cast me for the villain in this little play of yours, and yourself for the heroine. And you know it, you damned little mischief-maker! But don't you drive me too far! If I were one of your preposterous little tyrants that Greece is full of, you would be lying in a ditch this minute with your tongue pulled out and your body drawn and quartered. But you can see something in my face that makes me hesitate to send for the guards and turn you over to them. Instead, I let you go on arguing; and you taunt me, you take the offensive. (*He grasps her left wrist.*) What are you driving at, you she-devil?
ANTIGONE: Let me go. You are hurting my arm.
CREON (*gripping her tighter*): I will not let you go.
ANTIGONE (*moans*): Oh!
CREON: I was a fool to waste words. I should have done this from the beginning. (*He looks at her.*) I may be your uncle – but we are not a particularly affectionate family. Are we, eh? (*Through his teeth, as he twists.*) Are we? (CREON *propels* ANTIGONE *round below him to his side.*) What fun for you, eh? To be able to spit in the face of a king who has all the power in the world; a man who has seen people killed who were just as pitiable as you are – and who is still soft enough to go to all this trouble in order to keep you from being killed.

A pause.

ANTIGONE: Now you are squeezing my arm too tightly. It doesn't hurt any more.

CREON *stares at her, then drops her arm.*

CREON: I shall save you yet. (*He goes below the table to the chair at the end of the table, takes off his coat and places it on the chair.*) God knows, I have things enough to do today without wasting my time on an insect like you. There's plenty to do, I assure you, when you've just put down a revolution. But urgent things can wait. I am not going to let politics be the cause of your death. For it is a fact that this whole business is nothing but politics: the mournful shade of Polynices, the decomposing corpse, the sentimental weeping and the hysteria that you mistake for heroism – nothing but politics. Look here. I may not be soft, but I'm fastidious. I like things clean, ship-shape, well scrubbed. Don't think that I am not just as offended as you are by the thought of that meat rotting in the sun. In the evening, when the breeze comes in off the sea, you can smell it in the palace, and it nauseates me. But I refuse even to shut my window. It's vile; and I can tell you what I wouldn't tell anybody else: it's stupid, monstrously stupid. But the people of Thebes have got to have their noses rubbed into it a little longer. My God! If it was up to me, I should have had them bury your brother long ago as a mere matter of public hygiene. I admit that what I am doing is childish. But if the featherheaded rabble I govern are to understand what's what, that stench has got to fill the town for a month!

ANTIGONE (*turns to him*): You are a loathsome man!

CREON: I agree. My trade forces me to be. We could argue whether I ought or ought not to follow my trade; but once I take on the job, I must do it properly.

ANTIGONE: Why do you do it at all?

CREON: My dear, I woke up one morning and found myself King of Thebes. God knows, there were other things I loved in life more than power.

ANTIGONE: Then you should have said no.

CREON: Yes, I could have done that. Only, I felt that it would have been cowardly. I should have been like a workman who turns down a job that has to be done. So I said yes.

ANTIGONE: So much the worse for you, then. I didn't say yes. I can say no to anything I think vile, and I don't have to count the cost. But because you said yes, all that you can do, for all your crown and your trappings, and your guards – all that you can do is to have me killed.

CREON: Listen to me.

ANTIGONE: If I want to. I don't have to listen to you if I don't want to. You've said your *yes*. There is nothing more you can tell me that I don't know. You stand there, drinking in my words. (*She moves behind the chair.*) Why is it that you don't call your guards? I'll tell you why. You want to hear me out to the end; that's why.

CREON: You amuse me.

ANTIGONE: Oh, no, I don't. I frighten you. That is why you talk about saving me. Everything would be so much easier if you had a docile, tongue-tied little Antigone living in the palace. I'll tell you something, Uncle Creon: I'll give you back one of your own words. You are too fastidious to make a good tyrant. But you are going to have to put me to death today, and you know it. And that's what frightens you. God! Is there anything uglier than a frightened man!

CREON: Very well, I am afraid, then. Does that satisfy you? I am afraid that if you insist upon it, I shall have to have you killed. And I don't want to.

ANTIGONE: I don't have to do things that I think are wrong. If it comes to that, you didn't really want to leave my brother's body unburied, did you? Say it! Admit that you didn't.

CREON: I have said it already.

ANTIGONE: But you did it just the same. And now, though you don't want to do it, you are going to have me killed. And you call that being a king.

CREON: Yes, I call that being a king.

ANTIGONE: Poor Creon! My nails are broken, my fingers are

bleeding, my arms are covered with the welts left by the paws of your guards – but I am a queen!

CREON: Then why not have pity on me, and live? Isn't your brother's corpse, rotting there under my windows, payment enough for peace and order in Thebes? My son loves you. Don't make me add your life to the payment. I've paid enough.

ANTIGONE: No, Creon! You said yes, and made yourself king. Now you will never stop paying.

CREON: But God in Heaven! Won't you try to understand me! I'm trying hard enough to understand you! There had to be one man who said yes. Somebody had to agree to captain the ship. She had sprung a hundred leaks; she was loaded to the water-line with crime, ignorance, poverty. The wheel was swinging with the wind. The crew refused to work and were looting the cargo. The officers were building a raft, ready to slip overboard and desert the ship. The mast was splitting, the wind was howling, the sails were beginning to rip. Every man-jack on board was about to drown – and only because the only thing they thought of was their own skins and their cheap little day-to-day traffic. Was that a time, do you think, for playing with words like yes and no? Was that a time for a man to be weighing the pros and cons, wondering if he wasn't going to pay too dearly later on; if he wasn't going to lose his life, or his family, or his touch with other men? You grab the wheel, you right the ship in the face of a mountain of water. You shout an order, and if one man refuses to obey, you shoot straight into the mob. Into the mob, I say! The beast as nameless as the wave that crashes down upon your deck: as nameless as the whipping wind. The thing that drops when you shoot may be someone who poured you a drink the night before: but it has no name. And you, braced at the wheel, you have no name, either. Nothing has a name – except the ship, and the storm. (*A pause as he looks at her.*) Now do you understand?

ANTIGONE: I am not here to understand. That's all very well for you. I am here to say no to you, and die.

CREON: It is easy to say no.

ANTIGONE: Not always.

CREON: It is easy to say no. To say yes, you have to sweat and roll up your sleeves and plunge both hands into life up to the elbows. It is easy to say no, even if saying no means death. All you have to do is to sit still and wait. Wait to go on living; wait to be killed. That is the coward's part. *No* is one of your man-made words. Can you imagine a world in which trees say *no* to the sap? In which beasts say *no* to hunger or to propagation? Animals are good, simple, tough. They move in droves, nudging one another onwards, all travelling the same road. Some of them keel over; but the rest go on; and no matter how many may fall by the wayside, there are always those few left which go on bringing their young into the world, travelling the same road with the same obstinate will, unchanged from those who went before.

ANTIGONE: Animals, eh, Creon! What a king you could be if only men were animals!

A pause. CREON *turns and looks at her.*

CREON: You despise me, don't you? (ANTIGONE *is silent.* CREON *goes on, as if to himself:*) Strange. Again and again, I have imagined myself holding this conversation with a pale young man I have never seen in the flesh. He would have come to assassinate me, and would have failed. I would be trying to find out from him why he wanted to kill me. But with all my logic and all my powers of debate, the only thing I could get out of him would be that he despised me. Who would have thought that the white-faced boy would turn out to be you? And that the debate would arise out of something so meaningless as the burial of your brother?

ANTIGONE (*repeats contemptuously*): Meaningless!

CREON (*earnestly, almost desperately*): And yet, you must hear me out. My part is not a heroic one, but I shall play my part. I shall have you put to death. Only, before I do, I want to make one last appeal. I want to be sure that you know what you are doing as well as I know what I am doing. Antigone, do you know what you are dying for? Do you know the sordid story to which you are going to sign your name in blood, for all time to come?

ANTIGONE: What story?

CREON: The story of Eteocles and Polynices, the story of your brothers. You think you know it, but you don't. Nobody in Thebes knows that story but me. And it seems to me, this afternoon, that you have a right to know it, too. (*A pause as* ANTIGONE *moves to the chair and sits.*) It's not a pretty story. (*He turns, gets a stool from behind the table and places it between the table and the chair.*) You'll see. (*He looks at her for a moment.*) Tell me, first. What do you remember about your brothers? They were older than you, so they must have looked down on you. And I imagine that they tormented you – pulled your pigtails, broke your dolls, whispered secrets to each other to put you in a rage.

ANTIGONE: They were big and I was little.

CREON: And later on, when they came home wearing evening clothes, smoking cigarettes, they would have nothing to do with you; and you thought they were wonderful.

ANTIGONE: They were boys and I was a girl.

CREON: You didn't know why, exactly, but you knew that they were making your mother unhappy. You saw her in tears over them; and your father would fly into a rage because of them. You heard them come in, slamming doors, laughing noisily in the corridors – insolent, spineless, unruly, smelling of drink.

ANTIGONE (*staring outwards*): Once, it was very early and we had just got up. I saw them coming home, and hid behind a door. Polynices was very pale and his eyes were shining. He was so handsome in his evening clothes. He saw me, and said: 'Here, this is for you'; and he gave me a big paper flower that he had brought home from his night out.

CREON: And of course you still have that flower. Last night, before you crept out, you opened a drawer and looked at it for a time, to give yourself courage.

ANTIGONE: Who told you so?

CREON: Poor Antigone! With her night-club flower. Do you know what your brother was?

ANTIGONE: Whatever he was, I know that you will say vile things about him.

CREON: A cheap, idiotic bounder, that is what he was. A cruel, vicious little voluptuary. A little beast with just wit enough to drive a car faster and throw more money away than any of his pals. I was with your father one day when Polynices, having lost a lot of money gambling, asked him to settle the debt; and when your father refused, the boy raised his hand against him and called him a vile name.

ANTIGONE: That's a lie!

CREON: He struck your father in the face with his fist. It was pitiful. Your father sat at his desk with his head in his hands. His nose was bleeding. He was weeping with anguish. And in a corner of your father's study, Polynices stood sneering and lighting a cigarette.

ANTIGONE: That's a lie.

A pause.

CREON: When did you last see Polynices alive? When you were twelve years old. *That's* true, isn't it?

ANTIGONE: Yes, that's true.

CREON: Now you know why. Oedipus was too chicken-hearted to have the boy locked up. Polynices was allowed to go off and join the Argive army. And as soon as he reached Argos, the attempts upon your father's life began – upon the life of an old man who couldn't make up his mind to die, couldn't bear to be parted from his kingship. One after another, men slipped into Thebes from Argos for the purpose of assassinating him, and every killer we caught always ended by confessing who had put him up to it, who had paid him to try it. And it wasn't only Polynices. That is really what I am trying to tell you. I want you to know what went on in the back room, in the kitchen of politics; I want you to know what took place in the wings of this drama in which you are burning to play a part.

Yesterday, I gave Eteocles a State funeral, with pomp and honours. Today, Eteocles is a saint and a hero in the eyes of all Thebes. The whole city turned out to bury him. The schoolchildren emptied their savings-boxes to buy wreaths for him. Old men, orating in quavering, hypocritical voices, glorified the virtues of the great-hearted brother, the devoted son, the loyal prince. I made a speech myself; and every temple priest was present with an appropriate show of sorrow and solemnity in his stupid face. And military honours were accorded the dead hero.

Well, what else could I have done? People had taken sides in the civil war. Both sides couldn't be wrong; that would be too much. I couldn't have made them swallow the truth. Two gangsters was more of a luxury than I could afford. (*He pauses for a moment.*) And this is the whole point of my story. Eteocles, that virtuous brother, was just as rotten as Polynices. That great-hearted son had done his best, too, to procure the assassination of his father. That loyal prince had also offered to sell out Thebes to the highest bidder.

Funny, isn't it? Polynices lies rotting in the sun while Eteocles is given a hero's funeral and will be housed in a marble vault. Yet I have absolute proof that everything that Polynices did, Eteocles had plotted to do. They were a pair of blackguards – both engaged in selling out Thebes, and both engaged in selling out each other; and they died like the cheap gangsters they were, over a division of the spoils. But, as I told you a moment ago, I had to make a martyr of one of them. I sent out to the holocaust for their bodies; they were found clasped in one another's arms – for the first time in their lives, I imagine. Each had been spitted on the other's sword, and the Argive cavalry had trampled them down. They were mashed to a pulp, Antigone. I had the prettier of the two carcasses brought in, and gave it a State funeral; and I left the other to rot. I don't know which was which. And I assure you, I don't care. (*Long silence, neither looking at the other.*)

ANTIGONE (*in a mild voice*): Why do you tell me all this?

CREON: Would it have been better to let you die a victim to that obscene story?

ANTIGONE: It might have been. I had my faith.

CREON: What are you going to do now?

ANTIGONE (*rises to her feet in a daze*): I shall go up to my room.

CREON: Don't stay alone. Go and find Haemon. And get married quickly.

ANTIGONE (*in a whisper*): Yes.

CREON: All this is really beside the point. You have your whole life ahead of you – and life is a treasure.

ANTIGONE: Yes.

CREON: And you were about to throw it away. Don't think me fatuous if I say that I understand you; and that at your age I should have done the same thing. A moment ago, when we were quarrelling, you said I was drinking in your words. I was. But it wasn't you I was listening to; it was a lad named Creon who lived here in Thebes many years ago. He was thin and pale, as you are. His mind, too, was filled with thoughts of self-sacrifice. Go and find Haemon. And get married quickly, Antigone. Be happy. Life flows like water, and you young people let it run away through your fingers. Shut your hands; hold on to it, Antigone. Life is not what you think it is. Life is a child playing round your feet, a tool you hold firmly in your grip, a bench you sit down upon in the evening, in your garden. People will tell you that that's not life, that life is something else. They will tell you that because they need your strength and your fire, and they will want to make use of you. Don't listen to them. Believe me, the only poor consolation that we have in our old age is to discover that what I have just said to you is true. Life is nothing more than the happiness that you get out of it.

ANTIGONE (*murmurs, lost in thought*): Happiness . . .

CREON (*suddenly a little self-conscious*): Not much of a word, is it?

ANTIGONE (*quietly*): What kind of happiness do you foresee for me? Paint me the picture of your happy Antigone. What are the unimportant little sins that I shall have to commit before I am allowed to sink my teeth into life and tear happiness from it? Tell me: to whom shall I have to lie? Upon whom shall I have to fawn? To whom must I sell myself? Whom do you want me to leave dying, while I turn away my eyes?

CREON: Antigone, be quiet.

ANTIGONE: Why do you tell me to be quiet when all I want to know is what I have to do to be happy? This minute; since it is this very minute that I must make my choice. You tell me that life is so wonderful. I want to know what I have to do in order to be able to say that myself.

CREON: Do you love Haemon?

ANTIGONE: Yes, I love Haemon. The Haemon I love is hard and young, faithful and difficult to satisfy, just as I am. But if what I love in Haemon is to be worn away like a stone step by the tread of the thing you call life, the thing you call happiness; if Haemon reaches the point where he stops growing pale with fear when I grow pale, stops thinking that I must have been killed in an accident when I am five minutes late, stops feeling that he is alone on earth when I laugh and he doesn't know why – if he, too, has to learn to say yes to everything – why, no, then, no! I do not love Haemon!

CREON: You don't know what you are talking about!

ANTIGONE: I do know what I am talking about! Now it is you who have stopped understanding. I am too far away from you now, talking to you from a kingdom you can't get into, with your quick tongue and your hollow heart. (*Laughs.*) I laugh, Creon, because I see you suddenly as you must have been at fifteen: the same look of impotence in your face and the same inner conviction that there was nothing you couldn't do. What has life added to you, except those lines in your face, and that fat on your stomach?

CREON: Be quiet, I tell you!

ANTIGONE: Why do you want me to be quiet? Because you know that I am right? Do you think I can't see in your face that what I am saying is true? You can't admit it, of course; you have to go on growling and defending the bone you call happiness.

CREON: It is your happiness, too, you little fool!

ANTIGONE: I spit on your happiness! I spit on your idea of life – that life that must go on, come what may. You are all like dogs that lick everything they smell. You with your promise of a humdrum happiness – provided a person doesn't ask too much of life. I want everything of life, I do; and I want it now! I want it total, complete: otherwise I reject it! I will *not* be moderate. I will *not* be satisfied with the bit of cake you offer me if I promise to be a good little girl. I want to be sure of everything this very day; sure that everything will be as beautiful as when I was a little girl. If not, I want to die!

CREON: Scream on, daughter of Oedipus! Scream on, in your father's own voice!

ANTIGONE: In my father's own voice, yes! We are of the tribe that asks questions, and we ask them to the bitter end. Until no tiniest chance of hope remains to be strangled by our hands. We are of the tribe that hates your filthy hope, your docile, female hope; hope, your whore—

CREON (*grasps her by her arms*): Shut up! If you could see how ugly you are, shrieking those words!

ANTIGONE: Yes, I am ugly! Father was ugly, too. (CREON *releases her arms, turns and moves away. He stands with his back to* ANTIGONE.) But Father became beautiful. And do you know when? (*She follows him to behind the table.*) At the very end. When all his questions had been answered. When he could no longer doubt that he *had* killed his own father; that he *had* gone to bed with his own mother. When all hope was gone. When it was absolutely certain that nothing, nothing could save him. Then he was at peace; then he could smile, almost; then he became beautiful. . . . Whereas you! Ah, those faces of yours, you candidates for election to happiness! It's you who are the ugly ones, even the handsomest of you – with that ugly glint in the corner of your eyes, that ugly crease at the corner of your mouths. Creon, you spoke the word a moment ago: the kitchen of politics. You look it and you smell of it.

CREON (*struggles to put his hand over her mouth*): I order you to shut up! Do you hear me!

ANTIGONE: *You* order me? Cook! Do you really believe that you can give me orders?

CREON: Antigone! The ante-room is full of people! Do you want them to hear you?

ANTIGONE: Open the doors! Let us make sure that they can hear me!

CREON: By God! You shut up, I tell you!

ISMENE *enters through the arch.*

ISMENE (*distraught*): Antigone!

ANTIGONE (*turns to* ISMENE): You, too? What do you want?

ISMENE: Oh, forgive me, Antigone. I've come back. I'll be brave. I'll go with you now.

ANTIGONE: Where will you go with me?

ISMENE (*to* CREON): Creon! If you kill her, you'll have to kill me, too.

ANTIGONE: Oh, no. Ismene. Not a bit of it. I die alone. You don't think I'm going to let you die with me after what I've been through? You don't deserve it.

ISMENE: If you die, I don't want to live. I don't want to be left behind, alone.

ANTIGONE: You chose life and I chose death. Now stop blubbering. You had your chance to come with me in the black night, creeping on your hands and knees. You had your chance to claw up the earth with your nails, as I did; to get yourself caught like a thief, as I did. And you refused it.

ISMENE: Not any more. I'll do it alone tonight.

ANTIGONE (*turns round towards* CREON): You hear that, Creon? The thing is catching! Who knows but that lots of people will catch the disease from me! What are you waiting for? Call in your guards! Come on, Creon! Show a little courage! It only hurts for a minute! Come on, cook!

CREON (*turns towards the arch and calls*): Guard!

The GUARDS *enter through the arch.*

ANTIGONE (*in a great cry of relief*): At last, Creon!

CHORUS *enters through the left arch.*

CREON (*to the* GUARDS): Take her away! (CREON *goes up on the top step.*)

GUARDS *grasp* ANTIGONE *by her arms, turn and hustle her towards the arch, right, and exit.*

ISMENE *mimes horror, backs away towards the arch, left, then turns and runs out through the arch.*

A long pause, as CREON *moves slowly downstage.*

CHORUS (*behind* CREON. *He speaks in a deliberate voice*): You are out of your mind, Creon. What have you done?

CREON (*his back to* CHORUS): She had to die.

CHORUS: You must not let Antigone die. We shall carry the scar of her death for centuries.

CREON: She insisted. No man on earth was strong enough to dissuade her. Death was her purpose, whether she knew it or not. Polynices was a mere pretext. When she had to give up that pretext, she found another one – that life and happiness were tawdry things and not worth possessing. She was bent upon only one thing: to reject life and to die.

CHORUS: She is a mere child, Creon.

CREON: What do you want me to do for her? Condemn her to live?

HAEMON (*calls from offstage*): Father! (HAEMON *enters through the arch, right.* CREON *turns towards him.*)

CREON: Haemon, forget Antigone. Forget her, my dearest boy.

HAEMON: How can you talk like that?

CREON (*grasps* HAEMON *by the hands*): I did everything I could to save her, Haemon. I used every argument. I swear I did. The girl doesn't love you. She could have gone on living for you; but she refused. She wanted it this way; she wanted to die.

HAEMON: Father! The guards are dragging Antigone away! You've got to stop them! (*He breaks away from* CREON.)

CREON (*looks away from* HAEMON): I can't stop them. It's too late. Antigone has spoken. The story is all over Thebes. I cannot save her now.

CHORUS: Creon, you must find a way. Lock her up. Say that she has gone out of her mind.

CREON: Everybody will know it isn't so. The people will say that I am making an exception of her because my son loves her. I cannot.

CHORUS: You can still gain time. Let her out of Thebes.

CREON: The mob already knows the truth. It is howling round the palace. I can do nothing.

HAEMON: But, Father, you are master in Thebes!

CREON: I am master under the law. Not above the law.

HAEMON: You cannot let Antigone be taken from me. I am your son!

CREON: I cannot do anything else, my poor boy. She must die and you must live.

HAEMON: Live, you say! Live a life without Antigone? A life in which I am to go on admiring you as you busy yourself about your kingdom, make your persuasive speeches, strike your attitudes? Not without Antigone. I love Antigone. I will not live without Antigone!

CREON: Haemon – you will have to resign yourself to life without Antigone. (*He moves to the left of* HAEMON.) Sooner or later there comes a day of sorrow in each man's life when he must cease to be a child and take up the burden of manhood. That day has come for you.

HAEMON (*backs away a step*): That giant strength, that courage. That massive god who used to pick me up in his arms and shelter me from shadows and monsters – was that you, Father? Was it of you I stood in awe? Was that man you?

CREON: For God's sake, Haemon, do not judge me! Not you, too!

HAEMON (*pleading now*): This is all a bad dream, Father. You are not yourself. It isn't true that we have been backed up against a wall, forced to surrender. We don't have to say *yes* to this terrible thing. You are still King. You are still the father I revered. You have no right to desert me, to shrink into nothingness. The world will be too bare, I shall be too alone in the world, if you force me to disown you.

CREON: The world *is* bare, Haemon, and you *are* alone. You must cease to think your father all-powerful. Look straight at me. See your father as he is. That is what it means to grow up and be a man.

HAEMON (*stares at* CREON *for a moment*): I tell you that I will not live without Antigone. (*He turns and goes quickly out through the arch.*)

CHORUS: Creon, the boy will go mad.

CREON: Poor boy! He loves her.

CHORUS: Creon, the boy is wounded to death.

CREON: We are all wounded to death.

FIRST GUARD *enters through the arch, right, followed by* SECOND *and* THIRD GUARDS *pulling* ANTIGONE *along with them.*

FIRST GUARD: Sir, the people are crowding into the palace!

ANTIGONE: Creon, I don't want to see their faces. I don't want to hear them howl. You are going to kill me; let that be enough. I want to be alone until it is over.

CREON: Empty the palace! Guards at the gates! (CREON *quickly crosses towards the arch and exits. Two* GUARDS *release* ANTIGONE *and exit behind* CREON. CHORUS *goes out through the arch, left.*)

The lighting dims so that only the area about the table is lighted. The cyclorama is covered with a dark blue colour. The scene is intended to suggest a prison cell, filled with shadows and dimly lit. ANTIGONE *moves to the stool and sits. The* FIRST GUARD *stands upstage. He watches* ANTIGONE, *and as she sits, he begins pacing slowly downstage, then upstage.*
A pause.

ANTIGONE (*turns and looks at the* GUARD): It's you, is it?

GUARD: What do you mean, me?

ANTIGONE: The last human face that I shall see. (*A pause as they look at each other, then the* GUARD *paces upstage; and turns and crosses behind the table.*) Was it you that arrested me this morning?

GUARD: Yes, that was me.

ANTIGONE: You hurt me. There was no need for you to hurt me. Did I act as if I was trying to escape?

GUARD: Come on now, miss. It was my business to bring you in. I did it. (*A pause. He paces to and fro upstage. Only the sound of his boots is heard.*)

ANTIGONE: How old are you?

GUARD: Thirty-nine.

ANTIGONE: Have you any children?

GUARD: Yes. Two.

ANTIGONE: Do you love your children?

GUARD: What's that got to do with you? (*A pause. He paces upstage and downstage.*)

ANTIGONE: How long have you been in the Guard?

GUARD: Since the war. I was in the army. Sergeant. Then I joined the Guard.

ANTIGONE: Does one have to have been an army sergeant to get into the Guard?

GUARD: Supposed to be. Either that or on special detail. But when they make you a guard, you lose your stripes.

ANTIGONE (*murmurs*): I see.

GUARD: Yes. Of course, if you're a guard, everybody knows you're something special; they know you're an old N.C.O. Take pay, for instance. When you're a guard you get your pay, and on top of that you get six months' extra pay, to make sure you don't lose anything by not being a sergeant any more. And of course you do better than that. You get a house, coal, rations, extras for the wife and kids. If you've got two kids, like me, you draw better than a sergeant.

ANTIGONE (*barely audible*): I see.

GUARD: That's why sergeants, now, they don't like guards. Maybe you noticed they try to make out they're better than us? Promotion, that's what it is. In the army, anybody can get promoted. All you need is good conduct. Now in the Guard, it's slow, and you have to know your business – like how to make out a report and the like of that. But when you're an N.C.O. in the Guard, you've got something that even a sergeant-major ain't got. For instance—

ANTIGONE (*breaking him off*): Listen.

GUARD: Yes, miss.

ANTIGONE: I'm going to die soon.

The GUARD *looks at her for a moment, then turns and moves away.*

GUARD: For instance, people have a lot of respect for guards, they have. A guard may be a soldier, but he's kind of in the civil service, too.

ANTIGONE: Do you think it hurts to die?

GUARD: How should I know? Of course, if somebody sticks a sabre in your guts and turns it round, it hurts.

ANTIGONE: How are they going to put me to death?

GUARD: Well, I'll tell you. I heard the proclamation all right. Wait a minute. How did it go now? (*He stares into space and recites from memory:*) 'In order that our fair city shall not be pol-luted with her sinful blood, she shall be im-mured – immured.' That means, they shove you in a cave and wall up the cave.

ANTIGONE: Alive?

GUARD: Yes. . . . (*He moves away a few steps.*)

ANTIGONE (*murmurs*): O tomb! O bridal bed! Alone! (ANTIGONE *sits there, a tiny figure in the middle of the stage. You would say she felt a little chilly. She wraps her arms round herself.*)

GUARD: Yes! Outside the south-east gate of the town. In the Cave of Hades. In broad daylight. Some detail, eh, for them that's on the job! First they thought maybe it was a job for the army. Now it looks like it's going to be the Guard. There's an outfit for you! Nothing the Guard can't do. No wonder the army's jealous.

ANTIGONE: A pair of animals.

GUARD: What do you mean, a pair of animals?

ANTIGONE: When the winds blow cold, all they need do is to press close against one another. I am all alone.

GUARD: Is there anything you want? I can send out for it, you know.

ANTIGONE: You are very kind. (*A pause.* ANTIGONE *looks up at the* GUARD.) Yes, there is something I want. I want you to give someone a letter from me, when I am dead.

GUARD: How's that again? A letter?

ANTIGONE: Yes, I want to write a letter; and I want you to give it to someone for me.

GUARD (*straightens up*): Now, wait a minute. Take it easy. It's as much as my job is worth to go handing out letters from prisoners.

ANTIGONE (*removes a ring from her finger and holds it out towards him*): I'll give you this ring if you will do it.

GUARD: Is it gold? (*He takes the ring from her.*)

ANTIGONE: Yes, it is gold.

GUARD (*shakes his head*): Uh-uh. Suppose they go through my pockets. I might be court-martialled for a thing like that. (*He stares at the ring, then glances off right, to make sure that he is not being watched.*) Listen, tell you what I'll do. You tell me what you want to say, and I'll write it down in my book. Then, afterwards, I'll tear out the pages and give them to the party, see? If it's in my handwriting, it's all right.

ANTIGONE (*winces*): In your handwriting? (*She shudders slightly*).) No. That would be awful. The poor darling! In your handwriting.

GUARD (*offers back the ring*): O.K. It's not my letter.

ANTIGONE (*quickly*): Of course, of course. No, keep the ring. But hurry. Time is getting short. Where is your notebook?

The GUARD *pockets the ring, takes out his notebook and pencil from his pocket, puts his foot up on the chair, rests the notebook on his knee, and licks his pencil.*

Ready?

(*He nods.*) Write, now. 'My darling . . .'

GUARD (*writes as he mutters*): The boy friend, eh?

ANTIGONE: 'My darling. I wanted to die, and perhaps you will not love me any more . . .'

GUARD (*mutters as he writes*): '. . . will not love me any more.'

ANTIGONE: Creon was right. It is terrible to die.'

GUARD (*repeats as he writes*): '. . . terrible to die.'

ANTIGONE: 'And I don't even know what I am dying for. I am afraid . . .'

GUARD (*looks at her*): Wait a minute! How fast do you think I can write?

ANTIGONE (*takes hold of herself*): Where are you?

GUARD (*reads from his notebook*): 'And I don't even know what I am dying for.'

ANTIGONE: No. Scratch that out. Nobody must know that. They have no right to know. It's as if they saw me naked and touched me, after I was dead. Scratch it all out. Just write: 'Forgive me.'

GUARD (*looks at* ANTIGONE): I cut out everything you said there at the end, and I put down, 'Forgive me'?

ANTIGONE: Yes. 'Forgive me, my darling. You would all have been so happy except for Antigone. I love you.'

GUARD (*finishes the letter*): '. . . I love you.' (*He looks at her.*) Is that all?

ANTIGONE: That's all.

GUARD (*straightens up, looks at notebook*): Damn funny letter.

ANTIGONE: I know.

GUARD (*looks at her*): Who is it to? (*A sudden roll of drums begins and continues until after* ANTIGONE *exits. The* FIRST GUARD *pockets the notebook and shouts at* ANTIGONE:) O.K. That's enough out of you! Come on!

At the sound of the drum roll, the SECOND *and* THIRD GUARDS *enter through the right arch.* ANTIGONE *rises. The* GUARDS *seize her and exit with her.*
The lighting moves up to suggest late afternoon.

CHORUS *enters.*

CHORUS: And now it is Creon's turn.

The MESSENGER *runs through the arch, right.*

MESSENGER: The Queen . . . the Queen! Where is the Queen?

CHORUS: What do you want with the Queen? What have you to tell the Queen?

MESSENGER: News to break her heart. Antigone had just been thrust into the cave. They hadn't finished heaving the last blocks of stone into place when Creon and the rest heard a sudden moaning from the tomb. A hush fell over us all, for it was not the voice of Antigone. It was Haemon's voice that came forth from the tomb. Everybody looked at Creon; and he howled like a man demented: 'Take away the stones! Take away the stones!' The slaves leaped at the wall of stones, and Creon worked with them, sweating and tearing at the blocks with his bleeding hands. Finally a narrow opening was forced, and into it slipped the smallest guard.
Antigone had hanged herself by the cord of her robe, by the red and golden twisted cord of her robe. The cord was round her neck like a child's collar. Haemon was on his knees, holding her in his arms and moaning, his face buried in her robe. More stones were removed, and Creon went into the tomb. He tried to raise Haemon to his feet. I could hear him begging Haemon to rise to his feet. Haemon was deaf to his father's voice, till suddenly he stood up of his own accord, his eyes dark and burning. Anguish was in his face, but it was the face of a little boy. He stared at his father. Then suddenly he struck him – hard; and he drew his sword. Creon leaped out of range. Haemon went on staring at him, his eyes full of contempt – a glance that was like a knife, and that Creon couldn't escape. The King stood trembling in the far corner of the tomb, and Haemon went on staring. Then, without a word, he stabbed himself and lay down beside Antigone, embracing her in a great pool of blood.

A pause as CREON *and the* PAGE *enter through the arch on the* MESSENGER'S *last words.* CHORUS *and the* MESSENGER *both turn to look at* CREON, *then the* MESSENGER *exits through the curtain.*

CREON: I have had them laid out side by side. They are together at last, and at peace. Two lovers on the morrow of their burial. Their work is done.

CHORUS: But not yours, Creon. You have still one thing to learn. Eurydice, the Queen, your wife—

CREON: A good woman. Always busy with her garden, her preserves, her jerseys – those jerseys she never stopped knitting for the poor. Strange, how the poor never stop needing jerseys. One would almost think that was all they needed.

CHORUS: The poor in Thebes are going to be cold this winter, Creon. When the Queen was told of her son's death, she waited carefully until she had finished her row, then put down her knitting calmly – as she did everything. She went up to her room, her lavender-scented room, with its embroidered doilies and its pictures framed in plush; and there, Creon, she cut her throat. She is laid out now in one of those two old-fashioned twin beds, exactly where you went to her one night when she was still a maiden. Her smile is still the same, scarcely a shade more melancholy. And if it were not for that great red blot on the bed linen by her neck, one might think she was asleep.

CREON (*in a dull voice*): She, too. They are all asleep. (*Pause.*) It must be good to sleep.

CHORUS: And now you are alone, Creon.

CREON: Yes, all alone. (*To the* PAGE.) My lad.

PAGE: Sir?

CREON: Listen to me. They don't know it, but the truth is the work is there to be done, and a man can't fold his arms and refuse to do it. They say it's dirty work. But if we didn't do it, who would?

PAGE: I don't know, sir.

CREON: Of course you don't. You'll be lucky if you never find out. In a hurry to grow up, aren't you?

PAGE: Oh yes, sir.

CREON: I shouldn't be if I were you. Never grow up if you can help it. (*He is lost in thought as the hour chimes.*) What time is it?

PAGE: Five o'clock, sir.
CREON: What have we on at five o'clock?
PAGE: Cabinet meeting, sir.
CREON: Cabinet meeting. Then we had better go along to it.

CREON *and the* PAGE *exit slowly through the arch, left, and* CHORUS *moves downstage.*

CHORUS: And there we are. It is quite true that if it had not been for Antigone they would all have been at peace. But that is over now. And they are all at peace. All those who were meant to die have died: those who believed one thing, those who believed the contrary thing, and even those who believed nothing at all, yet were caught up in the web without knowing why. All dead: stiff, useless, rotting. And those who have survived will now begin quietly to forget the dead: they won't remember who was who or which was which. It is all over. Antigone is calm tonight and we shall never know the name of the fever that consumed her. She has played her part.

Three GUARDS *enter, resume their places on the steps as at the rise of the curtain, and begin to play cards.*

A great melancholy wave of peace now settles down upon Thebes, upon the empty palace, upon Creon, who can now begin to wait for his own death.
Only the guards are left, and none of this matters to them. It's no skin off their noses. They go on playing cards.

CHORUS *walks towards the arch, left, as*

the Curtain falls

Romeo and Jeannette

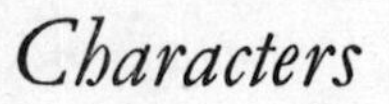

FREDERIC

JULIA

LUCIEN

JEANNETTE

THE MOTHER
(*of Frederic*)

THE FATHER
(*of Julia, Lucien and Jeannette*)

POSTMAN

Original Title: Roméo et Jeannette

Translator: Miriam John

First produced in 1945

Act One

A huge, badly furnished room in a large dilapidated house. It is in a state of the utmost disorder. It opens, at the back of the stage, on to dark corridors leading to a kitchen and the bottom of a staircase. The curtains are drawn over the french windows, but are parted to let in JULIA, FREDERIC, *his* MOTHER, *and a little light.* FREDERIC *and his* MOTHER *are rich country people, dressed in Sunday black.*

JULIA: They always leave everything open. (*Calling.*) Anybody there? (*There is no reply. She disappears into the dark passage at the back and can still be heard calling.*) Is anybody there?

FREDERIC *and his* MOTHER *remain on stage. The* MOTHER *looks around her.*

MOTHER: They don't seem to be expecting us.

As she says this, JULIA *comes back. One has the feeling she is frightened. She stammers.*

JULIA: But they had my letter. I posted it on Monday. (*She goes briskly to the table and removes some of the sordid odds and ends that are cluttering it.*) They're terribly untidy, all three of them.

MOTHER: So I see. (*She looks around her again suspiciously, an upright, black-clad figure, leaning on her umbrella.*) May we sit down?

JULIA (*hastily*): But of course. . . . (*She goes to a chair and tries it.*) No. That one's broken. The stool's all right. I bought it myself in the market before I went. It's quite new. (*She takes hold of the stool.*) No. That's broken, too.

MOTHER (*still standing*): What do they do with the chairs?

JULIA: I don't know. Stand on them . . . knock them about. . . .

MOTHER: Why should they knock them about?

JULIA (*with a desperate glance at* FREDERIC, *stammering*): I don't know. I wonder myself, sometimes.

FREDERIC (*coming to the rescue*): Why should you worry, Mother?

MOTHER: I don't, except that I should like to sit down.

JULIA *and* FREDERIC *look around.* JULIA *is beside herself.* FREDERIC *goes to an arm-chair snowed under with dirty linen.*

FREDERIC: Here's a chair! (*He tests it and pushes it towards her.*) A good solid one at that. Sit down, Mother.

Watched anxiously by JULIA, *his* MOTHER *seats herself after having tried the chair. She looks at the clock.*

MOTHER: It's ten to twelve.

JULIA (*blushing if possible even more furiously than before*): Yes. I don't understand it. (*She has taken up the pile of laundry which* FREDERIC *has thrown on the floor and wanders around the room with it, not knowing how to disguise it, talking as she does so.*) They know very well the train's at eleven.

FREDERIC: Maybe they went another way to meet us.

JULIA: No. At low tide they always go by the beach, across the bay. We should have met them.

MOTHER: Besides, if your father and brother had come to meet us at the station, your sister should have stayed behind to look after luncheon, surely.

JULIA (*still wandering about with her bundle of linen*): Yes, of course she should. I can't understand it.

MOTHER: True, there was probably no luncheon to look after. Have you been into the kitchen?

JULIA: Yes. There's nothing there.

She has at last succeeded in cramming the linen into a sideboard. She leans against the doors, panting like a hunted criminal. The MOTHER *has noticed nothing.*

FREDERIC (*amused at* JULIA'S *fears, and attempting to find a solution*): Maybe they intended to take us out to a restaurant.

JULIA (*uneasier than ever*): There isn't a restaurant in the village. Only a sort of buffet bar at the grocer's.

MOTHER: So we shall have to go back across the bay? (*Pause.*) It is five to twelve.

JULIA (*stammering*): Yes, but . . . now that the tide's coming in, it would be dangerous . . . we'd have to go by the road, and that takes longer.

MOTHER: Much longer?

JULIA (*after a second's hesitation*): Yes. Nearly twice as long.

The MOTHER *does not reply. There is a terrible silence. She looks slowly around her.* JULIA *begins to tidy up surreptitiously behind her back. Then, as the* MOTHER *looks down and pokes at some rubbish with her umbrella,* JULIA *bursts into tears and, snatching off her hat and throwing it down, she seizes a broom.*

I think I'd better sweep up!

MOTHER: Yes indeed. There's need of it.

FREDERIC (*sorry for* JULIA, *going to his* MOTHER): I'll help you, Julia. And you can drop your disapproving air, Mother, and go to the grocer's and buy some tinned stuff for lunch.

MOTHER (*eyes turned upward*): Tins – on a fifteenth of August!

JULIA (*taking a step towards her*): I'm terribly sorry, Mother. I really can't imagine what's going on. Please don't bother. I'll go to the grocer's.

MOTHER: No, Julia, you're more use where you are. And if you look hard enough you may even find a saucepan and some water. I'll get some noodles.

FREDERIC: That's right. And some pâté. And you can get some tinned lobster and some butter and jam. We don't all have to be on dry bread.

MOTHER (*from the doorway*): Shall I get enough for them?

JULIA (*in agony*): I— I don't know. I don't see where they could be having lunch.

MOTHER: They must have guessed we were inviting them to a picnic.

FREDERIC (*pushing her gently out*): Probably. Make it snappy, Mother. We'll lay the table while you're gone.

When she has gone, JULIA *lets go of the broom and falls weeping into a chair.*

JULIA: I knew this would happen. I knew it! They're terrible!
FREDERIC: D'you think they got your letter?
JULIA: Of course they did.
FREDERIC: In fact, they don't want to meet us.
JULIA: It isn't that. It's just that they'll all have gone their own sweet ways this morning, each counting on the others.
FREDERIC: Your sister as well? Do the two men usually help her with the house?
JULIA (*with a desolate gesture, tearfully indicating the disorder around her*): Look at it.

FREDERIC *bursts out laughing.*

Oh, don't laugh! Don't laugh! I'm so ashamed.
FREDERIC: Why ashamed?
JULIA: I didn't tell you. I thought I needn't. Why did your mother want us to come here? As though there were any need to ask permission to marry me – me! If we hadn't come, I needn't have said anything.
FREDERIC: About what, Julia?
JULIA: Everything. All the things I'm ashamed of.
FREDERIC (*smiling*): Are you really as ashamed of them as that?
JULIA: I always have been, ever since I was little.
FREDERIC: What's so extraordinary about them?
JULIA: You'll see soon enough. (*Suddenly she bursts out furiously:*) They haven't got a meal ready! They haven't even swept the place! They've all gone their own sweet ways, and they'll come back any old time, dressed any old how. And there will be your mother with nothing to eat.
FREDERIC: Don't worry about her. She's just getting some food, anyway.

JULIA: It's not as though I didn't warn them. I told them in my letter; I said, 'I'm coming with my fiancé and my future mother-in-law, so we must have a good lunch.' I even sent them some money.

FREDERIC: Perhaps they usually have lunch late.

JULIA: There's nothing in the kitchen but a drop of sour milk and a hunk of stale bread. Oh, and as for the money – I know what will have happened to that!

FREDERIC: Poor Julia.

JULIA: I wrote them in so many words – I said: 'Clean the house up a bit so that I'm not ashamed of it. My mother-in-law loves things to be tidy.' And look at it!

FREDERIC: We'll tidy it up between us. Up you get.

JULIA (*shouting through her tears*): No! I just want to lie on the floor and cry!

FREDERIC: Julia!

JULIA: I want them to find me here in the mess they've accumulated for over a week, with my fiancé and his mother. Let them be ashamed for once. It's their turn!

FREDERIC: Get up, Julia.

JULIA: Only of course they wouldn't even be ashamed. I know them. They wouldn't care. They don't care about anything. (*She sits up.*) You see, you wanted to meet them, and now you won't love me any more!

FREDERIC (*laughing*): It's already happened. I don't love you any more.

JULIA (*throwing herself into his arms*): I'm not like them! Even when I was a little girl, I was the one who swept and polished while my sister did nothing but look at herself in the glass. I was the one that made Papa shave and put on clean collars. You'll see, you'll see – he won't even have shaved!

FREDERIC: You never know. It is the fifteenth of August!

JULIA: He couldn't care less about holidays and Sundays and things. And as for what he does the rest of the time— They none of them care about anything. Eating scrap meals at all hours and living in squalor. So long as Papa can have his card parties at the bar and *she* can run about the woods or sunbathe on the sand all day. Too bad if the house is in chaos!

FREDERIC: And what about the winter?

JULIA: She just lies there, on what she calls her divan, smoking. Or she makes hats and dresses out of bits of old material, the way she did when she was small. You should see them, too. And of course none of them ever has a penny, or when they do, they spend it immediately. She makes most of her frocks out of old curtains. And no sooner are they finished than there's a dirty mark or a tear somewhere, and if her behind shows through or her knees poke out of her stockings – well, so what?

FREDERIC: Julia, Julia, so you can be bitchy!

JULIA: You hate that sort of thing so much – you're going to be so miserable.

FREDERIC (*gently*): But I'm not marrying your sister.

JULIA: I know you laugh at me sometimes. You call me a maniac, a busy bee, because I go around picking up litter and rubbing like mad every time I see a spot on something. But it's just that I have the feeling there's always something to tidy up; something that's got to be cleaned up after them.

FREDERIC: And your brother – what does he have to say?

JULIA: He wasn't like them, before. But when his wife left him and he came to live here he soon went the same way. He reads all day long, shut up in his room. I don't like him, either, now. Before, he was just a boy like any other boy, working hard, coming out top at school, wanting to earn his living. Now, it's as though a door had been shut between us. He looks at me the same way as she does, with a sort of sneer on his face, and refuses to have anything to do with anything. After all, it's not our fault if his wife doesn't love him any more.

FREDERIC: What about your mother, when she was alive?

JULIA (*shrinking*): Mother isn't dead. I lied to you. She went off with a travelling dentist who used to pull teeth in the street – to music – with a top-hat on. (*Pause.*) There. I've told you that, too, now. Now hate me.

FREDERIC (*taking her in his arms*): Idiot! Dear, sweet idiot!

JULIA: I shall never, never look you in the face again.

FREDERIC: That'll be very convenient for the next fifty years – I should say we'd both have about that long to go, with luck.

JULIA: Oh, Frederic, do you think you'll go on loving me in spite of them? Don't you think it would be better to get out right away? I'm so frightened.

FREDERIC (*holding her to him*): Why? I'm here.

JULIA: I don't know. Just *because* you're there. You're so clear, such miles away from them, so pure. Supposing you began to think I was like them?

FREDERIC: I know my busy bee.

JULIA: Your busy bee's going to die of shame.

FREDERIC: No. People don't die of shame.

JULIA: That's what you say. You say they don't die of love, either. What do they die of?

FREDERIC: I wonder.

He kisses her. LUCIEN *has appeared in the doorway, having come downstairs from the floor above. His shirt collar is undone and he has a book in his hand. He watches in silence while they kiss. Suddenly* JULIA *sees him and breaks away from* FREDERIC.

JULIA: Oh! Were you there?

LUCIEN: I'm always there when there's kissing going on. It's a plot against me. Ever since I became a cuckold I haven't been able to move a step without running across love. . . . And naturally I have a horror of kissing couples. I seem to find them all over the place. However, do go ahead. Don't let me embarrass you. Actually, it's not true. As a matter of fact, I enjoy it – in a sort of gruesome way. I say to myself: 'Well, well! Another two that won't be together long!'

JULIA: Is that the way you introduce yourself? I bring my fiancé here, whom you've never met, and that's the way you greet him.

LUCIEN (*icily*): Hullo.

FREDERIC (*holding out his hand*): Hullo.

LUCIEN (*recording*): He's polite, your friend. He holds out his hand and smiles nicely.

FREDERIC: It's a habit I have. I knew a character like you in the army.

LUCIEN: A cuckold?

FREDERIC: No. Just embittered.

LUCIEN: And I suppose with your nice smiles and your frank handshakes you finally softened him up, this embittered character?

FREDERIC: No, but I got used to him. We became the best of friends.

JULIA: Did you hear me call just now?

LUCIEN: Yes.

JULIA: And of course you didn't budge.

LUCIEN: Wrong again. I budged when everything went quiet, hoping that you'd given up and gone. Also, I budged because I was hungry. Do you suppose there's going to be any lunch?

JULIA: Lunch! Oh, yes, talking of lunch . . . where are the others?

LUCIEN (*with a wave of the hand*): One never knows where the others are – one hardly knows where one is oneself in this place. Don't you agree, Monsieur – er— You seem the well-educated type, as they call it. I like you a lot. Frank, loyal, honest, clear, go-ahead, and all the rest of it. A proper little soldier. You'll make an excellent cuckold.

JULIA: Lucien!

LUCIEN: A merry little cuckold. They're the best. I'm the doleful sort.

JULIA (*going to him and shaking him*): Lucien! You think you're funny, but you're just loathsome. You think you're being original, but you're vulgar, too vulgar for words. The commonest, drabbest little guttersnipe I've ever struck.

LUCIEN: I'm not a little guttersnipe; I'm a melancholy cuckold.

JULIA (*taking him by the arm*): Melancholy or not, you're damn well going to shut up!

LUCIEN: So we're not allowed to be unhappy, now? Compulsory happiness, is it? That's great.

JULIA: You forget it was me that used to wipe your nose for you and wash your dirty feet and spoonfeed you before you could walk. I know you. You're a little beast, but you're not as wicked as you'd have people think. So just you listen to me. Just because you've been miserable, because Denise left you and made you unhappy, that doesn't mean you're going to stop *me* being happy. I came here with my fiancé and his mother to tell you I'm getting married. Frederic's worth more than you and me, he understands everything. But there's his mother, and she certainly won't be able to understand you. Not even if we explain to her that you really have been hurt. She belongs to a kind that gets hurt more discreetly. So try to look a bit tidier when she comes back, and comb your hair, and behave decently. (*Suddenly, pitifully.*) *Please,* Lucien! Please don't spoil my happiness!

LUCIEN (*gently*): When people ask me nicely, I can't say no. I'll go and put a suit on. (*From the doorway, amiably, to* FREDERIC.) You're lucky. She's a brave kid. Tiresome, but brave. (*Exit.*)

FREDERIC: Poor chap. He must have suffered a lot.

JULIA: He's hateful!

FREDERIC: No, he's nice.

JULIA: Oh, you! Samson! Always stronger than anyone else. You laugh at everything, excuse everything. But *I'd* have preferred a brother with decent manners.

Enter FREDERIC'S MOTHER *and* JULIA'S FATHER, *their arms loaded with tins of food.*

FATHER (*with a theatrical gesture*): Sensation! . . . We met at the grocer's I was having a drink at the bar with Prosper. Then when Prosper says, 'Look who's here', I take one look at the silk dress and the umbrella and I have a presentiment. I get up. 'Mother-in-law, delighted to be presented to you!' I say. A manner of speaking, you understand, since I was presenting myself. The whole lot of 'em had their eyes popping out of their heads. (*To* JULIA.) I had to let her pay for the food – I hadn't a sou on me. Be a good girl and pay her back, Julie. No, no, I insist, you're my guest! Thank you, kind sir, delighted.

JULIA: Papa's very talkative.

MOTHER (*putting down the tins*): So I've noticed.

FATHER: What's this? Table not laid? Wine not chilled? Nothing ready? What's all this?

JULIA: I was going to ask you, Papa.

FATHER: Ask me? Ask *me*? (*Storming.*) Where's Jeannette?

JULIA: I was going to ask that, too.

FATHER: It's astonishing! (*He turns to the* MOTHER, *whom he waves towards the sofa with a large gesture, and in quite a different voice says:*) Without wishing to be indiscreet, how many children have you made, dear lady?

MOTHER: Eleven. Eight living.

FATHER: Eight living. Not to mention the others. That still leaves seven more. But no doubt you can keep track of yours. I've only made three, but I never seem to be able to lay hands on one of them. (*Shouting thunderously.*) Where is Lucien?

JULIA: In his room.

FATHER: You see. That's the end of it. No warning. No one else about. There's nobody I can rely on any more. You can carry on, that's your strength. But I'm all alone. It's very sad for an old man. Fortunately I have this one – she's the prop of my old age. Although if she goes and marries your son, she'll be yours. That'll make nine for you. Nine props. Well now, are you going to see to everything, Julie, make us a nice lunch?

JULIA (*sternly*): Is there any wine?

FATHER (*humbly*): Er— I'll tell you— I can cool it for you. . . . I don't know what I could have been thinking of. . . . Besides, my hands were full.

FREDERIC (*laughing*): Don't worry. I'll go and get some. Chin up, Julia!

FATHER (*watching him go out*): He's a charming young fellow, your son, congratulations! (*He stretches himself out on the divan.*) Well, Julie, are you pleased to see your old father again?

JULIA (*who is taking the tins to the kitchen*): I should have been even more glad to find the table laid and the house cleaned up.

FATHER (*with a wink at the* MOTHER): You mustn't believe her when she says things like that. She doesn't mean a word of it. She's delighted. Got a heart of gold. (*He picks something up off the floor and pushes it under the sofa.*) Besides, the place isn't so untidy. Few papers lying about, of course, and as for the dust, well, never mind that; you can't do anything about it, it comes back every day anyway. A bit of old lace. . . . It might strike you as untidy, but it isn't real untidiness. Just confusion. I used to be an artist. I need a certain amount of confusion around me.

MOTHER (*rising*): I'm going to lay the table.

FATHER: That's an idea. I'll help you. It'll make me feel young again. When I was twenty I always used to lay the table, to tease the maid.

MOTHER: Where are the plates?

FATHER: I don't know – here, there, and everywhere, I suppose.

MOTHER: How do you mean, you don't know? What do you do when you want to eat?

FATHER: Look for them. Here – here are three. They're dirty, though. Oh, never mind, it's only cheese. Just throw away the rind.

The MOTHER *snatches the plates from him and makes for the kitchen, calling to him.*

MOTHER: Find me some more.

FATHER: I'll do my best. (*Left alone, he hunts around for a while, then suddenly gets discouraged and throws himself full length on the sofa, pulls a cigar out of his pocket, and bites off the end, grumbling.*) Find me some more . . . find me some more! Hard nut, that. Proper dragon. Pity. Handsome woman, too.

The MOTHER *returns and finds him there. She tries to wither him with a glance, but he meets it stoically and goes on smoking beatifically. She seizes a broom and begins to sweep up round him.*

(*After a short silence:*) You know, I'm an optimist. It's a principle of mine that everything always sorts itself out.

MOTHER (*sourly*): Yes, when other people take over.

FATHER: Indeed, yes. But I've always observed that other people were rather willing to take over. It's extraordinary the number of people there must be on this planet that are determined to take action at all costs. If there weren't a few of us philosophers about, keeping ourselves to ourselves, there'd be no elbowroom for the scrimmage.

MOTHER (*stopping suddenly*): I've got four farms at home, not counting the town house. My boy has just qualified as a notary – he'll have his own practice one day. Maybe you're wondering why I should let him go to Julia, who hasn't a sou to bless herself with?

FATHER: Me? I'm not wondering anything. I'm delighted.

MOTHER: Julia is a good, hard-working girl. Honest, economical . . .

FATHER: Spit image of me.

MOTHER: Her aunt has been my friend for fifty years. She's told me she's leaving her everything when she goes.

FATHER: Poor Irma. How is she?

MOTHER: She's fine. I know she won't get anything from you.

FATHER (*with a start*): Who, Irma?

MOTHER: No, your daughter.

FATHER (*firmly*): Dear lady, I believe in marriages for love. They always go bad, of course, but all the same, before they fail they're a better bet than any other sort. A few years, even a few months of good going, and there's always that to your advantage. And I think you've got to be happy whatever happens, don't you?

MOTHER: The most important thing is to be a worker. To be serious.

FATHER: And don't you think happiness is serious? Don't

you think it takes hard work? Damnation, dear lady, I think people are bird-witted not to have only that in their heads, day and night, and be content with the price of a drink, a smile, the slightest thing. We're none of us ever happy enough, for heaven's sake. What are you talking about? One should demand happiness fiercely. (*To* JULIA, *as she comes in with plates, glasses, and a cloth.*) Aren't I right, Julie?

JULIA: What is it now?

FATHER: Why the 'now'? I was just saying to your mother-in-law that people are never happy enough. *You* intend to be happy, I hope?

JULIA: Yes, Papa, I do. And it would be nice if you would all help.

FATHER: Count on me, Julie. I may look like a comic, but my heart's in the right place. That's what your mother-in-law-to-be doesn't realize.

Enter LUCIEN, *dressed in a suit too big for him.*

MOTHER: Who is this?

FATHER (*with a bow*): This is my son, madame.

MOTHER: Is he a waiter?

FATHER: What's that? No, he's a lawyer. Oh, yes, well, come to think of it, where *did* you get that suit?

LUCIEN (*unsmiling*): It's yours. I'm wearing it in honour of the lady.

MOTHER (*guardedly*): That's very nice of you.

LUCIEN (*bowing respectfully*): My compliments, madame. (*To* JULIA, *who is watching him somewhat anxiously:*) Am I sufficiently elegant in Father's tails?

MOTHER (*to* JULIA): He seems very polite, your brother.

JULIA (*vaguely*): Yes, he does seem polite.

LUCIEN: You see – she said it herself!

MOTHER: Is this the one that's married? Where's his wife?

LUCIEN: On her honeymoon.

JULIA (*crying out*): Lucien!

LUCIEN: No, I was joking. She's at Lourdes, on a pilgrimage. She wants to have a baby.

The MOTHER *looks at him, wondering if he is serious.* JULIA *pulls her away hastily.*

JULIA: Mother, will you come and help me? I need some advice in the kitchen. Lay the table, you two!

LUCIEN (*to his* FATHER, *when they have gone*): I seem to have made a big impression on her. The outfit, maybe . . .

FATHER: Oh, she's a personality, but I think she's pretty dumb. All the same, to do her justice, she still has a very pretty bust. I have a weakness for that type.

LUCIEN: You're slipping. She's a hundred.

FATHER: You've no imagination. I can just see her, say, in about 1912, with a huge feathery hat. . . . Ah well, forget it; it's too late now.

JULIA (*coming in and going up to them*): Listen, both of you. We've probably only got a minute alone. Let's say no more about there being no lunch and the place being in a state.

FATHER: But I was the first to be upset about that! You saw for yourself.

JULIA: I'll have a word with Jeannette about it when she comes in. If she comes in. You spent the money just the same?

FATHER (*with a tragic gesture*): The milk bill had to be paid. Money just gets swallowed up in this house! There were only 120 francs left after that. I wanted to buy myself a made-up tie so as to look respectable today. . . . I had nothing decent to wear. I say I wanted to . . . but as a matter of fact I did and it's already messed up. They're no good, these gadgets. Now look at the one I had before the war. Just one snap and you were all set. Oh well, I've rigged up an old one now with string. Does it show?

JULIA: No, but you might have changed your collar.

FATHER: My collar? It's celluloid. You don't seem to realize. It's patent. You don't have to change it.

JULIA: You could wash it. And you could brush the dandruff off your jacket, and clean your nails, and not fasten your first button into your second buttonhole.

FATHER: Bah! You attach too much importance to details. You must look at the thing as a whole.

JULIA: And of course you didn't shave this morning?

FATHER (*innocent*): No. How did you know?

JULIA (*who has managed to button the jacket properly*): And don't spend the whole of lunch complaining that you haven't a bean.

FATHER: What do you take me for? I've taken some knocks, but I'm a good loser. On the contrary, I want to crush her beneath the weight of luxury, this woman. Get out all the silver, Julie!

LUCIEN (*in his corner*): It's been up the spout for years.

FATHER (*rounding on him, superb*): I can get it out whenever I wish! I've got all the tickets.

LUCIEN: Maybe we could lay the table with those.

FATHER: In any case, supposing we do have to give up the idea of luxury for the moment, at least let's be dignified, behave in style. Patriarchal simplicity. We are receiving her in the family house which misfortune has not spared, but which still stands solidly on its foundations. . . .

LUCIEN: Talking of that, it's raining in all the rooms, and the plumber wants an advance before he'll start on the repairs. Anything you can do about it?

JULIA: Always me! Me! You make me sick!

FATHER: Is it our fault if the roof's caving in? It's the plumber who should make you sick. Advance indeed! Little whipper-snapper I knew when he was that high.

LUCIEN: That's right. He knows you.

FATHER: He doesn't know me yet. I'll call in a rival.

LUCIEN: There aren't any.

FATHER: Rubbish. I'll get one from Paris. You can go so far and no farther with me. (*He lights another cigar and stretches himself out on the divan, suddenly calming down.*) Now what about this lunch, is anyone seeing to it?

JULIA: I sent you all I could. Now I've got to think about my wedding and my trousseau.

FATHER: Quite right. Do things in style. I don't want it said that we didn't give you anything. I suppose you earn your keep with your teaching? Do you give any private lessons? I met one of the Academy inspectors at a funeral, incidentally, and he told me you'd done very well in your exams.

JULIA: I'll do my best, don't worry. I just want you to realize that now I'm getting married you mustn't rely on me any more.

FATHER: Obviously. In fact, believe me, if times had been different, I'd have given you a handsome dowry.

JULIA (*to* LUCIEN): What about you?

LUCIEN: I'm waiting for an answer from the Ivory Coast.

JULIA: And supposing the Ivory Coast doesn't answer? It seems to me that with all your degrees you ought to be able to find a job nearer home than Africa.

LUCIEN (*with a jeer*): What, work here, among the cuckolds, in an office full of cuckolds, who'll spend all day talking about their love lives? Not likely. The wilds for me, and good, black, primitive Negroes with heads thick as boulders and no idea, but absolutely no idea, what love is. Not a white within four hundred miles. I've made that a condition. So if they do answer, it's yes right away and off I shall go with not so much as a good-bye. There's a little bag all ready by the coat rack, so I shan't lose a minute. As soon as the letter arrives – hat, kit, vamoose! And don't bother too much about letters. I shan't even open them.

FATHER (*calm*): Children are all ungrateful. (*After a pause.*) Anyway, I never write letters.

JULIA: What I sent you couldn't have been enough, though. What have you been living on this winter?

LUCIEN: Tinned stuff.

JULIA: Answer me – what have you been living on?

FATHER (*who has had enough*): *I* don't know! Jeannette managed somehow.

JULIA: Is she working? What does she do?

FATHER (*with a vague gesture*): You know what's she's like – one never sees her.

JULIA: You must know by experience that money doesn't grow in these parts. Did she get a job in town?

FATHER: No, no. She's been staying here.

JULIA: But I don't understand. Did she advance you much?

FATHER (*with another wave of the hand*): Oh! You know what I'm like about money. . . .

JULIA: Lucien! You know something about this. Let's have it.

LUCIEN: It's quite simple. I fully believe, my sweet, that we've been living all this winter on the generosity of Monsieur Azarias.

JULIA: You mean the Azarias up at the little château?

LUCIEN: Yes. The little lamb skips off at nightfall and doesn't come back till dawn. And I have the impression she goes that way, through the woods. All the same, every one of them! I'm delighted.

JULIA (*bursting out*): Oh, I'm so ashamed, so ashamed! And you never said a word! You didn't even write to me so that I could try to do something about it! That's all I need just now. Just before my wedding. Everybody'll know about it.

LUCIEN (*derisively*): Wrong tense. Everybody knows.

JULIA: Is that all you can find to say? Your sister has a lover, a lover that pays her. She visits him every night, and you just joke about it. You're delighted because everyone knows about it.

FATHER (*smoking on the divan, with a grand gesture*): I beg your pardon. I don't know about it.

Just then FREDERIC *comes in with some bottles.* JULIA *goes to him, as though calling for help.*

JULIA: Frederic! Frederic!

FREDERIC: What is it?

JULIA: Let's go away – now!

FREDERIC: Why?

JULIA: Go and find your mother in the kitchen – tell her you're sick, that you've got to go home. Tell her anything, but let's get out of here.

FREDERIC (*to the others*): Have you been quarrelling?

LUCIEN: Who, us? Not in the least.

FATHER: Leave her alone. The child's a bundle of nerves.

JULIA (*buried against him*): Frederic, you're so strong. You go through life smiling and thinking that everything's all right, that it's all easy. Oh, Frederic, you're so sure of yourself, but you don't know anything. Ever since you were a little boy there's been your mother to scold you and clear up in a neat and tidy house. How can you know—? But I'll be like her, Frederic, I'll be like her, I swear. I'll make you just as happy as you were when you were little. And you'll always find everything in its right place when you come home – things, feelings, everything.

FREDERIC (*rocking her*): Yes, Julia.

JULIA: And when we have a child, it'll have a real mother, like yours, with an apron on, and bread-and-butter cut thin, and a slap when it's naughty, and the same old things going on day in day out like the ticking of a clock. . . . But *I* know there's nothing but squalor and nastiness and cold nights in empty houses, and shame.

FREDERIC (*gently*): Yes, Julia.

FATHER: Charming! . . . Ah, love! Love! . . . I was just the same. Jumpy, nervous, suspicious, irritable. I would never believe I was loved enough. . . . And yet, God knows— (*Waving his hand and calling to* JULIA.) He adores you, child, he adores you! There's no need to cry; you can see it blindfold.

JULIA (*pressing herself closer to* FREDERIC): Let's get out, Frederic. I'm frightened.

FREDERIC (*smiling*): Frightened of what? You're with your Samson now, your strong man. You shouldn't be afraid of anything. Come, now, dry your eyes. Be sensible. Smile.

JULIA (*trying to smile*): I can't. I'm too frightened.

The MOTHER *comes in. She still has her hat on, but has put on an apron over her silk dress and is carrying in her hand a chicken which she has half plucked.*

MOTHER: Julia! We may yet succeed in making a decent meal. I've found a chicken in the garden. I've just bled it.

There is a stupefied silence from LUCIEN *and his* FATHER. *Then suddenly* LUCIEN *leaps up, yelping.*

LUCIEN: Leon! She's killed Leon!

MOTHER (*looking at the chicken*): Leon, who's that?

FATHER: Great jumping snakes! This is going to cause a riot!

LUCIEN (*yelling like a mad thing*): Leon murdered! Leon slain by the in-laws! Stupendous, unique moment!

MOTHER: But it's only a chicken! I'll send you a couple tomorrow – the biggest I've got.

LUCIEN: She says it's only a chicken. She says Leon's only a chicken. She has absolutely no conception of what she's done!

JULIA: I assure you, Lucien, nobody thinks you're funny.

LUCIEN: Who said anything about being funny? Nobody thinks it's funny. Look at Papa.

FATHER (*who seems to have lost his own*): Keep your heads, now. We must all keep our heads. Couldn't we revive it somehow? Artificial respiration . . .?

LUCIEN: Too late. It's bleeding. I see the blood of Leon flowing! Leon has perished at unworthy hands. And we are like a Greek chorus, helpless, ashen, dumb . . .

MOTHER: Make him be quiet, the lunatic, we can't hear ourselves speak!

LUCIEN (*standing on the sofa, still in his tails, declaiming*): Too late, madame, too late! The clouds are gathering round us. Listen. I hear the gate grinding on the hinge; the pine needles cracking beneath a footstep. Fate is about to burst upon this house! It is going to burst, my children. I tell you I have had a warning; it is definitely going to burst!

JEANNETTE *has appeared at the back. She stops as she suddenly sees the chicken in the* MOTHER'S *hand. They are all looking at her, but she is staring at the chicken.* LUCIEN *is heard to murmur in the silence.*

There we are. It's burst. . . .

JEANNETTE *looks at the* MOTHER *and suddenly makes towards her. The* FATHER *calls out in a strangled voice.*

FATHER: Be polite now, child!

JEANNETTE *has snatched the chicken away from the other woman and is holding it against her, teeth clenched, terrible. She speaks as if in a dream, in a scarcely audible voice.*

Who is this woman? What is she doing here with an apron over her stomach and blood all over her hands?

FATHER: I'll explain it all, child; there's been a terrible misunderstanding.

JEANNETTE: Who is this woman all in black with her low forehead and her big eyes and her respectability? Who brought her here, with her widow's weeds and her ear-rings and her strangler's hands?

JULIA: Jeannette, I forbid you. This is my fiancé's mother.

JEANNETTE (*still staring at the* MOTHER): Ah! So she's your fiancé's mother. So you forbid me. Did you forbid her to lay hands on my Leon just now?

JULIA (*shouting*): There was nothing to eat here – whose fault was that?

JEANNETTE (*shouting, but not looking at her*): There were tinned peas and sardines at the grocer's! I told Papa to get some.

FATHER (*feigning astonishment*): Me? You told me to get some? What with?

JEANNETTE (*not hearing him*): But no. She had to eat well, didn't she, your mother-in-law, so as not to let the family down? She had to feel nice and smug over coffee, didn't she, and be able to belch politely in her stays. That's hospitality. So she chased him with her knife and you let her do it. (*She turns on the* FATHER *like a Fury.*) You let her do it! What a coward you are! I can just see you, dancing attendance on her: 'But of course, madame, by all means!' And to think he used to know you; he used to come and perch on your shoulder and eat out of your hand!

FATHER: I was lying on the divan here. I didn't hear a thing. I was just smoking. . . .

JEANNETTE (*pressing the chicken against her*): I hope you'll all of you die like he did – slaughtered in bed one fine night. I hope you'll be frightened, the way he must have been frightened!

JULIA: Jeannette, stop being stupid now and shut up!

FATHER (*to the* MOTHER): Forgive her. She's just a child. Underneath, she's a fine kid. You just have to get to know her.

MOTHER: Get to know her? Thanks very much, I know her already! (*She unties her apron.*) Julia, my child, I do finally believe you were right. We could have done without meeting your family. Come along, Frederic, we're leaving. (*She makes for the kitchen. The* FATHER *runs after her, calling.*)

FATHER: But what about lunch? Now please, dear lady, compose yourself. . . . We were about to have a meal at last.

MOTHER (*going out*): Thank you. We shall dine when we get back. At home, we're free to kill chickens when we like.

The FATHER *watches her go with a gesture of despair.*

JULIA (*to* JEANNETTE, *before following the* MOTHER *out*): I detest you.

FATHER (*beside himself, to* JEANNETTE): A chicken! After all, it was just like any other chicken, you stupid little fool! Just because you called it Leon. . . . Admittedly it was a nice creature, but we're all nice . . . that doesn't prevent us from coming to an end one day!

He goes out. There remains only JEANNETTE, *standing motionless with the chicken pressed close against her;* LUCIEN, *still standing on the sofa; and* FREDERIC, *who has not taken his eyes off* JEANNETTE *since she came in. There is a short silence after all the uproar. Suddenly, without moving,* FREDERIC *addresses her gently.*

FREDERIC: I'm sorry. (JEANNETTE *looks at him; he smiles*

slightly): But your father is right. We're all mortal. He could have been run over.

JEANNETTE: That wouldn't be the same. I'm sure he was frightened. He saw the knife and he understood, I'm sure of it. He was so intelligent.

FREDERIC (*without smiling*): Maybe he didn't have time to understand exactly what she was going to do.

JEANNETTE (*in despair*): Oh, yes. I'm sure he knew he was going to die. As though it was his fault lunch wasn't ready. All he thought of was running about in the grass just quietly looking for little worms and being afraid of the wind blowing the shadows about. Their stomachs, their beastly stomachs, that's all they think of. (*She looks at* FREDERIC *and draws back a little.*) But who are you? I don't know you either.

FREDERIC: I'm Julia's fiancé.

JEANNETTE (*regarding him mistrustfully*): Oh, so you're *her* son?

FREDERIC: Yes, but you mustn't be unfair. It's not my fault.

JEANNETTE (*looking heart-brokenly at the chicken*): Poor Leon. He did so want to grow into a big, strong cockerel. A real cockerel with a proper red crest, waking everybody up in the morning.

FREDERIC (*gently*): Don't you ever eat chicken?

JEANNETTE (*lowering her head*): Yes. When I don't know them. I know that's just as unfair, but I've tried to give up eating meat altogether, and I can't – I like it too much.

FREDERIC: So you see, you can't help it either.

JEANNETTE (*shaking her head*): Yes, I can. When I'm old and understand everything like other people I shall say that, too, I know. That nothing is anyone's fault. It must be fine to become suddenly tolerant about everything; to go about excusing everything; not to kick any more. Don't you find getting old takes a long time?

FREDERIC (*smiling*): You just have to have a bit of patience.

JEANNETTE: I don't like patience. I don't want to be resigned and accept things. She must have told you things about me, my sister.

FREDERIC (*smiles*): Yes. Lots.

JEANNETTE: Well, it's all true. And worse. And it's all my fault. I'm the black sheep of the family – you must have heard; the one that does all the things that aren't done. You're supposed to detest me.

FREDERIC: I know.

JEANNETTE: And you don't have to smile at me as if I were a child and needed humouring. I don't like people to snivel and be soft, either. You're right. I eat other birds; why shouldn't I eat this one now that it's dead? Because I loved him? That's stupid. I'll go and give it back to the ogress! (*She goes into the kitchen, calling:*) Here you are, here's your chicken, you two! Pluck it in your old kitchen and cook it it if you want to!

She has disappeared. FREDERIC *turns to* LUCIEN, *who has been watching motionless, with his ambiguous smile.*

FREDERIC (*in a voice that tries to be bright, but does not succeed*): She's amazing!

LUCIEN *looks at him for a second without a word, then comes down off the sofa, smiling.*

LUCIEN: Yes. She'll go on amazing you, too.

FREDERIC, *surprised at his tone, stands staring at him.*

Curtain

Act Two

SCENE – *The same, except that the house is now in order. It is evening, after dinner. The room is already shadowy. At the back, in the lighted kitchen,* JULIA *and the* MOTHER *can be seen busying themselves with chores. Onstage the* FATHER *is sleeping in an armchair, a dead cigar in his hand.* FREDERIC *and* JEANNETTE *are seated at some distance from each other, looking at each other across the half-cleared table. Farther back, leaning against the windows, a shadow:* LUCIEN *looking out into the night.*

The FATHER *suddenly begins to snore noisily, then stops as* LUCIEN *begins furiously whistling a military bugle call.* FREDERIC *and* JEANNETTE *look at the* FATHER, *then at each other. They smile at each other for the first time. A clock sounds the half-hour somewhere. Their smiles fade.*

FREDERIC: The train's at half past ten, isn't it?
JEANNETTE: Yes.

Pause.

FREDERIC: How quickly today has gone.
JEANNETTE: Yes.
FREDERIC: When shall we see each other again?
JEANNETTE: At the wedding.

Silence. LUCIEN *moves suddenly and disappears into the darkness. He can be heard whistling the curfew as he wanders off.*

FREDERIC: This could be an evening a long time from now, when we come to spend a few days here with Julia. It'll be just like this. . . . Your father will be asleep in his chair, letting his cigar go out. Julia will be busy in the kitchen. We shall forget to light the lamp, just like this evening, and we shall sit and listen to the night coming on.

JEANNETTE: You'll never come back here, you know that.

FREDERIC: Why?

JEANNETTE: Julia will never want to come back.

FREDERIC (*after a pause*): Well, then, it's an evening a long time ago. An old, old evening that doesn't want to come to an end. We must be very old now, worn out, battered, together again after years and years apart; and we're reminding each other of that quiet evening when no one thought of lighting the lamp, when we sat waiting, waiting, not knowing what for.

JEANNETTE (*pulling herself up and crying out*): *I* shan't remember. I hate memories. They're cowardly and useless.

FATHER (*waking with a start and trying to look as though he has not been asleep*): What were you saying, child? I didn't quite catch.

JEANNETTE: Nothing, Papa. I wasn't saying anything. Go back to sleep.

FATHER (*dropping off again*): I'm not sleeping. I can hear everything.

JEANNETTE (*behind him, too softly to wake him up, and gazing somewhere into space*): All right, then, Papa. If you can hear everything, listen to this. Listen with all your ears. Listen to what your daughter has to say. Your bad daughter. Not the other one. *She* never says shameful things that burn when they're spoken. She always does the right thing, your other daughter, and she's going to get her reward. She's going to be happy. She won't need just the memory of one evening, later on. She'll have the right to every evening, every day, every minute – the right to a whole lifetime. And when she's dead, and there's life everlasting, she'll have the right to remember her own life all over again, for all time, sitting at the right hand of God the Father Almighty!

FREDERIC (*rising and breaking in*): Be quiet!

JEANNETTE (*shouting at first*): No, I won't be quiet! (*Then she looks troubled and says gently:*) Why should I obey you? What are you to me?

At this moment an old man in a dark cloak appears on the threshold with a telegram in his hand.

POSTMAN (*shouts*): Children! Children!

FATHER (*turning in his sleep*): Post, children, post! Postman's here!

LUCIEN (*he has loomed up out of the night, and falls upon the* POSTMAN): Is that you, postman? Is it for me?

POSTMAN: No, boy. It's for your sister. Telegram – night rate.

LUCIEN: When will it be for me, postman?

POSTMAN: When I get it, son.

He disappears into the night. There is the sound of the gate slamming, then, after a second, LUCIEN *goes up to* JEANNETTE *and holds out the telegram.*

LUCIEN: Well! Night rate, my love. Someone has something urgent to say to you. (*Pause. He waits.* JEANNETTE *has taken the telegram, but does not open it.*) Aren't you going to open it?

JEANNETTE: No. I know what's in it.

LUCIEN (*with a grimace, curious*): You're lucky! I'd like to know. . . . (*He goes off whistling a military call, after emptying a glass of wine that is standing on the table.*)

FREDERIC (*suddenly, dully*): What is in the telegram?

JEANNETTE: Nothing.

FREDERIC: Why don't you open it?

JEANNETTE (*tearing it up without looking at it*): I already know everything it says.

FREDERIC: Anyway, you're right. What business is it of mine? I've known you since this morning, and I'm leaving in an hour.

JEANNETTE: And marrying my sister next month.

FREDERIC: Yes.

They look at each other.

JEANNETTE (*suddenly, after a pause*): It's a telegram from my lover.

FREDERIC: The man who was following us in the woods this afternoon?

JEANNETTE: Oh, did you see him? No, not that one, poor lad. He doesn't dare write to me. Maybe he can't even write. This is another one, who thinks he has the right. I visit him every evening.

FREDERIC: And he's writing because he won't be seeing you this evening.

JEANNETTE: Not this evening or ever again, I sent him a note by hand this morning to tell him I wouldn't be seeing him any more.

Pause.

FREDERIC (*with an effort*): Why are you leaving him?

JEANNETTE: Because I don't love him. Because I suddenly felt ashamed of belonging to him.

FREDERIC: And yesterday?

JEANNETTE: Yesterday I didn't care. I didn't care about anything – about having a lover like him or about going about with bare legs and a torn frock and being plain.

FREDERIC (*dully*): You're not plain.

JEANNETTE: Yes. Julia's more beautiful than I am. Julia's pure, and I'm— I know what I'm worth. That man that was following us – he's been my lover, too, and I didn't love him either. And there were others before that, ever since I was fifteen, and I didn't love any of them.

FREDERIC: Why do you deliberately smear yourself?

JEANNETTE: So that you'll hate me. So that you'll go away tonight hating me. So that you'll marry Julia hating me.

FREDERIC: You knew perfectly well I shan't be able to.

JEANNETTE (*softly*): And also so that you'll never be able to forget this moment, when I told you everything bad about myself here in the dark.

FREDERIC: It's bad to tell someone everything like that, deliberately.

JEANNETTE: I've only got one evening – not even that, just

an hour – hardly that even now. There'll be plenty of time to be quiet after that.

FREDERIC: Why do you talk like that, when there's nothing we can do?

JEANNETTE: There's nothing we can do tomorrow, nothing we can do for the rest of our lives. But we can still do something for this one hour if they leave us alone. An hour is a long time when it's all you've got.

FREDERIC: What can we do?

JEANNETTE: Tell each other straight out what bad luck we've had. Tell each other about that secret bit of bad luck that we'll have to hush up for ever afterwards. Tell each other how stupid it is to deprive oneself of a single day, of a single minute, that might pass us by for ever and ever.

FREDERIC: But this morning I loved Julia!

JEANNETTE: Yes. And I expect you still love her. You're going away with her soon, anyway. She'll have you for the rest of her life. That's why I'm daring to say this, because she's better off than me.

FREDERIC: Julia's good. She mustn't be hurt!

JEANNETTE: I know. And I know that *my* hurt is too new, it doesn't carry the same weight. I know it's *my* memory that must fade like an old photograph, getting fainter and fainter day after day. I know there's got to come a day when you won't remember any more exactly what my eyes are like – you've hardly looked at them. And then another day, the day Julia's first son is born, or perhaps the day of the christening, when you'll forget them altogether.

FREDERIC (*with a muffled cry*): No.

JEANNETTE: Yes. That's why I dare say all this. I'm talking the way people talk when they're going to die. Not for a good cause, but shamefully, with nobody much to regret them.

FREDERIC: I shall go away with Julia in a little while, and marry her, I know. But I shall never forget you.

Silence.

JEANNETTE (*softly, with eyes closed*): I must say thank you, mustn't I, like poor people have to?

Another silence.

FREDERIC: This pain, this agony we've both been feeling today, it can't be love – that's impossible. But I shall never be able to get rid of it now.

JEANNETTE (*teeth clenched*): I shall. Tomorrow. I swear it.

FREDERIC: Will you?

JEANNETTE: I must be able to! I must tear the pain out of me all by myself, like an animal tearing a thorn out of its pad with its teeth. I don't want to go on loving with empty arms. I don't want to go on loving one and being with another.

FREDERIC: But we don't love each other! We scarcely know each other!

JEANNETTE (*shaking her head*): It's true. I can't love you, I hate you too much. What did you come here for? Couldn't you have married her at home, your Julia, without my knowing? Yesterday I could laugh. Yesterday I had a lover I wasn't sure I loved and I didn't care. He said he loved me, and I still liked to hear him say so – yesterday.

FREDERIC: Why did you write and tell him you were leaving him tonight?

JEANNETTE: No reason. So that I could be free when I said good-bye to you. And if I could have left the others as well, the ones before him, and wiped out the marks of their hands on me, I'd have done it.

FATHER (*turning in his chair as he sleeps, with a sigh*): Yes, but of course I'm not doing the paying.

FREDERIC (*smiling in spite of himself*): What's he dreaming about?

JEANNETTE (*also smiling*): I don't know. The wedding breakfast, maybe. . . . Poor Papa. When Lucien goes as well, we'll be alone, the two of us. Funny sort of set-up that'll be.

FREDERIC (*suddenly, gently*): I'm sorry.

JEANNETTE: Why? You've already said you were sorry for no reason once before, this morning, about the chicken. . . .

After all, everything's as it should be. The other way round would be terrible. Julia's a real woman. I'm not. You've loved her for months and months, but you've only loved me since this morning, and it's still not certain if you do. I'm the one that's a fool, to have said what I've said. What's happened to us must be going on every day, but other people just give a deep sigh and think, 'What a pity it's too late', and go on looking at each other in a special sort of way for years afterwards. It adds a little mystery to family life. . . .

LUCIEN *can be heard whistling outside. He suddenly looms out of the darkness behind them.*

LUCIEN: Well, children? Watching Papa having forty winks? (*Going up to him.*) Doesn't it give you the shudders, rather, this open-mouthed corpse? How surprised it looks. So that was life, was it? They should have told me. Too late, my dear friend, much too late. Sleep away. Have your little foretaste of death. Don't snore, though, or I'll whistle. I like the dead to be discreet. (*He looks at the others.*) Not bored with each other, I hope, all alone here? (*He watches the other two passing to and fro in the lighted kitchen.*) Look at them, busy little bees. Scrubbing and scouring away in the kitchen, thinking they hold the key to Truth like the handle of a saucepan, not suspecting a thing. They hate us, both of them. They know that from tomorrow on our squalor will win the day. It may even make them miss their train, but no matter. They don't want it said that they left our kitchen dirty. . . . We all have our own notion of honour, don't we? What's yours, Jeannie? (*Silence. The others do not answer. He goes to the table and pours himself a glass of wine.*) I'm mad about housewives. The image of death. How absurd it must look from a distance – all these unfortunate women rubbing away tirelessly at the same little corner, day in, day out, for years and years, being thwarted every night by the same dust. . . . There she is, this housewife, wearing herself out, drying herself up, getting wrinkled and ugly, until one fine night she crumples up and pegs out, all in after the last round of chores. And next day, on that same little corner that's still there – you bet – plenty of time ahead – there falls another layer of dust. And this time it stays. (*He stretches, yawns, and takes another drink.*) True, if they didn't do that, what would they do, poor dears? Make love? (*He gets up.*) Not everybody can make love, though – that wouldn't be right and proper. Would it, dear brother-in-law-to-be? (*He can be heard laughing mockingly in the shadows, even when he can no longer be seen. He whistles another military bugle call as he wanders off into the garden.*)

FREDERIC (*suddenly, in a dull voice*): Love. Does he really not believe that that's a day-to-day struggle, too?

JEANNETTE (*smiling a little tiredly*): Not so hard as today, though. I could never keep it up.

FREDERIC (*smiling, also rather tiredly*): Yes, today's been tough going. (*Pause.*) And there's still tonight to come. And having to wake up.

JEANNETTE: I'm a bad lot, so I shan't budge from my unmade bed. I shall pull the bedclothes up to my eyes. . . . Papa will come and shout at my door for a bit and then he'll go and warm up the stale coffee himself. Later on, around midday, I shall hear him calling me because he can't find a key to open a tin of sardines. And I shall go on lying low until night comes.

FREDERIC: Then when we've killed the first day, there'll be the others. (*Suddenly, he cries:*) I can't do it! (JEANNETTE *looks at him.*) I want to struggle, yes, but not against this part of me that's crying out. I want to struggle, but not against this joy. (*Looking at her, he exclaims:*) How far away you are on the other side of this table! How far away you've been all day. . . .

JEANNETTE: It had to be like that. What would have happened if you had so much as brushed against me?

FREDERIC: We've been fighting each other all day without touching, without even daring to look at each other. We've been rolling on the ground, stifling each other, without a word or a movement, while other people have been talking.

. . . Oh, how far away you are still. And yet you'll never be so close again.

JEANNETTE: Never again.

FREDERIC: Never again, even in thought. . . . It must be like that, mustn't it, if we want to be strong? We must never for a moment imagine ourselves in each other's arms. . . .

JEANNETTE (*motionless, eyes closed*): Not tomorrow. But tonight I'm in your arms.

There is a pause, then FREDERIC *sighs, also with eyes closed.*

FREDERIC: I couldn't keep it up. . . . Don't move! It's so good suddenly – it can't be wrong.

They both continue talking with their eyes closed, not moving.

JEANNETTE: Yes. It's good.

Pause.

FREDERIC (*in a whisper*): So it was possible. I feel as though I were drinking water. How thirsty I was.

JEANNETTE: I was thirsty, too. (*Pause, then dully:*) Maybe we ought to call them now. Wake Papa or go out after Lucien, but we ought to have someone with us.

FREDERIC (*suddenly*): Wait! It hurts too much. I didn't know what it was like to be hurt. (*He opens his eyes, takes a step towards her, and asks:*) Who is this man?

JEANNETTE: What man?

FREDERIC: Your lover.

JEANNETTE (*recoiling a little into the darkness*): What lover? I haven't got a lover.

FREDERIC: You just told me you had. Who is this man you go to see every night?

JEANNETTE (*loudly*): Who told you I went to see him every night? Do you listen to what other people say?

FREDERIC: You told me yourself.

JEANNETTE: I was lying! It wasn't true. Did you believe it? I haven't got a lover.

FREDERIC: Then why did you tell me you had? I believe everything you say.

JEANNETTE: To make you listen to me. Your one thought was to get away; you were trying with all your strength not to love me!

FREDERIC: And all my strength said no. All my strength went over to the enemy, battalion by battalion. How different it seems tonight, too. Like a host of strange faces that I don't recognize – and no one to offer me a helping hand in the darkness. What did the telegram say?

JEANNETTE: What telegram?

FREDERIC: The one you just tore up.

JEANNETTE: You frighten me. You sound like a judge. Remembering I had a telegram and tore it up. You remember everything.

FREDERIC: Yes. I used to forget everything. Names of streets, numbers, insults, faces. Julia used to laugh at me. Now I don't forget anything any more. Everything is in its place, with a label, a question mark. Life has become a nerve-racking survey of one's accounts. What was in that telegram? Answer me.

JEANNETTE: How can I answer you? You saw for yourself. I tore it up without opening it.

FREDERIC: Pick up the pieces and read them.

JEANNETTE: I don't know where they are any more.

FREDERIC: I do – they're by your feet.

JEANNETTE: It's dark. I shouldn't be able to see.

FREDERIC: I'll put the light on.

JEANNETTE (*suddenly, in a loud voice*): Oh, no! Please don't put the light on! Don't make me read it. Don't make me look you in the face. Just believe me. It would be so easy to believe me in the dark.

FREDERIC: But that's all I ask! To believe you, like a child, like a slave. Everything's crying out inside me that I want to believe you. Can't you hear it? But I can't. You tell lies all time.

JEANNETTE: Yes, I tell lies all the time, but you must believe me just the same. They're not real lies. With a little luck they might all have been true. They would all become true, if you wanted it that way. Oh, *please*! It's so much simpler for you. You need only want it.

FREDERIC: I do want it, I do want it, with all my might, as you do in dreams, but I can't. Who sent you that telegram?

JEANNETTE: You see, you're questioning me again. So I have to lie to you, to gain time.

FREDERIC: Why should you want to gain time?

JEANNETTE: Everything's so fragile still. It's too early to talk yet. Tomorrow we shall know each other. Tomorrow we may be stronger than words. . . . Oh, if you would only wait, if you would only wait a little. I'm so poor as you see me tonight. I've so few possessions yet. I'm just a beggar. Give me a little, just a little bit of quiet.

FREDERIC (*in a dull voice*): I can't.

JEANNETTE: Or ask me some other questions. Ask me why I'm trembling as I talk to you, why I cry when I tell you lies, why I'm getting so mixed up – me, the one that's so sure of everything and laughs all the time!

FREDERIC: I can't. I want to know who the others are. I want to know all the things that'll hurt me.

JEANNETTE (*with a sudden desperate gesture, out loud*): All right, then, you'll have asked for it. Take me or leave me with all my faults. You'll have to take half of them now, though. I can't go on alone. We must share and share alike. It was all true just now – I did have a lover, and he did write to me, to beg me not to leave him, I suppose. And there were others before him that I didn't love. Before I knew I ought to wait, that somewhere on this earth there was someone I didn't know yet, someone I was already about to steal. . . . There, you know everything now. Lying is the only way I know of defending myself. (*Pause.*) You don't say anything. You're standing there close to me; I can hear you breathing in the dark. I can feel that Julia must be like a great patch of light inside you now. You'll never be able to love this fraud as you love her, will you? (*She goes on in a low voice.*) And yet for all my bad ways and my goings-on and my wickedness of heart I'm like a virgin standing here in front of you at this moment – something the others will never know. But there's no bouquet, no white veil, no innocence, no little bridesmaids to carry the train – a bride all in black. . . . (*Her voice lower still.*) And all for you, if you would deign to look at her.

FREDERIC *has stepped towards her suddenly. He takes her in his arms and kisses her. She frees herself with the cry of a hurt animal and runs off. He remains alone and motionless in the dark room. The* MOTHER *comes in and lights the hanging lamp, which casts a gloomy light.*

MOTHER: You can't see a thing here. What are you doing in the dark? (*She stows some things away in the sideboard.*) There. The kitchen has probably never been so clean. Poor Julia! She was in tears about it, and I can well understand it. She's so unlike them. It was only for her sake I stayed this morning. Thank heavens it's over now. We've done what had to be done and now we'll all three pack up and be off and not come back any sooner than we can help. What's the matter? You're so pale. Are you tired?

FREDERIC: No, Mother.

MOTHER: It's this light. (*Looking at the* FATHER.) He's asleep, the old good-for-nothing. Still, he's a bit better than the other two. You saw the other girl, I suppose, leaving everything to Julia and me? The cheek of it! We'll try not to invite her to the wedding. Julia agrees with me. Your uncles would never understand how I could let you marry the sister of a girl like that. Poor Julia! She's suffered enough already on her account. (*She goes back to the kitchen, calling out to* JULIA, *who is just visible.*) We shall have to leave the rest, my dear, if we don't want to miss the train.

She has disappeared with JULIA. FREDERIC *has not stirred. A door opens suddenly.* JEANNETTE *appears. They talk in low voices, like criminals.*

JEANNETTE: What are we going to do?

FREDERIC: We must tell her.

JEANNETTE: Now that I'm the rich one, I feel ashamed. You call her.

FREDERIC (*calling, but scarcely raising his voice*): Julia.

JEANNETTE: Louder. She can't hear. . . . (*Suddenly crying out.*) Wait! It's wrong, what we're doing.

FREDERIC: Yes.

JEANNETTE: Nobody will ever be able to understand, nobody will ever forgive us, will they?

FREDERIC: No, nobody.

JEANNETTE: We're like two murderers that daren't look each other in the face. But we've got to do it. It would be shabbier still not to say anything.

FREDERIC: And tomorrow it will be too late. (*He calls again, still not loudly enough.*) Julia.

JEANNETTE (*coming up to him and putting her arms round him*): Wait! She's going to lose you. She's suddenly not going to have you in her arms any more. I'm trying to imagine what it's like to have nothing in your arms any more.

FREDERIC: It's like it was just now.

JEANNETTE (*with a cry*): I don't remember any more! Oh, how good it is to be together! When was it – yesterday? – that we didn't know each other?

FREDERIC: I don't know. We must call her.

JEANNETTE: Wait! Oh, if only you'd never known her! If only you'd known me first. I'm touching you. I'm really touching you. Forgive me, Julia – it's so good!

FREDERIC (*looking ahead of him into the distance*): We mustn't ask her to forgive us. We mustn't try to explain. We must tell her quickly, like cutting something with a knife. We must kill her quickly and get out.

JEANNETTE: How you love her still!

FREDERIC: Yes. (*He calls, louder this time.*) Julia!

JULIA (*appears, a cloth in her hand, at the kitchen door*): Are you calling me?

FREDERIC (*more softly*): Yes, Julia.

FREDERIC *and* JEANNETTE *have let go of each other and are standing close together looking straight ahead of them.*
JULIA *comes into the room and looks at them.*

JULIA: What is it?

FREDERIC (*making a beginning*): This is it, Julia. It's going to be difficult to say, and you won't be able to understand, I know. I'm not going to marry you, Julia.

JULIA (*does not move at first. Then she puts down the cloth on a chair. Looking at* JEANNETTE, *she asks*): What has she said to you?

FREDERIC: She hasn't said anything. You don't know. You can't ever know, you can't even understand. It's not our fault. We've both been fighting against it since this morning.

JULIA: Fighting . . . ? Who, you?

FREDERIC (*with a gesture of the hand*): Both of us. You must go with Mother, Julia. I'm staying here.

JULIA: Staying where?

FREDERIC: Or if you think it's better for you to stay, we'll go.

JULIA: 'We' . . . who's 'we'? (*They do not reply. She goes on in a lower voice:*) When you say 'we' . . . you don't mean us any more? Who do you mean you're going with? (*They do not answer.*) You're trying to frighten me, aren't you? And now you're going to laugh at me. Or maybe you want me to laugh first?

JEANNETTE: I'm going to hurt you. Julia. We've hated each other ever since we were little. But today I want to be humble with you. I want to be your servant.

JULIA: Stop trying to be nice to me. You're frightening me.

JEANNETTE: We've always quarrelled over everything – toys, clothes . . . everything. But today I'd willingly give you everything I have. Only I haven't got anything but my old shabby clothes and him – and I can't give you him. I wish I could make myself uglier, so that you didn't feel so hurt. I wish I could spoil my face, cut my hair. But then I don't want to be ugly either, because of him.

JULIA: Do you really think he can love you? You're everything he hates most in the world!

JEANNETTE (*humbly*): Yes, Julia.

JULIA: A slattern, a liar, and bone lazy!

JEANNETTE: Yes.

JULIA: He's so pure, so hard to please, the soul of honour – how can he love you? Is this a joke or something? Have you told him about your lovers?

JEANNETTE: Yes, I have.

JULIA: What about this last one – the one that pays you – does he know about him? I bet he doesn't.

JEANNETTE (*suddenly transfigured*): Thank you, Julia!

JULIA: What for?

JEANNETTE: At last you've been wicked!

JULIA: You weren't actually hoping I wouldn't defend myself? She got round you, I suppose? Rubbed herself against you as with the others? Kissed you full on the mouth in a dark corner, or better still, out on the sands?

FREDERIC (*loudly*): We've never been alone. We haven't even talked to each other!

JULIA: Oh, it doesn't take her long and she doesn't need much conversation. Ask her how she's done it before with the fisherboys at night, lying on the nets at the bottom of a boat in the stink of fish!

JEANNETTE: Thank you, Julia, thank you!

JULIA: Keep your thanks, you sneak thief!

JEANNETTE: Now that you're fighting back, I'm not ashamed. Thank you, Julia.

FREDERIC (*trying to pull her away*): Be quiet! Leave her alone!

JEANNETTE: You might have cried or burst into tears, and he might have taken pity on you. But you started defending yourself like a woman about to be robbed.

JULIA: Yes. Thief! Thief!

FREDERIC: Be quiet, both of you!

JULIA: Quiet? So I've got to be quiet, too? She's taking you away, and I've got to be quiet!

JEANNETTE: How clumsy you are. All stiff and dignified. You're only thinking of how much you hate me. You're only thinking of the harm we're doing you. You should be crying. Go on, cry! Melt his heart!

JULIA: You'd like me to cry, wouldn't you? But don't be too sure.

JEANNETTE: Cry! He's only waiting for that to take you back! He loves you still, you can see he does. Look at him at least!

JULIA: No.

JEANNETTE: Now, while I'm shouting and ugly and, my hair's all over the place! He hates me like this. He's beginning to miss you already. Cry, quick, Julia, cry!

JULIA: No! I've got all the time I need to cry in. That'll do for when I'm alone.

JEANNETTE: Tear my eyes out, then! Scratch me, hit me – I shan't defend myself. But do something horrible – you've got to, too, so that I'm not the only one! He's only thinking of you now; he's only listening to you. Do something mean and horrible or I shall kill you, I shall spit in your face!

She throws herself on JULIA. FREDERIC *tears her away, hurting her as he does so, and pushes her away from him.*

FREDERIC: Leave her alone now. I'm telling you to!

JEANNETTE (*with a cry of triumph*): He hurt me! Did you see? He hurt me, *me*! *I'm* his wife!

FREDERIC (*gently*): Please go now, Julia. You're worth more than she is, I realize that, and she's probably done all the things you said she had, but she's right; she's my wife now.

JULIA (*turning suddenly and running to the kitchen, calling*): Help! Mother! Help!

JEANNETTE (*with eyes closed, her voice hoarse*): How you must hate me at this moment!

FREDERIC (*hard, without looking at her*): Go up to your room. Get what you want to take with you and wait for me outside.

JEANNETTE *goes out.* LUCIEN *appears suddenly.*

LUCIEN: You're not going to do it?

FREDERIC: Yes. Now, this minute.

LUCIEN: Don't. It always goes wrong.

FREDERIC: Why?

LUCIEN: It's too good. And everything that's good is forbidden, didn't you know? (*He pours a glass of red wine.*) Take this glass of wine, for example; it isn't much, but it warms you up a bit on its way down. . . . That's forbidden. You have to take advantage when He's not looking. (*He empties the glass at a gulp.*) There! He didn't notice that one.

FREDERIC: Who?

LUCIEN (*pointing upward*): That One up there. Every time anyone's happy, He gets in a frightful rage. Doesn't like it.

FREDERIC: You're drunk.

LUCIEN: Not yet, alas. That doesn't happen till much later. You're not going to do this, are you? You'll never get away with it.

FREDERIC: We'll see.

LUCIEN: I can see already. I can see you a week from now, the two of you, in a month, a year. It's all unrolling in front of me like a little film. A terrible little film. But there's still time. Go and find Julia and your mother in the kitchen and tell them you were dreaming.

FREDERIC: I wasn't dreaming!

LUCIEN: Look at me, dear boy. I don't look the sensitive type, do I? Don't do it. Even if only for Julia's sake.

FREDERIC: I mustn't think of Julia any more!

LUCIEN: What's love? Nothing. Mockery, lies, wind. I tell you, she'll die now. Don't do it. It's not worth the trouble you cause yourself, let alone the trouble you cause other people. It's not worth a baby crying. Don't do it.

FREDERIC: I've been over all that. It's too late now.

LUCIEN: You can't have been over it all; you don't know it all. I know. I know it all! I've completed my education. It cost me somewhat dearly, my dear little education, and I'm still paying. I had to do it on the never-never; lifelong instalments . . . but now at least I can talk. I'm fully qualified in love. I've got my doctorate in cuckoldry. That makes me an authority. Don't do it, dear boy. The game's up in advance.

FREDERIC: But why?

LUCIEN: For no reason at all. Because she's a woman. Because we're alone in the world. Because one night in a month or a year or ten years from now, when you think you're holding your little mate in your arms, you'll suddenly realize you're like everybody else; that it's only a woman you've got in your arms, there's nothing there.

FREDERIC: That's enough. You shut up, too.

LUCIEN: Marry Julia. Have children. Become a man. A man with a profession, with money, with a girl friend later on – nobody'll mind that – a real man. Don't try to be clever. It's so easy to be happy! There's a formula; men have spent centuries perfecting it. Cheat, old man. Cheat at everything. Above all, cheat yourself. It's the only way of getting that One up there to leave you alone. He's got a weakness for tricksters, or else He's short-sighted. Or maybe He's asleep. (*He indicates the* FATHER.) Like him, with his mouth open. And if you don't make too much noise, he won't interfere. . . . But He's got a nose, a terribly keen sense of smell, and the whiff – just the merest whiff – of love, and He's on to it. And He doesn't like it. He doesn't like it at all. So He wakes up and starts taking an interest in you. He pounces on you like a sergeant-major. About turn! No good trying to be smart with me, my fine friend. Don't care for refractory types. Brought plenty like you to heel. You'll be a cuckold. What's that? What? Not satisfied? You can die of it, then, that'll teach you! Death! Death! Death! Death! You've read that little page at the back of your service certificate, where they promise you it served up in all sorts of different ways when you're a new recruit? That's love.

JEANNETTE (*appearing with a coat, hat and small bundle*): I'm ready.

FREDERIC: Let's go.

He takes her hand and they go out and disappear into the darkness. LUCIEN *has not moved. He helps himself to the rest of the wine, lifts his glass ceilingwards.*

LUCIEN: Here's to them. Do you mind?

FATHER (*awakened by the silence, and trying to look as though he has not been asleep*): Well, now, where are we, children? I hope this is going to be over soon.

LUCIEN (*smiling*): Quite soon. It's just beginning.

Curtain

Act Three

SCENE – *A deserted summer-house in the woods. The room is quite empty. At the back the bottom of a staircase is just visible. There is an overturned sofa lying on the floor. Hanging at the broken window is a dark curtain, bellying out in the wind. The room is in darkness. A storm can be heard outside.* JEANNETTE *comes in with* FREDERIC.

They are drenched with rain.

JEANNETTE: Let's come in here for a bit. At least we'll be out of the rain. (*They come in and shut the door. Everything suddenly seems quiet.*) It used to be used as a summer-house in the woods, but it's been neglected for a long time now. I shelter here now and again when I get caught in the rain. (*Silence. They stand in the middle of the dark room. She murmurs:*) It would be better to wait here.

Pause. A gale blows the curtains out again.

FREDERIC: What a storm!

JEANNETTE: Yes. The glass has all gone out of the windows. (*Short silence.*) There's a hurricane lamp in the corner there, if you've got any matches. (*He passes her a box of matches.*) The owner's very kind. He knows I come here sometimes and he leaves this for me.

FREDERIC: You know him?

JEANNETTE: Slightly. (*She pins back the flapping curtain with a plank.*) If we light up, we'd better draw the curtain. The light can be seen a long way off in the woods. (*He looks around him. She goes to the sofa and pulls it back into position.*) There's only an old rickety sofa, but it does stand up.

FREDERIC *has caught sight of the staircase.*

FREDERIC: What's up there?

JEANNETTE (*seeming to hesitate slightly*): It's a sort of hayloft. There's just an old mattress on the floor and some ancient moth-eaten curtains that I put up on the wall and an old trunk for a table. It's my home. I sleep there sometimes in the summer. I'll show it to you presently. (*Pause. They are standing face to face, not daring to move. She whispers:*) So here we are.

FREDERIC: So here we are.

Pause. They are embarrassed, and do not move. There is the sound of the storm outside.

JEANNETTE: Still, it is better to stay here than at the station.

FREDERIC: Are you shivering?

JEANNETTE: Yes.

FREDERIC: You're wet through. Are you cold?

JEANNETTE: No, I'm not cold. It's only my coat that's soaked. Take off your jacket and let it dry. I'll go upstairs and find you something. (*She runs lightly upstairs and can be heard walking about in the room above.* FREDERIC *takes off his jacket. She comes down again with a blanket which she throws over his shoulders.*) There! You look wonderful like that – like an old redskin chief. (*He goes to take her in his arms, but she disengages herself almost imperceptibly, murmuring.*) I'm frightened.

FREDERIC (*gently*): I'm frightened, too.

There is a short pause. She smiles.

JEANNETTE: I'm frightening you with my hair all wet like this. I'm so ugly.

FREDERIC: No, you're not.

JEANNETTE: They say I look like a mad thing when my hair's wet.

FREDERIC: Who are 'they'?

JEANNETTE: The others. (*Correcting herself.*) People.

FREDERIC: You look like a wood nymph.

JEANNETTE: I'd like to have been a real wood nymph, sitting all by myself up in the branches, with my hair all tangled, shouting insults at people. There were never any real ones, though, were there?

FREDERIC: I don't know.

JEANNETTE (*raising her eyes, suddenly serious*): Anyway, you probably like girls with their hair all tidy; the sort that brush it for ages and ages every morning in the bedroom. (*She passes her fingers through her hair, then runs suddenly to her little bundle and rummages feverishly in it. She gets up, vexed.*) No, I don't seem to have brought a comb with me. I'll buy a brush tomorrow. (*She is standing facing him; suddenly she cries:*) And I'll tidy my hair, properly, and make it smooth – the way I hate it and you like it. As smooth as Julia's! (*They stand looking at each other for a while, disconcerted, then she lowers her eyes, humble again.*) I'm sorry. But I should so much like to be beautiful. I do so want you to like me. (*Pause. She cries:*) Wait a minute! I haven't got a comb, but I did bring something else – in this box. (*She takes up a cardboard box, badly tied up with string, which she was carrying when she came in, and climbs upstairs. He remains alone on the stage, somewhat disconcerted. She can be heard calling from above.*) But you mustn't look! If you move an inch I shall come down again and you won't see a thing. I shall be rather a long time – it's dark up here.

FREDERIC: Do you want the lamp?

JEANNETTE: No, thanks. I don't need it. Don't move. Are you bored waiting?

FREDERIC: No.

JEANNETTE: Anyway, this will make up for it, I hope. (*There is a short pause, during which there is no sound from her, then suddenly she appears on the staircase in the eerie light of the hurricane lamp. She has hurriedly put on an unusual, flimsy white dress, but is still wearing her clumsy boy's shoes. She stands there for a while without a word.*) There. Now, I'm dying of shame. I'll go and take it off!

FREDERIC (*dully*): No. (*She stops.*) Did you bring that with you in your bundle?

JEANNETTE: No, not in that. In that big cardboard box that

I kept banging against the trees on the way. It's the only precious thing I have in the world.

FREDERIC: But it's a wedding dress. . . .

JEANNETTE: No. It's white, but it's a ball dress, a real ball dress, like the ones in the catalogues. . . . (*She looks slightly troubled.*) It's not new, though. . . . I bought it from a second-hand shop that was selling it for the material alone. I just managed to scrape up the money selling some of the wild-duck eggs I go nesting for in the reeds. They're very rare around here, you know. People have them hatched by their own hens, and get a much more valuable breed that way. (*She has the feeling he probably does not believe her and adds:*) I'd been selling eggs for a whole season, so I did have the money. Because, of course, the dealer wouldn't let me have a dress like this for nothing. It looks almost new, too, now that I've washed it. (*Her voice trails off. He says nothing, but stands looking at her. She turns back up the stairs, murmuring:*) I'll go and take it off.

FREDERIC (*tonelessly*): No. Keep it on. (*She comes down again and walks silently towards him, never taking her eyes off him. When she is close, he takes her in his arms.*) I don't care if it is new – or even if you got it as a present from someone.

JEANNETTE: Why don't you ever believe me? I'm sure you believe anything Julia tells you.

FREDERIC: Yes, I do.

JEANNETTE: But not me.

FREDERIC: No.

JEANNETTE (*disengaging herself*): Well, go and find her, then. *I* want to be believed, too! (*She comes back to his arms.*) No. Don't move. I'll tell you everything. Sit down. (*She makes him sit down and then sits at his feet.*) I didn't do it just with the wild-duck eggs, of course. I'd have needed much more than that. But it is true they paid for some of it. I didn't want you to know the rest, because I didn't think you'd like it. Papa had had some silver in pawn for ages and ages. He was always asking for renewals, but the time was running out. I stole the pawn ticket from a whole pile of them he keeps in a drawer and took the silver out, with the duck-egg money actually, and sold it to buy this dress. He'd never have had enough money to take the things out himself, and he'd just have lost the silver. Besides, there was a bit of money over, and I bought him a box of cigars with it. Only a small box, because this was expensive. (*Pause.*) I don't mind you knowing that, now that you know how I got the money. I bought it new in a big Paris shop. I chose it from the catalogue and they sent it through the post. So now you know. (*Another pause.*) Does that make you unhappy?

FREDERIC: No.

JEANNETTE: Do you believe me now?

FREDERIC: Yes.

JEANNETTE (*sighs and lays her head on his knee*): How simple it is to tell the truth. Somehow you just don't think of it.

FREDERIC: Do think of it, please, so that I don't get too hurt.

JEANNETTE: Are you hurt, truly? But you said just now you didn't care if the dress was new, or if someone had given it to me.

FREDERIC (*with his eyes closed*): It wasn't true.

JEANNETTE: Oh, good! I'm glad. Because if you only loved me that way, if you only desired me and didn't mind about anything else, I should be terribly unhappy. You must believe in me, make lots of demands on me.

FREDERIC: I want with all my might to believe in you; I shall go on asking you for the truth, every morning, like daily bread, to keep me going for the day.

JEANNETTE: That's right. Every morning when we wake up I shall tell you the truth. How good it'll be to give you all the truth I have in me, like a little piece of luggage to carry. It'll make me feel so light. And then at night I shall give you another little lot, before I go to sleep. But, of course, at night it will be a bit complicated.

FREDERIC: Why?

JEANNETTE (*sighing*): Because days are so long! Because I love you so much. Because I'm so afraid of hurting you.

FREDERIC: How else would you hurt me except by lying to me?

JEANNETTE: Oh! There are other ways. People are frightened of lies, but they're really only like little clouds; they pass without leaving any trace. And you mustn't think I can remember all mine, either. If I were to remember them all, if they were all to be stuck all over me like flies, then maybe it would be frightening. But when the cloud has passed, I feel all relaxed again; rather as if we'd been able to change the subject and I'd kept my mouth shut – all calm and innocent! Do you see?

FREDERIC (*sighing*): I'll try.

JEANNETTE: A step to the right – that's fine; a step to the left – that's bad. It's like being little again and not knowing quite which hand is which. (*Pause. Suddenly she asks:*) I'm not really the sort of woman you were thinking of as a wife, am I?

FREDERIC: Not altogether.

JEANNETTE: But here I am, with my head on your knee.

FREDERIC: Yes. Here you are.

JEANNETTE: I suppose that's what they call fate?

FREDERIC: I suppose it is.

JEANNETTE (*sighing happily*): What a good thing fate is.

FREDERIC (*after a pause, in a hard voice*): Yes. What a good thing. There's Julia, crying in her empty room back there, with everything around her shattered and insecure, but fate is good. And whatever it is inside me that's broken and will go on hurting for always – that's good, too. Everything's good. A terrible luxury, an appalling sweetness.

JEANNETTE: And me being the way I am?

FREDERIC: That's good, too. I suppose it was really the simplest thing in the world that we should be so unsuitable for each other, so full of contradictions, both of us. And that I should have to love Julia first, and meet you through her, and that you should be so different.

Silence.

JEANNETTE (*murmurs*): Even when we were small, we couldn't have been much alike.

FREDERIC: No.

JEANNETTE: Did you always come out top at school?

FREDERIC: Yes.

JEANNETTE: I can just see you, looking so tidy and clean with your school satchel over your shoulder. I was always dirty and tousled and covered with ink spots, with my hair falling into my eyes. I was always cutting school, to go and fight with the roughs.

FREDERIC (*smiling*): I can just see that, too!

JEANNETTE: There used to be a whole gang of us. We called ourselves the Kings of Trumps. They even said we killed a boy one night by throwing clogs at him. We were terrible. We had ink tattoo marks and real sabre cuts all over us. And we had a charm, too – a bit of red paper that we chewed to make us strong. We called it Mininistatfia. And all the while, there you were – I can just see you – with your clean white collar!

FREDERIC (*smiling*): I expect I pretended not to see any of you. I must have hated you all. We had a good crowd, too. We called ourselves the Dauntless. We had a system of military ranks, and we'd made up our minds to rid the world of roughs.

JEANNETTE: What a hope. Don't worry, they'll always be there.

FREDERIC: They used to steal fruit from our parents and show their backsides and pull our sisters' hair.

JEANNETTE: Yes, lovely plaits! Just made for pulling!

FREDERIC: We all agreed to put a stop to it once and for all and there was to be a big fight on the Fourteenth of July. We had a week's truce to get ourselves ready. Little bastards! They put knife blades on the ends of their sticks.

JEANNETTE: We had a big fight, too. One of the others got his arm broken. Ours was on Saint John's Day. We'd been dancing around bonfires like savages before it started. I'd made myself an American knuckle-duster with some nails. I buried it in the seat of the deputy mayor, because they'd brought in their parents to help them, the cowards, when they saw we were winning!

FREDERIC: Our crowd only had sticks and stones. We fought in the open with fair weapons. But we aimed better than they did. You should have heard the yelling when we got one of them in the dark!

JEANNETTE (*softly*): You threw a stone at me once. I've got a hole the size of a nut in my knee. Give me your hand. Look, it's there.

Pause. His hand is lying on her knee.

FREDERIC (*gravely*): I'm sorry.

JEANNETTE: That's all right – so long as you don't hurt me any more. (*Silence again. She sighs happily.*) It's nice to feel your hand there. Like being a horse that knows it'll never stumble. How quiet everything is all round us suddenly. Has the rain stopped?

FREDERIC: I don't know.

JEANNETTE (*after a pause*): It's as if something were being gently torn inside me. I have the feeling I shall never hurt you. Is that what they call tenderness, do you think?

FREDERIC: I don't know.

JEANNETTE: I didn't before, either. I'd only read about it in books. I thought it only happened after a very long time.

FREDERIC: I thought so, too.

JEANNETTE: It can't be true, can it? It's happened so quickly. I can desire you and be happy in your arms, but I can't love you like that, surely? How can I possibly? I don't even know you.

FREDERIC: I don't know you, either, but tonight you're going to be my wife. Wife and younger brother all in one, till death do us part – you, this little stranger with the shut face. How simple it is.

JEANNETTE: Holding hands is simple, and sitting like this with my head on your shoulder. But what about our real feelings . . . ?

FREDERIC: All we need to do is make ourselves think the opposite. I used to say to myself: She'll be very serious, and dressed in black like the girls where I come from. She'll have a shiny face with light eyes and hair brushed back – a little soldier bravely carrying her pack beside me. But no. It had to be your eyes, that I daren't look into; your straggly hair, your urchin face, and your lies. Everything I don't like I had to love.

JEANNETTE: Supposing I stop telling lies and brush back my hair, too?

FREDERIC: I used to tell myself: I'll have two children. The older one will be called Alain – he'll be a terror – and then there'll be the little one, Marie, and she'll be gentle as a bird. And every evening when I come home I shall go over their spelling with them, out of a book. But there aren't going to be any of those quiet evenings. It's as simple as that. No spelling by lamplight, no attentive little faces . . . only bare hotel rooms, lies, scenes, hurt.

JEANNETTE: You sound so contented when you say that.

FREDERIC: I am contented. Not the way I was hoping for – but differently. With the sort of contentment you feel when you've arrived somewhere, even if it should be the pit of despair; when you can say: Oh, good, this is it. I'm there.

JEANNETTE: And you think we're there?

FREDERIC: Yes. This time, we're there. It's taken a long time and we came a strange way around. But I can feel you all warm against me, and these few minutes before we take each other are almost like a bethrothal. I'm there all right.

JEANNETTE: Am I really there, too?

FREDERIC (*smiling*): You should know.

JEANNETTE: And it's too late to go back? You've finished with all the things you wanted before? That means you feel responsible. If I'm hurt, you'll have to feel guilty about me, and if I'm unhappy, no matter what for, you'll share it?

FREDERIC: Yes, no matter what for.

JEANNETTE: I can understand their being so solemn about it.

FREDERIC: Who?

JEANNETTE: Real fiancés. (*She gets up.*) But what I don't understand is that they cheat afterwards. They whisper things to each other in kitchens. If I'd once given a solemn oath like that, all dressed in white in a church with a bouquet, if I'd said to a boy, 'From now on I'm your wife, we share things – good and bad we both have to share', I'd be like a soldier with his captain; I'd rather cut my arm off! (*She turns away, saying in a loud voice:*) Why are you always thinking of Julia? Why are you always talking about Julia?

FREDERIC: Julia? Why, what have I said?

JEANNETTE: Can't you hear yourself? Every time you stop talking, you're calling 'Julia'. Every time your eyes look my way, they're looking at her, and I turn away in spite of myself. You know I shall never be like her. You know I'm just the opposite of her. Look at me. It's me, here, nobody else. Me, with the good and bad in me all tied up together in a knot. You have to take me as I am; it's no good trying to undo it.

FREDERIC: Be quiet!

JEANNETTE: What are you doing away from her, away from your mother and the lawyer and your own village, away from everything safe and good in your life? What are you doing here with this bedraggled woman that shouts and tells lies and makes you feel ashamed and will go on making your suffer? You want her, don't you? So take her quickly. She's yours for tonight. She'll co-operate. And in the morning, when you've had what you want, get back to Julia, quickly. She's the one you really care for.

FREDERIC (*taking her by the wrist*): We've been hurt quite enough. Now will you be quiet!

JEANNETTE (*struggling free*): That's right, hurt me! Twist my arm as you did just now to protect her! It's Julia you care for – always have and always will, my lad. If she'd had the courage to fight just now at the house, and forget about her clean apron and her nicely bound books and all the rest of it, she'd have been in the right camp now, I bet, along with the Dauntless against the Kings of Trumps.

FREDERIC: You're crazy!

JEANNETTE: And you'd have stood in front of her, wouldn't you, if I'd started throwing stones at her? So that she wouldn't be hurt and her dear sweet blood shouldn't flow? You would have, wouldn't you, like this evening, when I wanted to hit her?

FREDERIC (*hard, looking her full in the face*): Certainly!

JEANNETTE (*shouting like a child*): Well, I'd have let loose all my roughs on you. They'd have tied you to a tree and I'd have scalped her, your Julia! I'd have scalped her with all her pretty, well-groomed hair, before your very eyes! Oh, why aren't we kids any more? Why can't we have a good fight? (*She throws herself into his arms and cries out in anguish.*) Oh, if you could only take your knife out of your pocket and cut my heart in two, you'd see how good and red it is inside.

FREDERIC (*won over, pressing her against him*): How fast it's beating. . . .

JEANNETTE: Can you hear it? Oh, if I tell any more lies, if I can't undo all the strings I'm caught up in like a poor little fly, and if I hurt you and say wicked things, just think of my heart all helpless there in its prison. Because it's only my cunning or my wickedness or my pride that talks; I'm just a woman with all that she's done behind her and all that she's capable of in front of her, but my heart's like an animal that can only jump about to make itself understood. And it's jumping up at you now. Can you feel it? So whenever I push you away or laugh at you, even if I seem to want to hurt you, just listen to that. Don't take any notice of me. (*She presses herself against him.*) Hold me tight now – I shan't have your strength for long to boost mine up. (*She goes to the window, draws the curtain, and opens the door wide. The wind bursts into the room and makes the lamp flicker.*)

FREDERIC: What are you doing?

JEANNETTE: I'm opening everything so that the light can be seen right into the woods.

FREDERIC: Why?

JEANNETTE: So that no one can say I've given less than real

fiancés do. And since we're going to be together for better or worse, we can start now, can't we? It's like the swimming race across the bay on the fourteenth of July. There's always one left out. But anyone who isn't fit can easily not enter. (*She is standing at the open french window, facing the wind, in a state of exaltation.*)

FREDERIC: Shut that door. The lamp'll go out.

JEANNETTE: We'll light it again. We'll light it and wait until a man that's wandering about in the woods now like an old black sad owl sees it shining through the branches and comes knocking at the window. (FREDERIC *has taken a step towards her, but stops as she goes on.*) He knows he's lost me. He's looking for me, I feel sure. But he's just an animal. He's ugly and ashamed – maybe he won't dare come in. All right, so he doesn't come in – good! But I shall have done all I can to bring him here. It's like something I read somewhere at school – when the innocent and the guilty both had to take hold of the red-hot iron. After that it was just a question of courage and luck . . . it was well worth another trial.

FREDERIC: Do you want me to meet this man?

JEANNETTE: It's like an operation, Frederic. If I don't lose too much blood, if I'm not too mutilated, there may be just a chance I'll go on living. (*She adds, gravely:*) Only afterwards I want you to love me like Julia.

FREDERIC *suddenly goes to the window, shuts it, and turns towards her.*

FREDERIC: If that man comes in here – if I look him in the face – I may not be able to love you any more.

JEANNETTE: I know. With the red-hot iron there was always the risk you'd die of burns. But you had to take hold of it just the same.

FREDERIC: Isn't what we've done enough? Isn't it enough that she's been hurt?

JEANNETTE: No. Each of us has to pay his share.

FREDERIC: I love you, and we're alone at last after that interminable day. Don't let's wait any longer! The night's coming on so quickly. I've accepted it all – the wrong and the hurt we've caused, and your being so different – provided we're there now. (*He draws the curtain.*) Please, please don't ask any more. Don't look for any more ways of being hurt. Look, I'm not asking any more of you. Men fight and die for dreams, too, but there comes a time when they feel tired; when they want to call a halt, feel their wives near them, and snatch a bit of happiness at long last.

He has taken a step towards her. She draws back.

JEANNETTE: No, Frederic. When we were in the woods, I thought we should never be here quickly enough, I wanted you so much; but now if you touch me I think I shall call out.

FREDERIC: I don't recognize you any more. Who are you, so tense and pale all of a sudden, so on the defensive?

JEANNETTE: I'm their sister.

FREDERIC: Whose sister?

JEANNETTE: Of the women in your life – all that trail of women hanging on to each other's black skirts, stretching back over the generations and mounting guard over your heart. Aunts, cousins, grandmothers, and Julia, too. I'm not afraid of them any longer. I'm like them. It isn't difficult. It's love that does it.

The door opens suddenly. LUCIEN *appears on the threshold, his clothes streaming.*

LUCIEN: Excuse me. I'm disturbing you, I'm afraid. We shall have done quite a bit of walking in the rain tonight, all of us. Funny sort of weather for romance. (*He closes the door again.*) Azarias sent me. He daren't come in; he's shy. But he's not a bad chap, and I should think he loved you. He says I'm to tell you you can keep the dress. (JEANNETTE *has not moved.* FREDERIC *turns to her without a word.* LUCIEN *opens a box he has been carrying in his hand.*) And I'm to give you the veil you left behind. (*He calmly places the huge tulle veil on a chair.*)

JEANNETTE (*softly in the silence*): Yes, it was a wedding dress.
FREDERIC: And he gave it to you?
JEANNETTE: Yes. Yesterday.
FREDERIC (*after a silence*): Why did you bring it with you?
JEANNETTE (*like a child*): It was the only nice thing I had.

They stand facing each other, silent and motionless.

LUCIEN (*smiling*): Is that beyond your comprehension? Be fair, now. She was going away with you for ever and always – the great love. You must admit it was the best possible time to give a bit of thought to her appearance. It's a mere man's idea to wonder who bought her the dress. . . . Besides, I must point out that she left the veil behind – a very delicate sentiment. And, of course, a no less delicate sentiment prompted us to bring it back to her.
JEANNETTE (*softly*): I hate you, Lucien.
LUCIEN: Yes. It's a lousy part I'm playing in all this – not very clever, I must confess. (*He looks at the two of them standing there dumb and out of countenance. Then he says mockingly:*) Poor lambs! It's pitiful. Wanting the truth, the whole truth, and nothing but the truth, and then when it's there in front of them they just shut up and want to cry. You need to be hard-boiled like me to welcome the lady Truth.
FREDERIC (*suddenly*): Why did you lie to me?
JEANNETTE: You saw it was new, so I realized I'd never be able to tell you.
FREDERIC: Tell me what? That he'd given it you yesterday?
JEANNETTE: Yes.
FREDERIC: But you brought it with you just the same.
JEANNETTE: Yes.
FREDERIC: I was only offering you escape and poverty, you knew that. You followed me at once, with nothing. Like me you broke off with everything, left everything behind, and the crime we're guilty of was only excusable because we both abandoned everything, I wish I could tear it off you and rip it to pieces and dirty it all over.

He goes towards her but she draws back with a cry, holding the dress against her.

JEANNETTE: No!

The cry brings FREDERIC *to a standstill.*

LUCIEN (*softly*): It isn't nice to spoil things! Besides, she loves her dress, bless her. Not as much as you, of course, but very much. If you ask her to choose, she'll choose, and go and take it off. But we've been weeping over the catalogues for months now and we've dreamed of this dress for so long, with nothing but our shabby old sweaters to wear. Think of it, we might even have married Azarias, just for that.

FREDERIC (*loudly*): It's not true!

LUCIEN: Oh, but it is. What do you think women are made of, anyway? Steel, platinum, diamond? But of course that's something the law wouldn't teach you. They're nothing but sighs, dreams, whims; there's good and there's bad all mixed up together, and according to the chemical equation they either combine or cause an explosion. Women have a knack of taking on the aspect of something eternal, so that you want to die suddenly, they're so beautiful; and then one fine morning they become terrifying, monstrous. They've slipped through your fingers. Azarias is rich, and he loves her. She's leaving him tonight for you, with no regrets. And don't think for a minute she used to go to him for the sake of his cash – she's not a whore, my sister. She went to him because it amused her, and she's going off with you because it amuses her more, but she's taking her dress with her. That's all.

FREDERIC: Shut up!

LUCIEN: You'll be well away by the time you have to admit it yourself. It does me good, so leave me alone.

FREDERIC (*suddenly*): You were lying! You were lying again! You've been lying to me all the time. When am I going to be able to believe you now?

LUCIEN: Oh – tomorrow – in five minutes' time – or even now. You've only got to go away with her – just leave it to her.

From tomorrow on, you'll believe her. It's a solution, and no sillier than feeling hurt.

FREDERIC: I couldn't do it.

LUCIEN: I thought I couldn't either. But it's the solution, I assure you, however wise you are, or however silly.

FREDERIC: I wish I could understand!

LUCIEN: Understand what? What goes on in their flimsy little carcasses at such times? Nobody's ever understood that, not even themselves. What would be the good of it, anyway? It can't be so pretty. Give it up. You just have to get used to them. You might as well try to understand disease, stupidity, poverty, war, death. We're children at the game.

FREDERIC *has dropped on to the sofa, head in hands.* LUCIEN *seats himself beside him.*

Oh, we put up a good show with our manly exploits, explaining to all and sundry that we're scientists, poets, heroes, that we'd rather die than not live in freedom, that we are capable of abstract thought. Fat lot that has to do with anything. (*Silence for a while between them. He goes on:*) Better hang on to your mother, or a Julia if you can find one, or to the women in books. . . . (*He points to a picture, a huge engraving hanging in a large black frame and yellowed from exposure through the broken window.*) Take the wife of Poetus, for instance. This old summer-house has been very useful to our family. When my wife left me I used to come and hide myself away here many a time. And one day, when I'd been staring blindly at the wall, I discovered this engraving, hanging lopsided in the middle of a panel. The glass is dirty, so you can't see it very well. It's the wife of Poetus, a Roman condemned to death by Nero. She has just snatched the sword from the centurion's hand and, as Poetus hesitates, she stabs herself first, then hands the sword to her husband with a smile, saying, '*Non dolet.*'

FREDERIC *has glanced up at the picture, but lets his head fall into his hands again. Silence.* JEANNETTE *is the last to turn to the picture.*

JEANNETTE: What does it mean – *Non dolet*?

LUCIEN: It means 'It doesn't hurt'. First Empire style, you know. She's no beauty, of course, maybe a little rotund for aesthetes such as ourselves, but all the same . . . (*He sighs, half wistfully, half mockingly.*) Lucky Poetus!

Pause.

JEANNETTE (*softly*): Frederic, I just want to tell you something. I opened the door myself just now so that this man should come in and tell you more or less the same as Lucien has just told you. I'm a liar, it's true, and I'm not worth much, and it's true I brought the dress with me, too. (*Pause. She continues with an effort.*) You heard what he said. Julia, your mother, and now the ladies of Rome as well, they're all against me! All the women that have been strong and pure. Well, I can be that, too, more than they can. What has Julia given you, after all? Her little bit of goodness, or her fear of being compromised? And what about your mother? I suppose she used to rock you in her arms at night when you couldn't sleep? Do you think I wouldn't have done the same? Do you think I wouldn't have looked after you when you were sick and held you in my arms? I would have been ten mothers to you for a thousand nights! I'd have been like a mother hen that never pecks at a single grain for herself. I'd have been like a she wolf, standing in front of her young and fighting for them to the death. But *she's* had ten other children; she's done all the same things ten times over because it moved her guts to see a little piece of herself living and moving after it was born, the way it moves the guts of all animals!

LUCIEN: True, even the worst of women become mothers. Maybe it'll move you one day, the same as it did her, and then we'll all have to revere you.

JEANNETTE (*turning on him, ablaze*): No! I don't want to feel the way all mothers do about just any of their children! I don't want to be twelve times exalted in spite of myself, twelve times true to the death, twelve times unique! This isn't just some vague instinct I've given way to, something that makes it absolutely necessary for me to have a child to suckle. I love *him*! It's for him I want to sacrifice myself and die. This isn't the sort of love that'll come surging up again like sap every time my waistline gets thick. It's the first and last time, I know it, till the skin of my stomach clings to my spine. The last time I shall be ready to give my blood, here and now, and my milk, if it would come!

LUCIEN (*getting up, spitefully*): Your blood, your milk! You work fast. You've only known him a day.

JEANNETTE: That's all you can think of to say, all of you. Is it my fault it's only a day?

LUCIEN: Your blood. . . . Ah, they're good talkers if you listen with your eyes shut. Fortunately you only have to look at them, with their fluttering eyelids and their little nervous grin. You've given him your mouth and the taste of your skin on his tongue. That's all there is to it. You're just a girl he's picked for the night.

JEANNETTE: No! I'm his wife!

LUCIEN: His wife! You? Don't make me die laughing. Look at him. Firm, frank, reliable – a real honest-to-God little French soldier, fairly bursting with the right sentiments. You, his wife? You want him; he wants you. Good luck to you. Get on with it, quick. But don't start building a cathedral on it.

JEANNETTE: Supposing I were to become everything he loves in one night? Supposing that all of a sudden I stopped being lazy and untidy and a liar and became brave and honourable?

LUCIEN (*bursts out laughing*): All the same! Every one of them! They're quite capable of drowning Mama and Papa one fine night in order to make off with the dear boy; they're ready to steal for him, sell themselves at the street corner, descend to whatever depths may be necessary. But if he, the angel child, prefers modesty, sentiment, virtue, he has only to say so. It's so easy! They can turn that on, too. It's all one to them. And sincerely, what's more. Refusing to give themselves, lowering their eyes, blushing if one uses the wrong word, looking down from their pedestal. They can do anything, for as long as it lasts.

JEANNETTE: Yes, I can do anything, I can do anything!

LUCIEN: Only what they can't actually manage is to make it last.

JEANNETTE: That's a lie!

LUCIEN: What they can't do is to see that it's all still true next day. They're honest from day to day. It's a way the pretty little things have. And the unfortunate thing is that *we* need just that tomorrow. We couldn't care less about this love they offer us just for today. It doesn't mean a thing if tomorrow isn't safe. That's why we put all we've got into trying to be happy with them until in the end they leave us when they get tired and we have to take the blame.

JEANNETTE: He'll be happy! He'll believe me. You couldn't believe Denise, but I'll give him so much that he'll believe me!

LUCIEN: What'll you give him? You've nothing to give. You've none of you anything to give, except your body for a minute, and your everlasting changes of mood.

JEANNETTE: It isn't true!

LUCIEN: And he hasn't anything to give you, either. You're lovers. You've played your cards. You can dance the dance to the end, now. Throw yourself in the river in despair, kill yourselves for each other, nurse each other through leprosy, sell yourselves. It's all a sham, a mirage, nothing but show! You've nothing to give. . . . You've chosen love, you're chosen to take, always, to think of nothing but yourselves.

JEANNETTE: It's not true!

LUCIEN: Oh, yes. You've chosen love, and you're here to hate each other, to be revenged on each other, you'll never know what for. No need to beat your breast about it; it's always been the same, ever since there were men and women, pairing off like flies in the small hours.

JEANNETTE: No!

LUCIEN: Yes. And maybe you'll go off now into the wide

world, the two of you, hand in hand, but you'll be watching each other like two enemies in the desert. And people will say, 'What a sweet couple! How they must love each other.' Yes. Sweet couple of murderers! Capable of anything, dear ladies! Claws out and fangs bared. One of 'em's got to have the other's blood and the sooner the better. That's love for you!

JEANNETTE (*who has thrown herself on the sofa beside* FREDERIC): Oh, you're too horrible – you're too horrible!

LUCIEN (*coming up to her and speaking more softly*): What do you believe, then? That it's Philemon and Baucis for the asking? A pushover? Tenderness, devotion, confidence, the lot, day in, day out? You have to pay for that, my sweet, day after day, with sweat and boredom and petty scraping and fear all rolled into one. You pay for it with kids that are ill and you don't know whether they're going to live or die; with nights and nights of lying next to each other and listening to each other breathing, and all the time the wrinkles are getting deeper and deeper. . . .

JEANNETTE: I know I shall have wrinkles! I know I shall get old. And people will say, 'There are those two old people.' And when he dies, I shall die next day.

LUCIEN (*dropping down wearily beside them, muttering*): Die . . . die. . . . What is there in dying? You've got to begin by living. That's not so funny, and it lasts longer.

JEANNETTE: You're saying all this to stop us living.

LUCIEN (*suddenly strangely tired*): No. To stop you dying, silly kid. You get everything mixed up.

There is a short silence. All three of them are sitting sedately side by side, looking straight ahead of them.

JEANNETTE (*softly, humbly*): You hate love. But the women you've known aren't everything – you haven't known them all. There must be some who've loved with all their might, for ever. Isn't there just one? If there is, I can, too.

LUCIEN: I've never had her number.

JEANNETTE: That one you were talking about over there in the picture, was she in love?

LUCIEN: The wife of Poetus, you mean?

JEANNETTE: I don't know. Yes. What was it she said when she took the knife first, to give her husband courage?

LUCIEN: *Non dolet.*

JEANNETTE: *Non dolet.* Didn't that mean she loved him?

LUCIEN: Yes, I suppose so.

JEANNETTE (*getting up*): Well, if it's no more difficult than that . . .

LUCIEN: Where are you going?

JEANNETTE: To take off this dress. (*She disappears upstairs.*)

LUCIEN (*when he and* FREDERIC *are alone*): I've told you all I know, anyway. I've warned you about my own little experiences. Now maybe you'd better judge for yourself all the same.

There is the sound of glass breaking upstairs.

What's she doing now, the little lunatic? Smashing the windows?

After a minute or so, JEANNETTE *reappears, very pale in her white dress. She holds out her arm to* FREDERIC. *Blood is running freely from a jagged cut.*

JEANNETTE: Look. It doesn't hurt. I've forgotten how they say it in Latin.

The two men have got up. There is a second's stupefied silence, then FREDERIC *falls on her and wraps her arm in his handkerchief, kissing her and stammering.*

FREDERIC: Jeannette, my love . . . forgive me. I'll believe you. I'll always believe you!

They have their arms around each other. LUCIEN *raises his arms heavenwards.*

LUCIEN: Right, fine! If they're going to start lopping their arms off now, what can one say?

At this moment the door opens, the wind hurtles through the room again, the light almost goes out; and the old POSTMAN *is revealed, standing outside the door in the rain, hesitating on the threshold.*

POSTMAN (*softly*): Children, children!

LUCIEN (*going to him*): Is it for me, postman?

POSTMAN: No, boy. It's your father sent me, to tell you to go straight to the town to fetch the doctor. They're mighty worried at the house. Your sister's drunk something. They think she's poisoned herself.

FREDERICK *has disengaged himself from* JEANNETTE'S *embrace.* LUCIEN *turns to him.*

LUCIEN: Go on back. I'm taking Azarias's car to fetch the doctor. (FREDERIC *does not move immediately. He goes to him and takes him by the arm.*) Come on, quickly. This time it's the real thing.

He goes out, dragging FREDERIC *with him. The* POSTMAN *follows, leaving the door wide open. There is a long silence.* JEANNETTE *remains alone, motionless, looking very small in her white dress with the wind buffeting her and her arms clasped around her. Suddenly she turns her head towards the open door.*

JEANNETTE (*murmuring*): You can come in now.

A man appears like a shadow in the doorway, his coat streaming with rain. As the shadow advances into the room, the curtain falls.

Act Four

SCENE – *Same as in Act One. Late afternoon a week later.* FREDERIC *is stretched out on the sofa, his head buried in his arms. The* FATHER *is pacing up and down the room, watching him with an air of hostility. Enter* LUCIEN. *The* FATHER *goes towards him.*

FATHER: Is the trap there?

LUCIEN: Yes.

FATHER: Good. (*He takes him aside.*) I can't pretend I'm sorry to see the back of them. A week, I tell you. This boy's been here a whole week and not once has he opened his mouth. I'm old-fashioned. Politeness first, I say. My girl friend could have been at death's door, but as a man of the world first and foremost I'd at least have kept up the conversation. Not he.

LUCIEN: You can keep up both sides of a conversation.

FATHER: Julia nearly died. Right. But she's been out of danger since yesterday. . . . I said to myself. Now he'll make an effort. But still not a word.

LUCIEN (*softly*): Maybe he isn't out of danger.

FATHER: I'm delighted he's getting out of here. I make no secret of it. I'd rather talk to myself and have done with it. At least one knows where one is. (*There is a sound of music in the distance. He shouts suddenly:*) Stop that music!

LUCIEN: Not a hope.

FATHER: I may look calm, but my nerves are all in pieces.

He settles himself calmly in his chair and lights a cigar. LUCIEN *goes up to* FREDERIC.

LUCIEN: Not very delicate, I must admit, giving us the full orchestral works. What you probably don't know is that in the ordinary way one wouldn't be able to hear it – the house is too far away. She must have arranged to have it somewhere this end of the grounds, to make certain we'd hear. It should be a very smart weddding. There are five Citroens in front of the gate. Monsieur Azarias has connexions.

FATHER (*from his corner*): And not even a card from them. (*Pause. Then, in a detached voice:*) Where do you think they ordered the food?

LUCIEN: At Biron's.

FATHER (*contemptuously*): Pooh! Conventional stuff. Fish balls, lamb cutlets, chicken. I can feel myself swallowing it.

LUCIEN: Then what are you complaining of?

FATHER: The snub.

LUCIEN: You'll swallow that, too.

FATHER: Never. I'm a good chap, but I've got the memory of an elephant. I never forget and I never forgive. I don't say a word, and people think I'm easy-going, but fifty years afterwards the worm turns. (*Pause.*) Cheese, ice bombe, mocha cake, champagne. That fellow can only think of one menu. If they'd condescended to consult me, I'd have said, go to Thomas. Thomas is the only one in this part of the country that knows how to serve food. *Oeufs mimosa*, lobster Thermidor, stuffed shoulder . . . magnificent!

LUCIEN: It didn't make much difference to you, though, did it?

FATHER (*rattled*): True. (*Pause.*) Do you think I'd have been able to wear it if they'd invited me?

LUCIEN: Wear what?

FATHER: My dinner jacket.

LUCIEN: Certainly.

FATHER: It'd have been a great honour for them. After all – this Azarias fellow – I knew his father.

LUCIEN: And now he knows your daughter. That makes you quits.

FATHER: You ridicule everything. But with me, it's all engraved here. (*He points to his forehead. The music becomes louder. He leaps to his feet shouting:*) Make them stop that row!

LUCIEN: *You* make them stop it.

FATHER: That's just what they'd like. They can keep it up for a week, I'll play deaf as a post. The musicians'll be the first to tire. What do you suppose an orchestra like that costs a day? There must be at least six of them. Say about two thousand francs a day each, you see what this little bit of nonsense adds up to? (*He goes out into the garden.*)

LUCIEN (*coming back to* FREDERIC): She just wanted us to hear her wedding. Julia's got to hear it in bed, Mama's got to hear it in the kitchen, the whole village has got to hear it. The bells this morning weren't enough. She's scattered fiddlers all over the shrubbery. She must hate them all up there, but I can just see her in the thick of it. She'll make 'em all dance until morning, drive 'em to a standstill, and all for our benefit.

FREDERIC: Julia's going to get up. In an hour from now we shall be gone.

LUCIEN: We'll try to let her know. That may shut it up. I imagine these waves of harmony are aimed more particularly at you.

FREDERIC: Possibly.

LUCIEN: She wants to be quite sure you're suffering at the same time. She adores you, that kid. You saw how nicely she cut her arm. What was it? 'I've forgotten how they say it in Latin.' Splendid entrance, that.

FREDERIC: But then why? Why immediately after . . . ?

LUCIEN: You really are incorrigible, old man. You want to know everything! You must get out of this terrible habit. Nobody will ever know why. She doesn't know herself. (FREDERIC *has thrown himself down with his face in the cushions.*) It hurts, doesn't it, at first? You have the feeling you just can't stand the pain another second. You ought really to yell out, or break something. But what? You can't break *them.* How about the furniture? Grotesque. It's when you realize there's nothing to break that you begin to grow up. (*Pause. He comes and sits beside* FREDERIC.) You can live quite comfortably with a pain, you know; you'll see when you get to know it. You find out the subtleties and hidden crevices of it. You become a specialist in it. You know what to feed it on every day, and what may not be good for it. You get to know the sort of whisper that stirs it and the sort of music that lulls it to sleep. And later, much later, when you stop being lonely at last and can talk about it to other people, you begin to show it off to the public, like a guide at a museum. You become the peak-capped employee of your own pain. You die just the same, but more gradually. (FREDERIC *gets up to escape him, and goes to look out of the window.*) Don't be in such a hurry to be unhappy. You've got all your life before you. What's so splendid about being a cuckold is that it gives you plenty of time. I'm not talking of the uncouth type that murder their wives at the first suspicion and then blow out their own brains. . . . I refer to the artist cuckold, the good craftsman that likes a job well done according to the rules, a job that does justice to him.

The music grows louder.

FATHER (*appearing at the french window*): That's splendid! They've brought in some brass, now. We're not going to get a wink of sleep tonight.

LUCIEN (*sharply*): We shouldn't have got that anyway. (*The* FATHER *goes away again.* LUCIEN *goes up to* FREDERIC, *suddenly harsh.*) A wink of sleep . . . funny expression, isn't it? You can just imagine a huge, dark, open eye that fills the room and watches you. And you can't get a wink out of it. You summon up all your strength and hang on like grim death to that enormous eyelid, but there it is, always open, watching you, thoughtless, vacant, imbecile, a real human eye. Do *you* sleep?

FREDERIC (*shrugging*): Yes.

LUCIEN (*shouting*): You'll never sleep again!

FREDERIC (*turning abruptly*): What are you getting at? What are you trying to do to me?

LUCIEN (*softly*): Watch you. Watch you being hurt. It does me good.

FREDERIC: Watch away. Is it pretty – the sight of someone being hurt?

LUCIEN: No. It's frightful, it's obscene. But when it's your own reflection in a mirror, it's worse. I used to look at myself in the glass the whole night long, you know, watching my death's-head grin and my idiot eyes. I used to watch my chin tremble and wait like a huntsman stalking his prey for hours and hours, just to see if that smackable cuckold's face would burst into tears. Now, at last, it's somebody else – that makes a nice change.

FREDERIC: Quick, then. Take a good look. I shan't be looking at myself in the glass. I'm a man, and tomorrow, whatever happens, I'm going to live.

LUCIEN (*jeering*): Bravo, little man!

FREDERIC: I shall have work to do. I shall marry Julia. I've got a whole house to decorate and a garden to clear and wood to cut for the winter.

LUCIEN (*one confidence deserving another*): I took up gym. Yes, I thought, this has only happened because you're thin and don't stand up straight. It's all because you've no muscles on your chest and arms to make a man of you. No muscles, no women. Everything quite suddenly became simple, and I set out to conquer the mighty muscle. I bought a book – ninety francs. The secret was cheap. And every morning by my open window, clad in my little singlet, more cuckold than ever, I would go through my Swedish drill. (*He goes through some motions.*) One, two, three, four. One, two— (*He stops suddenly, already exhausted.*) But believe me, it's all a lie – muscles take a long time to grow. What's more, if you look a little closer at the face of the instructor on the cover, you'll notice that in spite of his athletic body he was probably a cuckold, too. One piece of advice. Start right away with plenty of red wine. You get results much quicker that way. (*He helps himself, drinks, and offers wine to* FREDERIC.) Shall I pour you some?

FREDERIC: No, thanks.

LUCIEN: As you wish. But to have real class as a cuckold

means you have only one privilege – to suffer twice as much. And what's the point of being a cuckold with class, anyway? Is there such a thing as having cancer in style or wearing your leprosy with an air? You might as well writhe in your colic, spit out your phlegm, or cough up your lungs and yell when it hurts. Have a good moan, get on people's nerves. You might as well be a puny, cringing little cuckold, unseemly in the eyes of God – just to show Him. Know what I did the first day? I fell off my chair suddenly during dinner and lay still on the floor to make them think I was dead. For no reason. Just so that they'd be scared; so that something should happen. They dabbed my temples with vinegar, they tried to unclench my teeth with spoons, and I could hear them fussing and bustling about, and there I was all the time, breathing away quietly, I wasn't dead, but I was a cuckold. I'd have liked to go one better, too. Whip off my pants, piss all over the wall, black my face and walk the streets with a huge false nose so that people would say, 'What's he doing, that young man there with the big false nose?' 'Nothing. He's just a cuckold. That's a cuckold's nose!'

FREDERIC: Oh, shut up!

LUCIEN: Am I embarrassing you? The gentleman wants to suffer in peace, perhaps, in the grand manner? Maybe he wants to play cuckolds all by himself? Nasty, common cuckolds aren't quite his style? Maybe he's a special sort of cuckold. All the same, we are brothers, monsieur; we've drunk out of the same cup. And since there's nobody to kiss us, we shall have to kiss each other.

He goes to embrace FREDERIC *playfully, but* FREDERIC *pushes him away.*

FREDERIC: Let me go! You're drunk. You stink of alcohol.

LUCIEN: Maybe I do stink of alcohol, but drunk at five o'clock? Never. My dear chap, it's like that business of the muscles, it takes time. Everything takes time. No, I shan't be drunk until tonight, and then I shall be quite speechless; that's when I become respectable. (*Declaiming.*) The Count used to shut himself up alone every evening in his library, and the Countess would hear him staggering upstairs in the middle of the night. . . . I only stagger when I'm sober. I get drunk so as to be able to go up to the Countess every night without staggering. (*Short pause.*) Only there's always a slight disappointment awaiting me up there – no Countess.

FREDERIC (*after a while*): I'm not going to go back to my suffering like a dog to its vomit. Let it bleed itself away and have done with it. This juvenile world you've dragged me into, the two of you, doesn't belong to me. Neither my father nor my mother nor any of the people in my village have ever had time to pay much attention to their own troubles, though their children died of unknown diseases and their wives left them just the same. They simply had other things to do besides brooding over their own woes.

LUCIEN: Oh, a farmer's life for me!

MOTHER (*coming in*): Julia's up now. The journey will tire her a little, but she prefers to go tonight. Like me, she has only one desire – to get out of this place as soon as possible.

LUCIEN: But it's so pretty at this time of the year.

MOTHER (*to* FREDERIC, *paying no attention to* LUCIEN): Are you ready?

FREDERIC: Yes, Mother.

MOTHER: I'll call you to help Julia downstairs. I'm just going to get her a cup of coffee. (*She goes into the kitchen.*)

FATHER (*who has come back and is watching her go*): Ever since she cleared out the cupboards, she's been cutting me dead. I don't know what she could have found there.

LUCIEN (*in a low voice, to* FREDERIC, *as though continuing a conversation*): And if you're strong enough to get over the days (and you may manage that – you seem pretty tough) there'll always be the nights. Nights when the sleeping cuckold relives his agony. Even if I got her back, even if she stayed faithful to me after that and I managed to forget about it during the day, I'd still be a cuckold to the end of my nights. (*Pause.*) And yet it's the only chance of being no more than half a cuckold. That's why I've never given up waiting.

FREDERIC: How long is it now?

LUCIEN: Two years. She'd gone out to buy some stockings, if you please! I must say, I'm beginning to get a bit worried. . . .

FREDERIC: You'll forget her.

LUCIEN: No, brother. Another illusion to discard. You find someone else, maybe. But you don't forget. (*He gets up.*) Besides, cuckolds always tend to make themselves out more pathetic than they are. I'm not waiting for her any more exactly. Just a letter. A letter from the Ivory Coast with a beautiful green stamp on it. I'm told they're blacker and stupider there. I shall get on fine with the niggers.

FATHER (*getting up and going over to them*): I'm listening to you two talking away there. I don't understand you, my dear boys. There you are, torturing each other, frightening each other. Life and love have always seemed so much simpler to me. And don't go thinking I haven't been in love. When I was twenty I had three mistresses. A girl in the records department, a dizzy blonde who learned the whole thing from me from A to Z; then there was the little waitress at the restaurant where I had my meals; and a young girl from one of the best families in the town. A virgin, my dear boy, before she knew me. Used to take her to her room at night, a couple of steps from where her parents were sleeping. J.P. . . . Forgive me if I only tell you her initials. She got married later on to one of the district high-ups.

LUCIEN: I knew her. She was hunchbacked.

FATHER (*riled*): Not really. A slight malformation that didn't affect her charm in the least.

LUCIEN: She was plain, too!

FATHER (*concurring*): Her nose was rather prominent. But a fine pair of eyes! (*He goes up to* LUCIEN.) Anyway, dear boy, we're both men, aren't we, damn it all? I was a bit of a lad, too, you know. What's a hump or a nose once you're in bed? . . . (*He makes a vulgar gesture.*) One mustn't be romantic, after all. Love is just an enjoyable moment. Once the pleasure is past— (*This time the gesture is lofty.*) Careful! Utmost gallantry and politeness, of course. I've always respected women. But that's the end of it. I wouldn't have given up billiards with the boys on that account. I arranged my life so as never to suffer! And it was a principle of mine to be the first to clear out. Never more than three months. Once that was up, I was relentless. I've seen some of them howling like animals, running out naked into the street after me. But I was always deaf to prayers, threats, everything. Once, a big brunette – a dressmaker from Cahors – a Juno, dear boy, with breasts like that – leaped into the kitchen as I was on my way out, seized a bottle of bleach, and said if I took another step she'd drink it. I walked straight out.

LUCIEN: And did she?

FATHER: I'm convinced of it. I met her three weeks later, and she had got considerably thinner. But things always work out, hang it all! She married a gendarme. Now she has a grown-up son – a hairdresser. What do you think life's all about, anyway? The main thing is never to be taken in.

LUCIEN: And if you get hurt?

FATHER (*sincerely amazed*): But you don't get hurt! That's where I don't understand you!

MOTHER (*coming in with a cup in her hand*): There. I'll just take her her coffee, and we'll be off.

FATHER: We shall miss you, dear lady.

MOTHER: The mare's in good trim. Charles says we shall be back for dinner. It only took him three hours to get here. He's brought a blanket, but I'm afraid Julia may catch a chill in the night air. I'll take one with me from here and send it back to you.

FATHER (*in lordly manner*): Dear lady, the house is yours.

MOTHER: The wedding will take place on the date we arranged, but Julia thinks as I do that after what has happened it would be better not to ask anyone.

FATHER: But the family . . .

MOTHER: Julia prefers that neither of you should be there.

FATHER (*who dare not understand*): Neither of us . . . ?

MOTHER: Her brother or you.

FATHER (*out of countenance*): But, after all, her father . . .

MOTHER: Frederic's uncle will give her away. She wants to have only one family from now on.

FATHER (*abdicating, proud*): I was just having a jacket made . . .

The MOTHER *does not reply. Suddenly* LUCIEN *shouts.*

LUCIEN: If I marry a Negress out there, Papa, I'll invite you! It'll be magnificent. Everyone will be quite naked, quite black, and they'll all stink. And there you'll be, all alone in your dress suit, sweating away in the procession with my blonde inamorata on your arm. We, too, shall be thoroughly respectable; we, too, shall be snug in the bosom of the family, Papa, all among the blacks.

FATHER (*with a Shakespearean gesture, as an exit line*): I no longer have any children!

LUCIEN: Where are you going?

FATHER: To Prosper's. Lend me five hundred francs.

LUCIEN: Take a thousand, dear King Lear. Go and get drunk; it's well worth it.

The MOTHER *watches them go out, shrugs her shoulders, and goes upstairs again to* JULIA. FREDERIC *is left alone. Suddenly* JEANNETTE *appears in the doorway, dressed in white. She stands there for a while without moving, looking at* FREDERIC. *He sees her and gets up.*

JEANNETTE (*softly*): Yes, I got married in white, to infuriate the villagers. And, of course, I had to find some use for the dress. (*A momentary silence. He does not respond.*) Are you still going to have your wedding next month?

FREDERIC: Yes.

JEANNETTE: Mine's all over now. (*Pause.*) It's good when things are over and done with, when there are no more decisions to make, no turning back. That's why I came to say good-bye.

FREDERIC: Go away!

JEANNETTE (*gently*): Yes, I will. But don't say it so unkindly. I've already gone away, once and for all. I'm talking to you now from the other end of the earth. This is just one of those special moments granted by Fate sometimes when people can't turn back. We're like two trains that have gathered speed and go faster and faster in opposite directions as they pass. And we're giving each other a last little smile through a window. (*Pause. As though recording a finding.*) Not even a smile.

FREDERIC: No.

JEANNETTE: How solemn you are. Don't you know how to play at life?

FREDERIC: No.

JEANNETTE: I'm unhappy, too, but I play. I'm merry as a cricket up there at the house, making them all drink and dance. My husband's guests have never stopped paying me compliments. He's the only one who always knows everything in advance, and he's frightened.

FREDERIC: Frightened of what?

JEANNETTE: He's like a man who's won a raffle and isn't quite sure of his prize.

FREDERIC: Will you make him unhappy, too?

JEANNETTE: He's unhappy already.

FREDERIC: Does that amuse you?

JEANNETTE: I don't care one way or the other. I don't know him.

FREDERIC: And this morning you said in front of all those people that you were his wife.

JEANNETTE: That's what they thought they heard, but I said nothing of the sort. This morning, in front of the curé and the man with the sash, I said, not that I was taking this man for better or worse, for ever, but that I was giving you up till the end of my life and after. Yes, it's strange. The priest called out in church: 'Mademoiselle Jeannette Maurin, do you consent never to take Monsieur Frederic Larivière to be your lawful wedded husband?' And nobody moved a muscle; nobody seemed to think it unusual to put it that way or call out your name like that at someone else's wedding. It was the same at the town hall. Nobody was at all alarmed that there should have to be all that dressing up, that great fat man with the multi-coloured sash, all that prize-giving paraphernalia, and a husband rigged out like a sacrificial bull, just to tell me that I was never to love and honour you, never to follow you throughout the world.

FREDERIC: What the others heard was true. You've tied yourself for always to another man.

JEANNETTE: No. I've cut myself off from you for always. It's a solemn sacrament. The Church should have provided for it along with the others: the sacrament of renunciation. (*Silence. They stand looking at each other. She murmurs*): How far away you are!

FREDERIC: Yes. All this week I've been trying to pull myself up out of the pain, inch by inch, but I kept falling back into the pit. Now I'm at the top. With sweat running off me and my nails torn and bleeding. And I'm going to try not to fall back again.

JEANNETTE: It's a long climb.

FREDERIC: Yes. There isn't far to go, but it's a long climb.

JEANNETTE: I came to ask you to forgive me for hurting you, too.

FREDERIC (*with a gesture*): Never mind.

JEANNETTE: Did you go back to the summer-house in the night?

FREDERIC: Yes. As soon as the doctor said Julia would be all right.

JEANNETTE: Did you wait for me?

FREDERIC: Until morning.

JEANNETTE (*after a pause*): Perhaps I ought to have left you a note.

FREDERIC: Perhaps. (*Pause.*) When I went off with your brother, there was a man standing outside. Was that the one?

JEANNETTE: Yes.

FREDERIC: And did he come in when we'd gone?

JEANNETTE: I called him in.

FREDERIC: Why?

JEANNETTE: To tell him that if he wanted me, I'd marry him.

FREDERIC: And it was settled then and there?

JEANNETTE: Yes. We even cheated a bit over the banns. In a small place like this you can manage things like that. I hoped you'd still be here on my wedding day.

FREDERIC: Everything's turned out very well. We're only just going. (*Short silence.*) So all that remains is for me to wish you happiness.

JEANNETTE (*softly*): You're not serious.

FREDERIC: I wish I weren't. It must be good to be able to laugh.

JEANNETTE: They do say so.

FREDERIC (*suddenly, loudly*): But I shall laugh later on. Tomorrow, in a year, in ten years maybe, I swear to you I shall laugh. When the children begin to talk they're bound to say something funny; or the puppy we'll have bought them to play with will run away from a shadow in the garden; or perhaps for no reason – just because we suddenly get a hot day with the sun shining on the sea – then I'll laugh.

JEANNETTE: Yes.

FREDERIC: I've still got this pain, and everything's uncertain still. But there'll be a morning, a bright new morning without any memories, when I shall get up with the sun and everything will fall into place again. It'll be like waking from a bad dream, and I shall find the place all freshly painted, and my little black table by the study window, and the hours going slowly by and the shadow of the church growing longer and longer across the square, and Julia's smile, like quiet water at night. One day I shall be strong again and all the people and things around me will stop being a perpetual question mark and become an answer, a certainty.

JEANNETTE: Yes, my darling.

FREDERIC: Oh, I've asked far too many questions this last week! Let things speak for themselves from now on! Let the warm stones say, 'Look, it's summer, we're warm.' And the evening, creeping up over the bench in front of the house:

'I'm evening, full of the noise of birds, you must rest now.' And then afterwards the stillness of night: 'Don't think any more, I am peace.' I don't want to ask any more questions ever again!

JEANNETTE (*softly, after a pause*): You love so many things in this life. They'll answer you some time or other. Just be patient for a while. But I hate evening, and peace, and summer. I shan't wait for anything.

FREDERIC (*suddenly, without moving*): Why didn't I find you when I went back there in the night? (JEANNETTE *makes a small, weary gesture, but does not answer.*) I'd put my handkerchief around your hurt arm! I'd taken you in my arms. I'd said, 'I'll always believe you.' You told me you loved me.

JEANNETTE (*in her small voice*): You shouldn't have left me alone.

FREDERIC: I thought Julia was going to die.

JEANNETTE: Yes. It was very sensible and very good of you to go to her at once, but it was just precisely the moment when sensible things and good things aren't quite fair any more.

FREDERIC: She'd taken poison because of us.

JEANNETTE: Yes. A bit earlier maybe, or a bit later, I might have thought 'Poor Julia!' too. And I would have waited patiently all night, happy to know that you'd be reassured by morning. But we were unlucky. That was just the moment not to leave me.

FREDERIC: Why?

JEANNETTE (*with a sad little smile*): You always ask why. Do you think I know? All I know is that just at that moment I was like a bird in the topmost branches of a tree, ready either to fly away or to build my nest there.

FREDERIC: But you did love me?

JEANNETTE: Yes, I loved you. I still love you.

FREDERIC: And yet that man had only to come into the summer-house . . .

JEANNETTE: No, poor thing. You flatter him. . . . I called him in. It was already over by then.

FREDERIC: What was already over?

JEANNETTE: I can tell you exactly when it finished. You hadn't even left the room yet. It finished when you took your arms from around me.

FREDERIC: What finished?

JEANNETTE (*with eyes closed*): You're starting all over again, the way you did the first day. You're going all over it again, like a judge.

FREDERIC (*taking her by the wrist*): What was it that finished? I want to know.

JEANNETTE (*softly*): You won't make it easier for me to tell you by hurting me. (*He lets her go.*) I'm doing my best to explain, but its difficult for me, too. If you like, it was the certainty that I felt, deep inside me, that I was stronger than your mother, stronger than Julia and all those Roman women; that I deserved you more than anyone else. That was what came to an end after you'd gone. I'd just put my arm through that window; I could see my own blood running for you, and I was proud. You could have told me to jump out of the window, to enter into the fiery furnace, and I'd have done it. I could have been poor for always with you; I could have been faithful to you for ever. The only thing I couldn't bear was not to feel you touch me any more.

FREDERIC: Why didn't you call after me? Why did you let me go?

JEANNETTE: It was already too late. The very moment you took your hands away from me, I stopped being stronger. It was like falling down into an enormous chasm. There was no more I could do. You hadn't even quite let go of me, you hadn't even taken a step towards the door before I became the weaker one, the less certain, the one less right for you. Even if I'd wanted to, I couldn't have called you back.

FREDERIC: Did you think I would come back?

JEANNETTE: Yes. But to have waited for you would have been dishonest. I hadn't anything to give you any more. I couldn't be your mistress and lie to you afterwards, like the others, could I? Dead or alive, Julia would at once have been stronger in your thoughts than me. Once we'd made love, and that wouldn't have taken long, we'd have been a pretty sight, the two of us, wouldn't we?

FREDERIC: You could have run away, without calling him in.

JEANNETTE: Alone?

FREDERIC: Yes.

JEANNETTE: I can't be alone. And anyway I knew that Julia wouldn't die and that you'd finish up by marrying her. I wanted to get married right away, to be the first.

FREDERIC: But why?

JEANNETTE: To hurt you.

FREDERIC (*after a pause*): You have. Are you satisfied?

JEANNETTE: No. Whenever you suffer, I suffer, too. Every time I hurt you, I hurt myself the same way. And if you were to die of it, I'd die, too, at the same time.

Silence.

FREDERIC: Oh, if only I'd never met you! The world made sense before, for good or bad. Everything around me had its right place, and a name. It was all simple. Now, as I listen to you, I can't think as you do at all, and yet childish and false as your suffering is, I can't bear it.

JEANNETTE: Yes, the other one's pain always hurts.

FREDERIC: I want with everything I've got to believe you and understand you, but you must come a little way to meet me. Our chance of happiness together couldn't just have depended on that split second when I took my arms away. It's childish!

JEANNETTE (*smiling*): We're so different, my darling. We really did have only the tiniest chance, and only once.

FREDERIC: Oh, why do you look so sad when you smile? I don't ask you to be sensible like me – I only ask you not to shut yourself up in that dark little world where nobody can get at you. I feel so clumsy with my great, coarse man's hands; it's as though your secret were running away like water through my fingers. But maybe I could learn just the same, even if I don't really understand. There are games and languages that stupid people learn that way, without ever having understood the rules. I'll learn.

JEANNETTE (*smiling*): You won't.

FREDERIC: I'm strong, and patient, and humble. You're not the only human being I'm no good to, all the same. Let's forget all the things that go to make up my strength and justify my existence – they don't count any more.

JEANNETTE (*after a pause*): Do you think I would ever consent now to drag you along at my apron strings, with your face looking anxious or composed, according to my moods, and with all my ugly misdeeds caterwauling around me? I'm no longer the little soldier that cut her arm for you the other night. Do you think I'd ever consent to deceive you eventually, as I did the others, without any reason, and to have you forgive me till the next time because I looked unhappy? I'd rather die. (*Another silence while they stand looking at each other. She goes on, more gravely:*) That was what I came to tell you. That evening when I agreed to marry this man, I gave myself to him again. I've become weak and cowardly all over again, and lazy and untidy and a liar. I'm everything you hate again, and I can't even be your wife! (*She stops, and then continues in her small voice:*) But if you like, there is something I can do tonight, so as to make it last forever in spite of everything, and that's die with you.

Pause.

FREDERIC (*in a hard voice, without looking at her*): No. That's too cowardly. We've got to go on living.

JEANNETTE (*softly*): With all the ugliness and failure, until we're old and hideous and finally die in our beds, sweating and struggling like animals. The sea is so clean. It washes everything with its great big waves.

FREDERIC: No. (*Pause again.*) The sea isn't clean. It has thousands of bodies buried in it. Death isn't clean either. It doesn't solve anything. It filches part of you away, but it botches the job and leaves behind a great caricature of a body that decomposes and pollutes the air – an enormous, disgusting thing that has to be hidden quickly. Only children and people who've never watched over a dead body can still think of death as something to adorn with flowers, something to call on at the first sign of age or the first pang of suffering. People have to get old. They have to grow out of the world of childhood and accept the fact that things are not so pretty as when they were young.

JEANNETTE: I don't want to grow up. I don't want to learn to accept. Everything's so ugly.

FREDERIC: Maybe it is. But all this horror, this fuss about nothing, this absurd, grotesque adventure that life is – it belongs to us. We've got to live through it. Death's absurd as well.

The orchestra starts up again.

JEANNETTE (*softly*): Very well, then. I shall go back and dance. They must be waiting for me. (*She cries out suddenly.*) Forgive me for coming!

She runs into the garden and disappears. JULIA *appears, followed by the* MOTHER. FREDERIC *has not moved.*

JULIA: Are you ready, Frederic?

FREDERIC (*seeing her, replies after an almost imperceptible pause*): Yes.

JULIA: Do you think we can go?

FREDERIC: Come along. (*He goes to help her downstairs.*) Aren't you afraid of catching cold in the trap?

MOTHER: I've got a second rug for her.

FREDERIC: We won't go by Les Baux. We'll cut across the Marsh. They mended the road last winter. We'll be home before nightfall that way.

MOTHER: I must say, your father and brother might have been here to say good-bye to you, my dear. Do you know where they are? They're at that bar.

JULIA: So much the better. I'd rather not see them again.

They are walking across the stage as they talk. FREDERIC *stops in the doorway and takes a last look at the room, standing aside to let* JULIA *pass.*

FREDERIC (*mechanically*): Go ahead. Sure you haven't left anything behind?

JULIA (*stopping, suddenly*): How about you?

FREDERIC (*simply, with an absent look*): I didn't bring anything.

They go out. LUCIEN *bounds out of the kitchen like a demon, calling after them like one demented and making ridiculous farewell gestures from the sofa in front of the window, on which he is standing, throwing flowers after them.*

LUCIEN: Long live the bride! Health, wealth and happiness! Long live the bride!

FATHER (*dashing in like a whirlwind*): Did you see her?

LUCIEN: Who?

FATHER: Jeannette.

LUCIEN: Where?

FATHER: Down on the beach. (*He pulls him round to show him.* LUCIEN *looks, but says nothing.*) What does she think she's doing?

LUCIEN (*softly*): Going for a swim.

FATHER: Fully dressed?

LUCIEN: That's right, fully dressed.

FATHER: But the tide's coming in.

LUCIEN: The tide's coming in.

FATHER: Doesn't she realize that if she goes that way she'll be caught in the current?

LUCIEN: She knows the bay better than you do.

FATHER (*yelling*): Hey, there, Jeannette! Coo-ee-ee! Jeannette! Oh, my God!

LUCIEN (*softly*): She's running. She can't hear you against the wind. And even if she could, she'd take no notice. She's done for, Papa, the little sister's done for.

FATHER: What are you talking about? You mean you think she . . .

LUCIEN: Sure of it.

FATHER (*running wildly about the room*): God Almighty! We must do something! We've got to do something! Come on, fetch some ropes. We'll go up to the house and get help.

LUCIEN (*stopping him*): No.

FATHER: What d'you mean, 'no'?

LUCIEN: I tell you, there's nothing to be done. Leave her alone. First of all, it's too late and, secondly, you'll be doing her a favour.

FATHER (*pulling himself away*): You – you – that's monstrous! I'm going to cut down through the woods.

LUCIEN: You do that. It'll give you some exercise and it won't look so nasty as it does from here.

FATHER (*goes out and comes back immediately, shouting*): Hurrah! Hurrah! It's Frederic! He's seen her from the road and jumped out of the trap! Run for it! There's a man for you! He's got to the beach by the little bridge. He's cutting across by the lagoon; he's up to his knees in water. He'll never make it.

LUCIEN (*coming up to him and speaking softly*): He will.

FATHER: He's doing it! He's made it! Bravo there! Come on, now, come on! Oh, well done, my boy! What a sportsman! Come on! Come on!

LUCIEN (*shouting suddenly*): Shut up! What do you think you're watching – a football match?

FATHER: What do you mean, a football match?

LUCIEN: You're disgusting when you yell like that. I said shut up!

FATHER (*taken aback*): But I'm your father.

LUCIEN (*who has taken him by the lapels as if to start a fight and is shaking him*): I know that! Only you're so stupid and unsightly that there are times when I just can't bear it any more that you're my father. And this is one of them. So shut up! Do you hear me? Shut up, or I'll knock you cold!

FATHER (*who can see* FREDERIC *down on the beach, pulling himself away*): He's caught up with her! He's caught up with her! Let me go! If they run to the signal station, they'll be all right. There's a bend just there with a stretch of sand still uncovered. Jeannette knows about it, she must know! It's their last chance. . . . But they'll have to run for it, good grief! They'll have to put on a spurt. Why the hell aren't they running?

LUCIEN: You can see what they're doing. They're talking.

FATHER: But it's insane! But . . . they must both be mad! Why doesn't someone go after them and tell them? I'm too old! Holy Moses! This is no time for talking! (*He begins to shout grostesquely, cupping his hands into a megaphone.*) Stop talking there, both of you! Stop talking!

LUCIEN (*in a low voice*): Stop that or I'll strangle you! Let them talk. Let them talk while they can. They've got plenty to say to each other. (*Pause, while the two of them watch, breathing hard and clinging to one another.*) Now – do you see what they're doing, you old optimist? Do you? They're kissing. Kissing. With the sea galloping up behind them. You just don't understand it, do you, you scruffy old Don Juan, you old cuckold, you old rag-bag! (*He shakes him mercilessly.*)

FATHER (*at the top of his lungs, trying to tear himself free*): The tide! The tide! Oh, Jesus! (*Yelling helplessly, ridiculously.*) Mind the tide!

LUCIEN: A fat lot they care about your tide or your bawling or Julia or that woman watching from the road or any of us! They're in each other's arms and they've only got about a minute to go.

FATHER: They shan't say I didn't do anything about it. I'm going after them by the Customhouse path!

LUCIEN: That's right. Don't get your feet wet. (LUCIEN *is left looking far out to sea, perfectly still. Suddenly he says in a dull voice:*) Love. Unhappy love. Are you happy now? With your hearts and your bodies and your romance. Haven't we still got jobs to do, books to read, houses to build? Isn't it still good to feel the sun on one's skin, to drink wine freshly poured, to have water running in the streams, shade at noon, fires in winter, snow and rain even, and the wind and the trees and the clouds and the animals, such innocent creatures, and children; that is, before they get too ugly? Isn't that right, Love? Everything's good, isn't it? (*He turns abruptly away from the window, as though he does not want to see any more. He goes to the table, pours himself a glass of wine, and speaks softly, looking at the ceiling.*) Well, there it is. Are you satisfied? That's the way it had to be. But I told them you didn't like the idea. (*Pause. He pours another glass.*) Forgive me, Sir, but you make me thirsty!

He empties his glass at one gulp. The POSTMAN *appears in the doorway, dressed in a dark cloak.*

POSTMAN: Children! Children!

LUCIEN (*makes towards him precipitately*): Is it for me this time, at last?

He has snatched the letter from the old man's hands and opened it nervously. He scans through it and crams it in his pocket. Then, without a word, he goes to fetch his bag and hat from the stand.

POSTMAN: Well?

LUCIEN (*turns to him and speaks gently*): There are no more children, now. Good-bye, postman.

He gives him a friendly little shove and dives out into the darkness without looking back.

Curtain

Medea

Characters

MEDEA

JASON

CREON

THE NURSE

THE BOY

THE GUARDS

Original Title: Médée

Translated by: Luce and Arthur Klein

First produced in 1946

When the curtain rises MEDEA *and the* NURSE *are seen squatting on the ground before a wagon.*
Vague music and singing are heard in the distance.
They listen.

MEDEA: Do you hear it?
NURSE: What?
MEDEA: Happiness. Prowling around.
NURSE: They are singing in the village. Today may be a feast day for them.
MEDEA: I hate their feast days. I hate their joy.
NURSE: It does not concern us.

A silence.

At home our feast days came earlier. In June. The girls put flowers in their hair and the boys paint their faces red with their blood, and then in the small hours of the morning after the first sacrifices they begin to fight. How handsome our Colchis boys look when they fight!
MEDEA: Be quiet.
NURSE: Afterwards they spend all day taming wild animals. And in the evening they set large fires before your father's palace . . . large yellow bonfires made with herbs that smelled so strongly. Have you forgotten the fragrance of our native plants, child?
MEDEA: Be quiet. Not another word, good woman.
NURSE: Ah, I am old now and the way is so long . . . Why, why did we leave, Medea?
MEDEA (*shouts*): We left because I loved Jason, because I stole from my father for him, because I killed my brother for him!

Be quiet, good woman. Be quiet. Do you think it is wise to repeat these things over and over again?

NURSE: You had a palace with walls of gold and now we squat here like two beggars before a fire which is always going out.

MEDEA: Go and fetch some wood.

The NURSE *gets up moaning and walks away.*

(*Suddenly shouts:*) Listen!

She stands up.

Someone is coming up the road.

NURSE (*listens, then says*): No. It is the wind.

MEDEA *again crouches. The singing is once more heard in the distance.*

Do not wait for him any longer, my dove. You are eating your heart out. If it is true this is a feast day, they have surely invited him there. And your Jason is dancing now, dancing with the daughters of Pelasgus and here we are, you and I.

MEDEA (*in a hollow tone*): Be quiet, old woman.

NURSE: I won't say a word.

A pause. She bends down and blows on the fire. Music is heard.

MEDEA (*suddenly*): Smell!

NURSE: Smell what?

MEDEA: Their happiness stinks, even to this heath. Yet they have confined us far enough from their village! They were afraid we would steal their chickens during the night.

She stands up and cries out:

But what have they to sing and dance about? Do I sing? Do I dance?

NURSE: They are in their own homes. Their day's work is done.

A pause. She dreams.

Do you remember? How white the palace looked at the end

of the cypress road when we returned from our long rides. . . ? You would give your horse to the slave and you would throw yourself on a divan. Then I would call the maidens to bathe you and dress you. You were the mistress and the King's daughter and nothing was too beautiful for you. They would bring you dresses from the great chests and you would make your choice, calm and naked, while you were rubbed with oil.

MEDEA: Quiet, you fool. You are too stupid. Do you think I miss a palace, dresses and slaves?

NURSE: On the run, always on the run, ever since!

MEDEA: I could have gone on running away.

NURSE: Chased, beaten, scorned, without a country, without a home.

MEDEA: Scorned, chased, beaten, without a country, without a home, but not alone.

NURSE: And you drag me with you, old as I am. And if I die, where will you leave me?

MEDEA: In a hole, on the side of the road, anywhere, old hag. And I, too, I accepted that. But not alone.

NURSE: He is leaving you, Medea.

MEDEA (*cries out*): No.

She stops.

Listen.

NURSE: It is the wind. It is the feast day. He will not return tonight either.

MEDEA: But what is this feast day? What happiness is it that stinks even here from their sweat, their cheap wine, and their greasy food? People of Corinth, what have you to shout and dance about? What makes you so gay this evening while I am so choked and oppressed. . . . ? Nurse, Nurse . . . tonight I feel as if I were in labour. I suffer and I am afraid as when you helped me to pull a child from my womb . . . Help me, Nurse. Something stirs in me as it did then and it is something that says no to their joy over there, something that says no to happiness.

She clings to the old woman, trembling.

Nurse, if I cry out, you will put your hand over my mouth, and if I struggle, you will hold me tight, won't you? You won't let me suffer all alone . . . Oh, hold me, Nurse. Hold me with all your strength. Hold me as you did when I was a little girl, as you held me on the night when I almost died in childbirth. I still have something to bring into the world to-night, something bigger and more alive than myself, and I do not know if I will be strong enough . . .

A BOY *enters suddenly and stops.*

BOY: Are you Medea?
MEDEA (*shouts to him*): Yes! Speak up! I know!
BOY: Jason sent me.
MEDEA: He won't come back? He is wounded! He is dead?
BOY: He sends word that you are saved.
MEDEA: He won't return?
BOY: He sends word that he will come, and that you are to wait for him.
MEDEA: He won't return? Where is he?
BOY: He is with Creon, the King.
MEDEA: Imprisoned?
BOY: No.
MEDEA (*again shouts*): Yes! This feast day is for him? Speak! You can see that I know. It is for him?
BOY: Yes. It is for him.
MEDEA: What has he done? Come, tell me quickly. You have run all the way, your face is flushed, and you are anxious to go back. They are dancing, are they not?
BOY: Yes.
MEDEA: And drinking?
BOY: Six large barrels in front of the palace.
MEDEA: And they play games, and fireworks and guns light up the sky. Come, tell me, child, and you will have played your part and can return at once and enjoy yourself. You do not know me. What difference can it make to you in what

you are going to tell me? Why does my face frighten you? Do you want me to smile? There you are. I am smiling. Besides, it must be good news, since they are dancing. So tell me quickly, child, since I know!

BOY: He is marrying Creon's daughter, Creusa. The wedding is tomorrow morning.

MEDEA: Thank you, child! Go and dance now with the girls of Corinth. Dance all night long as much as you can. And when you are old remember that you were the one who broke the news to Medea.

BOY (*takes a step*): What shall I say to him?

MEDEA: To whom?

BOY: Jason.

MEDEA: Tell him that I thanked you.

The BOY *exits.*

(*Suddenly shouts:*) Thank you, Jason! Thank you, Creon! Thank you, night! Thank you, all of you! How simple it was. Now I am freed. . . !

NURSE (*approaches*): My proud eagle, my little vulture . . .

MEDEA: Leave me alone, woman! I no longer have need of your hands. This time my child has come by itself. Oh, my newly born hatred . . . ! How soft you are, how good you smell. Oh, little black girl, now you are the only thing I have left in the world to love.

NURSE: Come, Medea . . .

MEDEA (*stands up with folded arms*): Leave me alone. I am listening.

NURSE: Take no heed of their music, and let us go inside.

MEDEA: I do not hear it any more. I am listening to my hatred . . . Oh, sweetness! Oh, lost strength. . . ! What did he do to me, Nurse, with his great warm hands? He had only to enter my father's palace and touch me with a single caress. Ten years have gone by and Jason's hand no longer grips mine. I have found myself again. Have I been dreaming? Now I am Medea! I am no longer that woman bound to the smell of a man, that bitch in heat who waits. Oh, shame!

Shame! My cheeks are burning, Nurse. All day long I waited for him, my legs open, maimed . . . Humbly, that part of myself that he could take and give back, that middle of my womb was his . . . I had to obey him and smile at him and adorn myself to please him, since he took my life with him when he left every morning, only too happy when he returned in the evening and brought my life back to me. How could I help not giving him the Golden Fleece when he wanted it, and all my father's secrets. How could I help not killing my brother for him, and afterwards following him in his flight . . . poor and guilty with him. I did all I had to do, that is all, and I could have done even more. You know all that, good woman, for you, too, have loved.

NURSE: Yes, my vulture.

MEDEA (*shouts*): Maimed. . . ! Oh, sun, if it is true that I come from you, why was I born maimed? Why did you make me a girl? Why these breasts, this weakness, this open wound in the middle of myself? Would not the boy Medea have been handsome? Would he not have been strong? His body strong as stone, made to take and then go . . . firm, intact and complete. Ah! Then Jason could have come with his great powerful hands; then he could have tried to touch me with them! Each of us with his knife – yes! – and the stronger kills the other and walks away free; yes, free. Not this struggle where I only yearned to yield, this wound I was craving for. Woman! Woman! Bitch! Flesh made with a little mud and a man's rib! A mere piece of man! Whore!

NURSE (*kisses her*): Not you, Medea, not you!

MEDEA: I as well as the others. . . ! More cowardly and more open than the others. Ten years! But tonight it is over, Nurse. I have become Medea again. How good it is.

NURSE: Calm yourself, Medea.

MEDEA: I am calm, Nurse. I am subdued. Do you not hear how softly I speak. I am dying. I am killing everything in me softly. I am strangling everything.

NURSE: Come now. You frighten me. Let us go in.

MEDEA: I, too, am frightened.

NURSE: What are they going to do with us now?

MEDEA: Why bother about that? What you should rather ask is what are we going to do with them. Yes, I am frightened, too, but not of their music, their shouting, their wretched king, or their orders! I am afraid of myself! Jason, you put her to sleep, but now Medea is awakening again! Hatred! Hatred! You great bountiful wave, you are washing me and I am reborn.

NURSE: They are going to drive us away, Medea.

MEDEA: Perhaps they will.

NURSE: Where shall we go?

MEDEA: There will always be a country for us, good woman, where Medea will be queen. Either this side of life or the other. Oh, my black kingdom, you are mine once more.

NURSE (*moans*): Now we shall have to pack everything again.

MEDEA: Yes, we shall pack again, old woman. Afterwards!

NURSE: After what?

MEDEA: Must you ask?

NURSE: What do you want to do, Medea?

MEDEA: What I did for him when I betrayed my father, when I had to kill my brother so we could escape. What I did to old Pelias when I tried to make Jason king of his island. What I have done for him ten times over. But this time, at long last, I will do it for myself!

NURSE: You are mad! You cannot.

MEDEA: What can I not do, good woman? I am Medea, all alone in front of this wagon; abandoned on the shore of this strange sea, expelled, disgraced, hated! But nothing is too much for me!

The music grows stronger in the distance. MEDEA'S *voice drowns it.*

Let them sing, let them sing their wedding songs! And quickly, too! Let them be swift in adorning the bride in her palace! There is a long night before tomorrow's wedding . . . Ah! Jason, you know me though, you know what a virgin you took in Colchis. What could you imagine? Did you think I was going to cry? I followed you in blood and crime, and I need blood and crime to leave you.

NURSE (*throws herself on her*): No more, I beg you, say no more! Bury your moans in the bottom of your heart; bury your hatred. Endure it. Tonight they are stronger than we!

MEDEA: What difference does that make, Nurse?

NURSE: You will take your revenge, my little wolf; you will revenge yourself, my little vulture. One day you, too, will hurt them. We are nothing here. We are only two strangers in their wagon with their old mare. Two chicken thieves at whom the children throw stones. Wait one day, my child; wait a year and soon you will be the strongest.

MEDEA: Stronger than tonight? Never.

NURSE: But what can you do in this hostile island? Colchis is far away and even from there you were driven out. And now Jason, too, is leaving us. What have you left?

MEDEA: Myself!

NURSE: Poor child! Creon is king and it is only because he permitted it that we were allowed to stay on this heath. Were he to say a word, were he to give his permission, they could all be upon us with their knives and their spears. They could kill us.

MEDEA (*softly*): They will kill us. But too late.

NURSE (*throwing herself at her feet*): Medea, I am an old woman and I don't want to die! I followed you, I gave up everything for you. But the earth is still full of good things – the sun on our faces when we stop, the warm soup we sip at midday, the feel in our hands of the little coins we have earned, the nip which warms one's heart before going to sleep.

MEDEA (*pushes her aside with contempt*): Carcass! Yesterday I, too, wanted to live, but now it is no longer a matter of living or dying.

NURSE (*clinging to her legs*): I want to live, Medea!

MEDEA: I know. You all want to live. It is because Jason wants to live, too, that he is leaving.

NURSE (*suddenly nasty*): You no longer love him, Medea. You have not desired him for a long time now. One cannot help knowing everything squeezed together in this wagon. He was the first to tell you that he was too warm one night, and that he wanted to sleep outside. And you let him go and I heard you relax and heave a contented sigh to have the bed all to yourself that night. One kills for a man who still takes you, not for a man you let out of your bed at night.

MEDEA (*takes her by the neck and lifts her brutally before her face*): Take care, woman! You know too much. You say too much. I sucked your milk all right, and I have put up with your whinings. But it is not from milk that Medea has grown. I owe no more to you than I would to the goat I might have sucked in your place. So listen: you have said too much, you and your carcass, with your little nip and your sun on your rotten flesh . . . To your dishes, old hag. To your broom and your potato peelings with the others of your kind. The game we are playing is not for the likes of you. And if you happen to die by mischance and without knowing why, then it is your hard luck. And that is all.

She throws her on the ground. At that moment the old woman shouts.

NURSE: Look out, Medea! Someone is coming!

MEDEA *turns round.* CREON *is before her, accompanied by two or three men.*

CREON: Are you Medea?

MEDEA: I am.

CREON: I am Creon, the King of this village.

MEDEA: Greetings.

CREON: I have heard of your story. Your crimes are known here. In the evening – here as well as in all the islands off this shore – women tell them to their children to frighten them. I have put up with you and your wagon on this heath for several days. But now you will have to go.

MEDEA: What have I done to the people of Corinth? Have I looted their farms? Did I make their cattle sick? Have I poisoned their wells when I went and drew water for my meals?

CREON: No, not yet. But all that you might do one day. Go away.

MEDEA: My father, Creon, is also a king.

CREON: I know. Go to Colchis then and complain.

MEDEA: All right, I shall return there. I will not frighten the matrons of your village any longer; nor will my horse steal the scanty grass of your land any longer. I shall return to Colchis, but let the one who brought me here take me back there.

CREON: What do you mean?

MEDEA: Give Jason back to me.

CREON: Jason is my guest, the son of a king who was my friend. And he is free to do as he chooses.

MEDEA: What are they singing in your village? Why these brilliant displays in the sky, these dances, this wine given so freely to all? If tonight is the last evening they allow me to stay, why do these honest Corinthians prevent me from sleeping?

CREON: I have come to tell you that as well. Tonight they are celebrating my daughter's betrothal. Jason will marry her tomorrow.

MEDEA: Long life and long happiness to them both.

CREON: They have no need of your wishes.

MEDEA: Why refuse them, Creon? Invite me to the wedding. Introduce me to your daughter. I can be useful to her, don't you know? For ten years now I have been Jason's wife. I have quite a lot to teach your daughter, who has only known him ten days.

CREON: It is to avoid this scene that I have decided you will leave Corinth tonight. Harness your horse and pack. You have one hour to cross the border. These men will show you the way.

MEDEA: And if I should refuse?

CREON: The sons of old Pelias, whom you murdered, have asked all the kings of this shore for your head. If you remain I will deliver you into their hands.

MEDEA: They are your neighbours, and they are strong. Kings

do each other such good turns. Why are you waiting?

CREON: Jason asked me to let you go.

MEDEA: Kind Jason! I ought to thank him, don't you think? Can you imagine the Thessalians torturing me on the very day of his wedding? Can you see me at the trial, only a few leagues from Corinth, saying aloud for whom I had Pelias killed? 'For the son-in-law, honest Judges, for the honoured son-in-law of your kindly neighbouring king, with whom you maintain the best possible relationship!' You take the task of kingship very lightly, Creon. At my father's palace I had time to learn that one does not govern that way. Have me killed at once.

CREON (*in a hollow voice*): Yes, I know I ought to. But I promised to let you go. You have one hour.

MEDEA (*stands in front of him*): Creon, you are old. You have been king for a long time. You have seen enough men and slaves. You have played enough filthy tricks. Now look at me and recognize who I am. I am Medea. Medea, the daughter of Aeëtes, who had plenty of others slaughtered when it was necessary – and more innocent than myself, I can tell you that. I am one of your race. Of the race of those who judge and who decide, without ever reconsidering and without remorse. You do not behave like a king, Creon. If you want to give Jason to your daughter, have me killed at once . . . with the old woman and the children who are asleep in there . . . and the horse. Get two trustworthy men to burn all that on this heath and scatter the ashes afterwards. Let there be only one thing left of Medea: a big black spot on this grass and a tale to frighten the children of Corinth at night.

CREON: Why do you want to die?

MEDEA: Why do you want me to live now? Neither you, nor I, nor Jason has anything to gain in my living another hour. You know it well enough.

CREON (*gestures vaguely and suddenly says in a hollow voice*): I am weary of blood.

MEDEA (*shouts*): Then you are too old to be king! Let your

son reign in your stead, let him do the work as it ought to be done. And you go and tend your vineyards in the sun. That is all you are good for!

CREON: Arrogance! Fury! Do you think I came here to seek your advice?

MEDEA: You did not come for it, but I give it to you! It is my right. And yours is to silence me if you have the strength for it. That is all.

CREON: I promised Jason that you would leave unharmed.

MEDEA: Unharmed! I will not leave unharmed, as you say. That would be too easy a thing if on top of all that I were not even harmed! I am to vanish! To be annihilated! A shadow, a memory, an unfortunate mistake, this Medea who was dragged along for ten years. All that is only Jason's dream! He may conjure me away, hide himself among your guards in your palace, bury himself in your daughter's innocence and become King of Corinth when you die . . . he knows his name and mine are bound together for ever. Jason-Medea! That will never be severed any more. Drive me away, kill me; it will be the same. In marrying him your daughter marries me, and you accept me with him whether you like it or not.

She shouts.

Creon, be king! Do what must be done. Drive Jason away. He bears half my crimes. His hands which are going to touch your daughter's skin are red from the same blood. Give us one hour; even less for both of us. We are accustomed to flee after each of our evil deeds together. Believe me, it doesn't take long to pack.

CREON: No. Go alone.

MEDEA (*suddenly in a soft voice*): Creon, I do not want to beg from you. I cannot. My knees cannot bend, my voice cannot be humble. But you are human, since you could not bring yourself to have me killed. Do not let me go alone. Give the ship back to the exile. Give her companion back to her. I was not alone when I came. Why discriminate between us now? It is for Jason that I killed Pelias, betrayed my father, and slaughtered my innocent brother when I fled. I am Jason's woman. I belong to him and so does each of my crimes.

CREON: You are lying. I have thought it all out. Jason is innocent without you. Separated from yours, his case is defensible. You alone have soiled yourself . . . Jason is one of us, the son of one of our kings. His youth, like many another, may have been wild; now he is a man who thinks as we do. You alone come from afar; you alone are a stranger here with your hatred and your witchcraft. Go back to your Caucasus, find a man among your race, a barbarian like yourself; and leave us in this rational land, on the shore of this even sea which has no need for your frenzied passion and your screams.

MEDEA (*after a pause*): Very well, I will go. But my children, what is their race? The criminal's or Jason's?

CREON: Jason thought they would only hinder your flight. Leave them with us. They will grow up in my palace. I promise you they will have my protection.

MEDEA (*softly*): I have to say thank you again, don't I? On top of everything you are human, you are just, all of you, and without hatred.

CREON: Keep your thanks. Go. The hour is almost past, and when the moon is high in the sky nothing will protect you here any longer. My order has been given.

MEDEA: Though a barbarian and a stranger, Creon, and however rough the Caucasus from which I come may be, mothers there hold their children tightly against themselves like other mothers. And so do the beasts in the forests . . . They are asleep inside. These cries, these torches in the night, these unknown hands which take them and tear them from me – they may be too much to pay for their mother's crimes. Give me until tomorrow, I will awaken them in the morning as I always do and I will send them to you. Believe Medea, King! They will have hardly passed the bend in the road and I shall be gone.

CREON (*looks at her for a moment in silence, then says suddenly*): Agreed.

He adds in a hollow voice, still looking at her:

You see, I am getting old. One night is too much for you. It is enough time for ten of your crimes. I should deny your request . . . But I, too, Medea, have killed many. And children as well when I entered conquered villages at the head of my drunken soldiers . . . In exchange I give the peaceful night of these two children to Fate. And if she so desires, let her use the night to ruin me.

He exits, followed by his men.

The moment he disappears MEDEA'S *face lights up and she spits after him, shouting with all her might.*

MEDEA: Depend on it, Creon! Depend on Medea! Fate should be helped a little. You have lost your claws, old lion, if you are now reduced to saying prayers and atoning for little dead children . . . Ah! you want to let these two children sleep because something stirs in you when, alone at night in your empty palace after dinner, you think of all those you killed. It is your stomach, old beast, which is decaying. Nothing else! Eat gruel, Creon, take medicines, and do not become soft over yourself . . . who are so kind, the old Creon whom you know so well, such a good man at heart – only misunderstood – but who, nevertheless, slaughtered his share of innocent ones when he still had his teeth and solid legs. With animals, they kill the old wolves to keep them from these final tender tears. Don't expect them to count in your favour. I am Medea, old hyena! My scales are right, if only the gods, too, would accept them. I know what good and evil mean. I know one pays on the nail for what one does, and that all is fair, but that we have to help ourselves at once. And since your chilled blood and dead glands have made you cowardly enough to give me this night you are going to pay for it!

She shouts to the NURSE.

Go and pack, old hag! Gather your pots and pans, roll the blankets and harness the horse. We shall be gone in an hour.

JASON (*entering*): Where are you going?

MEDEA (*facing him*): I am running away, Jason! Running away! There is nothing new for me in changing my abode. Only the cause of my flight is new, for until now it was for you that I fled.

JASON: I came behind them. I waited until they had gone to see you alone.

MEDEA: Have you still something to say to me?

JASON: I have. And anyway I must listen to what you have to say before you go.

MEDEA: And you are not frightened?

JASON: Yes.

MEDEA (*goes softly towards him*): Let me look at you . . . I loved you! For ten years I slept next to you. Have I aged like you, Jason?

JASON: Yes.

MEDEA: I can still see you standing before me – like this – that first night in Colchis. That dark hero who had just landed, the spoiled child who wanted the gold of the Fleece and who had to be kept from dying . . . Was it you, do you think?

JASON: It was I.

MEDEA: I ought to have left you to face the bulls alone! Alone to face the giants rising armed from the earth, and the dragon who guarded the Fleece.

JASON: Perhaps.

MEDEA: You would be dead. How easy a world without Jason would be!

JASON: A world without Medea! I, too, have dreamed of it.

MEDEA: But this world includes both Jason and Medea, and we have to take it as it is. And you may ask your father-in-law for help and have me taken to the frontier by his men. One or two seas are not enough between us: you know that. Why did you prevent him from having me killed?

JASON: Because I loved you. Because you were mine for a long time, Medea.

MEDEA: And I no longer am?

JASON: No.

MEDEA: Happy Jason who is freed from Medea! Is it your sudden love for this little Corinthian goose, her young, sour smell and her locked maiden knees which have freed you from me?

JASON: No.

MEDEA: Who then?

JASON: You.

A pause. They stand face to face. Suddenly she shouts.

MEDEA: You will never be freed, Jason! Medea will always be your woman! You may have me exiled, may strangle me in a moment when you can no longer bear my shouting. Yet never, never will Medea leave your memory! Look at this face in which you read only hatred! Look at it with your own hatred. Resentment and time may deform it; vice may leave its mark on it. One day it will be the face of a vile old woman whom everyone will loathe. But to the very end you will keep reading in it the face of Medea!

JASON: No! I will forget it!

MEDEA: You think so? You will go and drink in other eyes, suck life from other mouths, take your little man's pleasure wherever you can. Oh! you will have plenty of other women, you need not worry. Now you will have thousands of them, you who were exhausted by having only a single one! You will never have enough of them to find this gleam in their eyes, this taste on their lips, and this smell of Medea in them.

JASON: I want to flee from all that.

MEDEA: Your head, your ugly man's head, may want to forget; in spite of yourself in the darkness your confused hands on those strange bodies will seek for the lost form of Medea. Your head will tell you they are a thousand times younger or more beautiful. Then do not close your eyes, Jason; do not let yourself go for even a second. In spite of yourself, your stubborn hands would seek for their remembered home . . . And in the end you will take women who resemble me, new Medeas for old Jason's bed, when the real Medea will be nothing but an old unrecognizable bag of bones. Anything . . . a mere fold of a hip or the tremble of a single muscle will be enough for the young hands of your old arms to remember, and be surprised at not finding her again. Cut off your hands, Jason. Cut off your hands at once, and change them if you still want to love.

JASON: Do you think I am leaving you to look for another love? Do you think it is to start all over again? It is not only you whom I hate: it is love.

A pause. They look at each other again.

MEDEA: Where do you want me to go? Where are you sending me? Shall I get to the Phasis, or Colchis, my father's kingdom, the fields soaked with my brother's blood? You are driving me away. To what country do you order me without you? What unexplored seas? To the Straits of Pontus, where I followed you, cheating, lying, stealing for you? Lemnos, where I am not likely to be forgotten? Thessaly, where they are waiting for me to revenge their father, killed for you? All the paths I opened for you I have closed for myself. I am Medea, loaded with horror and crimes. You may not know me any longer, but *they* all know me still. What a burden, an old accomplice! You see, you should have let them kill me.

JASON: I will save you.

MEDEA: You will save me! What will you save? This worn-out skin, this carcass of Medea good only to drag along in its boredom and its hatred no matter where? A little piece of bread and a house somewhere, and let her grow old in silence, and at last let no one speak of her any more! Is that your wish? Why are you such a coward, Jason? Why do you not go to the very end? There is only one place, only one dwelling where Medea will be silent at last. This peace you want me to have so that you can live, give it to me. Go and tell Creon that you accept. It will only be a little hard moment to bear. You have already killed Medea today; you know it. Medea is dead. What more, then, can a little blood of Medea mean? A puddle on the ground which will be washed, a caricature petrified in a grin of horror which will be hid somewhere in a hole. Nothing. Have done with it, Jason. I cannot bear to wait any longer. Go and tell Creon.

JASON: No.

MEDEA (*more softly*): Why not? Do you think a muscle which is torn, a skin which cracks is more?

JASON: I do not want your death either. Your death is still yourself. I want oblivion and peace.

MEDEA: You will never have them any more, Jason! You lost them in Colchis that night in the forest where you took me in your arms. Dead or alive, Medea is there, before your joy and your peace, standing guard. The dialogue you began with her will be finished now with your death. After the words of tenderness and love it was insults and scenes. Now, true enough, it is hate, but it is still with Medea that you speak. The world is Medea for you, for evermore.

JASON: Has the world always been Jason for you?

MEDEA: Yes.

JASON: You forgot quickly! I did not come back here for a last scene. But this couch to which you pretend we are bound for ever, who was the first to desert it? Who was the first to accept other hands on her skin, the weight of another man on her body?

MEDEA: I.

JASON: I thought you had also forgotten why we fled from Naxos.

MEDEA: You were already escaping. Your body rested near mine each night, but in your head, in your ugly man's head, closed up, you were already conjuring another happiness without me. Then I did try to be the first to escape from you!

JASON: 'Escape' is a convenient word.

MEDEA: Not so convenient, you see, for I have not been able to. I hated those hands, that other smell, even that pleasure you no longer gave me . . . I hated them at once. I helped you to kill him. I told you the time. I was your accomplice against him. I sold him to you. Have you forgotten the night I told you: 'Come, he is here. You can take him'?

JASON: Never speak of that night again!

MEDEA: I was vile that night, wasn't I? Twice vile. And you despised me, you hated me with all your might and I had nothing else to expect from you but that cold glance – yet all the same it was you I begged to take me away. Though you know, Jason, my shepherd from Naxos was handsome! He was young and he loved me!

JASON: Why did you not choose to tell him to kill me? I would be sleeping far from you now. It would all have been over.

MEDEA: I was unable to. I had to glue myself to your hatred again, like a fly, to resume my way with you. The very next day I had to lie down again against your bored body so that I could finally go to sleep. You think that I have not despised myself a thousand times more than you have? I howled before my mirror alone! I have torn myself with my nails for being that bitch who came back to sleep in her hole. Beasts forget each other and at least leave each other once their lust dies . . . Yet I know you, hero of the Corinthian girls! I weighed your worth. I know what you can give. But you see I am still here.

JASON: Perhaps you had your shepherd killed too soon!

MEDEA (*suddenly says brusquely*): I tried, Jason, didn't you know that? I tried with others, too, since then. I simply couldn't!

A pause. JASON *suddenly says more softly.*

JASON: Poor Medea . . .

MEDEA (*stands up before him like a fury*): I forbid you to pity me!

JASON: You allow me to feel contempt? Poor Medea, entangled with yourself! Poor Medea, for whom the world reflects only Medea. You may forbid pity. Nobody will ever have pity for you. Nor would I, were I to learn your story today. The man Jason judges you with other men. And your case is settled for ever. Medea! It is a beautiful name though, it will have been yours alone in this world. Proud one! There will never be other Medeas on this earth, ever: take that with you to the little dark corner where you hide your joys. Mothers will never give their daughters this name. You will be alone until the end of time, as you are at this moment.

MEDEA: I am glad!

JASON: You are glad! Stand up, clench your fists, spit, rage . . . The more we are able to judge you, to hate you, the better it will be, will it not? The larger the circle around you, the more alone you will be; the more you will suffer, the better it will be. Well, you are not alone tonight, so much the worse . . . I who suffered most by you, I whom you chose from all the others to devour, I pity you.

MEDEA: No!

JASON: I pity you, Medea, who know only yourself, who can give only to take. I pity you, bound to yourself for ever, surrounded by a world seen through yourself . . .

MEDEA: Keep your pity! Medea wounded is still a threat. Rather defend yourself.

JASON: You look like a little quartered beast who struggles entangled in its own intestines and still crouches to attack.

MEDEA: Hunters who allow themselves feelings of pity instead of recharging their weapon come to a bad end, Jason. You know all that I can do still?

JASON: Yes, I know.

MEDEA: You know that I will not be moved, that I will not start feeling pity at the last minute! You have seen me face and risk everything many times for much less, haven't you?

JASON: Yes.

MEDEA (*shouts*): Then what do you want? Why do you come so suddenly and confuse everything with your pity? I am vile; you know that. I betrayed you like the others. I only know how to do evil. You cannot endure me any more, and you sense what crime I am preparing. Beware then! Retreat! Call the others! Defend yourself instead of looking at me in this way!

JASON: No.

MEDEA: I am Medea! I am Medea, you are making a mistake! Medea, who never gave you anything, ever, except shame. I lied, cheated, stole. I am dirty . . . It is because of me that you are running away and that everything around you is stained with blood. I am your misery, Jason, and your ulcer. I am your wasted youth, your broken home, your wandering life, your solitude, your shameful sore. I am all the filthy gestures and all the filthy thoughts. I am pride, selfishness, lewdness, vice and crime. I stink! I stink, Jason! They are all afraid and draw back before me. You know I am all that, and that soon I will be decay and ugliness and old age full of hatred. All that is black and ugly on earth was entrusted to me . . . Then since you know all this, why do you not stop looking at me like that? I don't want your tenderness. I don't want the kindness in your eyes.

She shouts in his face.

Stop! Stop, Jason! or I kill you at once so that you won't look at me like that any more!

JASON (*softly*): Perhaps it would be best, Medea.

MEDEA (*looks at him and says simply*): No. Not you.

JASON (*goes to her and takes her by the arm*): Then listen to me. I cannot prevent you from being yourself. I cannot prevent you from doing the evil you bear within you. Besides, the die is cast. These unsolvable conflicts come to a head like others, and without doubt someone already knows how everything will end. I cannot prevent anything. I must simply go on playing the part which has fallen to me since the beginning of time. But what I can do is to say everything, once and for all. Words are nothing, but they must be said all the same. And if tonight I must be among the dead in this story, then I want to die washed clean of my words . . . I loved you, Medea, at first as a man loves a woman. You undoubtedly knew and enjoyed only that love, but I gave you more than a man's love – perhaps without your knowing it. I lost myself in you, like a little boy in the woman who

brought him into the world. For a very long time you were my country, my light. You were the air I breathed, the water I had to drink to live, and my daily bread.
When I took you in Colchis, you were only a girl more beautiful and harder than the others whom I had conquered with the Fleece and was taking away. Is that the Jason you regret? I took you away as I did your father's gold . . . to spend you quickly and to use you as merrily as I would that gold. And then, well, of course I still had my ship, my faithful companions and other adventures to pursue. At first I had the same kind of love as you, Medea; I loved you through myself . . . The world was Jason, Jason's joy, his courage and his strength – his hunger. And if we were both greedy, well, we would see which of us would devour the other . . .
And then one night, a night which looked like any other night, you fell asleep at the table like a little girl, your head against me. And that night, when perhaps you were only worn out from the long journey, I suddenly felt I had charge of you. A minute before I was still Jason and I had only my pleasure to follow in this world, as harshly as I liked. You had but to be silent, your head to slip on my shoulder, and all of that was finished . . . The others would go on laughing or talking around me, but I had just left them. The young man, Jason, was dead. I was your father and your mother. I was the one bearing the sleeping Medea's head on him. What were you dreaming of in your little woman's brain while I was thus taking charge of you? I carried you to our bed, and I did not love you, did not even desire you that night. I only watched you in your sleep. The night was still. For a long time now we had left your father's pursuers far behind, my companions in arms were standing guard around us, and yet I did not dare close my eyes. I defended you, Medea – indeed, against nothing – the entire night.
In the morning we resumed our flight and the days resembled each other. But little by little all those boys who had been the first to follow me on the unknown sea, all those young fellows from Iolcus who were ready to attack monsters with their

fragile weapons if I lifted my finger, little by little they grew afraid. They understood I was no longer their leader, that I would never bring them to look for anything anywhere again, now that I had found you. Their glances were sad and maybe a little scornful, but they never reproached me. We divided the gold and they left us. Then the world took its shape. The shape I thought it would always keep. The world became Medea . . .
Have you forgotten those days when we did nothing, thought of nothing without each other? Two accomplices before a life grown hard, two little brothers, both alike, carrying their knapsack side by side, sworn friends, each one dividing the pack, each with his knife to protect the other, each sharing the same fatigue and the same bread. I would have made you ashamed had I offered you my hand when the way was hard, had I offered to help you. Jason was in command of only one small Argonaut. My little fragile army with its hair raised in a kerchief, with clear honest eyes – that was you. But I could still conquer the world with my faithful little troop . . . ! I did not feel as strong the first morning on the *Argo*, with my thirty sailors who had given me their lives . . . And at night, at bivouac, the soldier and the captain would undress side by side, surprised at finding each other man and woman again under their identical tunics and at loving each other. We may be miserable now, Medea; we may tear each other and suffer. Those days were given us and no shame or blood can ever stain them.

A pause. He dreams a little. MEDEA *has squatted down on the ground while he was speaking, her arms round her knees; her head is hidden. He sits near her on the ground without looking at her.*

Afterwards, the little soldier put on her woman's face again, and again the captain had to become a man, and we began to hurt each other. Other girls passed in the street whom I could not help but look at. I was astonished to hear for the first time your laughter ring with other men and then you began to lie. One lie at first which followed us a long time like a venomous beast whose eyes we dared not meet when we looked back. Then others, more numerous each day. And at night, when we took each other silently, ashamed of our bodies, which were still accomplices, the whole herd of your lies would swarm and breathe round us in the darkness. Our hatred must have been born then from one of those struggles without tenderness. But why talk again of what is dead? My hatred, too, is dead . . .

He has stopped. MEDEA *says softly.*

MEDEA: If we are attending the wake of only dead things, Jason, why do both of us feel so much pain?

JASON: Because it is hard for all things to be born in this world and it is also hard for them to die.

MEDEA: Did you suffer?

JASON: Yes.

MEDEA: Doing what I did, I was no happier than you.

JASON: I know.

A pause.

MEDEA (*asks in a hollow voice*): Why did you remain so long?

JASON: I loved you, Medea. I loved our fierce life. I loved crime and adventure with you. And our embraces, our dirty and wild struggles, and this feeling of complicity we found again at night on the straw in the little corner of our wagon after our vileness. I loved your black world, your boldness, your revolt, your connivance with horror and death, your passion for destruction. I believed with you that one should always take and fight and that everything was permitted.

MEDEA: And you no longer believe it tonight?

JASON: No. I want to accept now.

MEDEA (*whispers*): Accept?

JASON: I want to be humble. I want the world, the chaos where you led me by the hand – I want it to take shape at last. You are probably right in saying there is no reason, no light, no resting-place, that we always have to search with bloodstained hands, strangle and throw away all that we have torn apart. But *I* want to stop now and be a man. Maybe behave without illusion, as those we used to despise. Just as my father did and my father's father and all those who accepted before us – and more simply than we – to clear a little piece of ground where man can stand in this confusion and this night.

MEDEA: You think you can do that?

JASON: Without you, without your poison drunk every day. Yes, I can.

MEDEA: Without me. Then *you* were able to imagine a world without me?

JASON: I am going to try with all my might. I am not young enough now to suffer. I answer the appalling contradictions, the abysses, the wounds by the simplest gesture man has invented in order to live: I discard them.

MEDEA: You speak softly, Jason, and you say terrible things. How sure of yourself you are! How strong!

JASON: Yes, I am strong!

MEDEA: Race of Abel, race of the just, race of the rich, how confidently you speak. It is good to have heaven on your side and the police as well, isn't it? It is good to find yourself thinking like your father and your father's father, like all those who have been right since the beginning of time. It is good to be good, to be noble, to be honest. And all that given to you one fine morning as if by chance, with the first weariness, the first wrinkles, the first gold. Play the game, Jason, give the signal. Say yes! *You* are preparing a splendid old age for yourself!

JASON: I would have loved to do that with you, Medea. I would have given everything to grow old with you in an appeased world. You are the one who refused.

MEDEA: No!

JASON: Follow your way. Turn around and around, tear yourself to pieces, beat yourself, scorn everything, insult, kill, deny all that is not yourself. As for me, I have had enough. I am content. I accept these appearances with the harshness and determination I had when I refused them with you before. And if I must continue fighting, it is for them I will fight now – and humbly, too – leaning against the futile wall I have built with my own hands between the absurd nothingness and myself.

A pause. He adds:

And when all is said and done, this is what it is to be a man, this and nothing else.

MEDEA: Have no doubt, Jason. You are a man now.

JASON: I accept your contempt, with this name.

He rises.

That young girl is beautiful. Less beautiful than you when you appeared to me the first night in Colchis, and I will never love her as I loved you. But she is new, she is simple, she is pure. I am going to receive her without smiling from her father's and mother's hands, in the morning sun, with her white dress and her train of little children . . . From the clumsy fingers of that little girl I expect humility and oblivion. And if the gods grant it, what you hate most in the world, what is farthest from you: happiness, poor happiness.

A silence. He has stopped. MEDEA *whispers.*

MEDEA: Happiness . . .

Another silence. Suddenly she says in a little humble voice, without moving:

Jason, this is hard to say, almost impossible. It chokes me and I am ashamed. If I told you that I am going to try with you now, would you believe me?

JASON: No.

MEDEA (*after a pause*): You would be right.

She adds in a toneless voice.

Well . . . we have said everything, haven't we?

JASON: Yes.

MEDEA: *You* have said your say. You have washed yourself clean. You can go now. Farewell, Jason.
JASON: Farewell, Medea. I cannot tell you: Be happy. Be yourself.

He has gone. MEDEA *murmurs again.*

MEDEA: Their happiness . . .

Suddenly she stands up and shouts to JASON, *who has disappeared.*

Jason! Do not leave this way! Turn round! Shout something! Hesitate! Feel some pain! Jason, I beg you, all you need is a single moment of bewilderment or doubt in your eyes to save us all. . . !

She runs after him, stops, and shouts again.

Jason! You are right, you are kind, you are just, and all the blame is mine for ever. But doubt it! for just a second, for just a little second! Look back and perhaps I will be freed . . .

Her arms fall down wearily. JASON *is now far away. She calls in another voice.*

Nurse.

The NURSE *appears on the threshold of the wagon.*

It will soon be daybreak. Awaken the children, dress them as if for a feast day. I want them to bring my wedding gift to Creon's daughter.
NURSE: Your gift, poor child! What have you left to give?
MEDEA: In the hiding-place, the black chest I brought from Colchis. Bring it.
NURSE: You had forbidden anyone to touch it! Even to let Jason know it existed.
MEDEA: Go and fetch it, old hag, and without a word. There is no longer time to listen to you. Everything must go terribly fast now. Give the chest to the children and lead them within sight of the city. Let them ask for the King's palace, and say that it is a gift from their mother, Medea, for the

bride . . . Let them deliver it into her hands and let them come back. Listen once more. The chest contains a gold veil and a diadem, remnants of the treasure of my race. But *they* must not open it!

She shouts, suddenly terrifying, at the hesitating old woman.

Obey!

The old woman disappears into the wagon. Later she will come out again, silently, with the children.

(*Alone.*) It is now, Medea, that you must be yourself . . . O, Evil! Great living beast who crawls on me and licks me, take me. I am yours tonight. I am your wife. Come into me, tear me, swell and burn in the middle of me. You see, I welcome you, help you, open myself to you . . . Weigh on me with your large hairy body, press me in your big calloused hands, your raucous breath on my mouth, choke me! At last I am alive! I am suffering and being born. This is my wedding. It is for this night of love with you that I have lived. And you, night, brooding night, night rustling with suppressed cries and struggles, night swarming with the leaping beasts which chase after each other, which take and kill each other . . . please wait a little longer; do not go away too fast . . . Oh, numberless beasts around me, obscure workers of this heath, terrible innocences, killers . . . That is what men call a quiet night, this gigantic swarming of silent matings and murders. But *I* feel you, I hear all of you for the first time tonight under water and grass, in the trees, under the earth . . .
The same blood beats in our veins. Beasts of the night, stranglers, my sisters! Medea is a beast like you! Medea is going to glow and kill like you! This plain touches other plains and those plains still others down to the limit of the shade, where millions of beasts who are alike take each other and slaughter at the same time. Beasts of the night! Medea is here, standing among you, yielding and betraying her race. I utter with you your obscure scream. I accept like you, with-

out wanting to understand any more, the black command. I trample, I put out the little light. I give the shameful signal. I take upon myself, I assume, I claim. Beasts, I am you! All that is hunting and killing tonight is Medea!

NURSE (*enters suddenly*): Medea! The children must have reached the palace and a great clamour is rising from the city. I do not know what your crime is, but the air already echoes with it. Harness the horse to the wagon; let us run away and reach the border.

MEDEA: I run away? But if I had already gone I would come back to enjoy the sight.

NURSE: What sight?

BOY (*rushes in*): All is lost! The kingdom, the State, have fallen. The King and his daughter are dead!

MEDEA: Dead so quickly? How?

BOY: Two children came at dawn bearing a gift for Creusa, a black chest containing a veil richly embroidered with gold and a precious diadem. Creusa had hardly touched them, hardly adorned herself with them like a little anxious girl in front of her mirror, when she suddenly changed colour and fell writhing in horrible sufferings, disfigured by the pain.

MEDEA (*shouting*): Ugly? Ugly like death, was she not?

BOY: Creon rushed in; he wanted to take her in his arms, to tear off the veil and the gold band which were killing his daughter! But hardly had he touched them when he, too, grew pale. He hesitated a moment with horror in his eyes, then collapsed, howling with pain. Now they are lying against each other, dying in convulsions and entangling their limbs, and no one dares to come near them. But the rumour is spreading that you are the one who sent the poison. The men have taken their sticks and their knives; they are hurrying towards the wagon. I have run before them! You will not even have time to defend yourself! Run, Medea!

MEDEA (*shouts*): No!

She shouts to the BOY, *who has fled.*

Thank you, boy! Thank you for the second time! You must

run! It is better not to know me. As long as men will remember, it will be better never to have known me!

She runs towards the NURSE.

Take your knife, Nurse, cut the horse's throat. Soon nothing must remain of Medea. Put wood under the wagon. We are going to make a bonfire as in Colchis. Come!

NURSE: Where are you dragging me?

MEDEA: You know where. Death, death is gentle. Follow me, you will see! You have finished whining and dragging your old aching bones. You are going to rest, at long last, for a long Sunday!

NURSE (*frees herself, howling*): I don't want to, Medea! I want to live!

MEDEA: How long, old bitch, with death on your back?

The two frightened children run in and throw themselves into MEDEA'S *arms.*

(*Stops.*) Ah! So here you are, you two? Are you frightened? All these people who are running and howling, these bells . . . Soon all will be quiet.

She pulls their heads backwards, looks into their eyes, and murmurs.

Innocence! Trap of children's eyes, sneaky little brutes, heads of men. Are you cold? I will not hurt you. I shall be quick. Just time for the surprise of death in your eyes.

She caresses them.

Come. Let me reassure you, let me hug you a minute, warm little bodies. You feel happy against your mother. You are no longer afraid. Warm little lives that came out of my womb, little wills to live and be happy. . . .

Suddenly she shouts.

Jason! Here is your family, tenderly united. Look at it. And may you always wonder whether Medea, too, would not have loved happiness and innocence. Whether she, too, might not have been faith and faithfulness. Soon when you suffer, and until the day you die, think that long ago there was a little girl, Medea, demanding and pure. A little Medea, tender and gagged, behind the other. Think that she will have struggled all alone, unknown, without a helping hand, and that *she* was your true woman! I would have wanted, Jason . . . perhaps I, too, would have wanted it to last for ever and be the way it is in stories! I want, I want still at this moment – as strongly as I used to when I was a child – everything to be light and kindness! But innocent Medea was chosen to be the prey and the place of the struggle . . . Others more frail or more mediocre can glide through the meshes of the net towards calmer waters or down to the slime; small fish do not concern the gods. Medea was game too big for the snare; she stays there. The gods do not have such a windfall every day – a soul strong enough for their battles, for their dirty games. They put the whole weight on my back and they look at me while I struggle. Look with them, Jason, at Medea's last efforts! I still have innocence to slaughter in that little girl who would have wanted so much and in these two warm little pieces of myself. They are waiting for this blood above. They cannot bear to wait any longer!

She drags the children towards the wagon.

Come, little ones, do not be frightened. You see, I am holding you, I am caressing you, and all three of us are going home now . . .

They are inside the wagon. The stage remains empty for a moment. The NURSE *reappears, wild-eyed, like a beast in hiding. She calls out.*

NURSE: Medea! Medea! Where are you? They are coming!

She draws back and suddenly shouts.

Medea!

Flames are shooting out from everywhere. They envelop the wagon. JASON *enters quickly at the head of his armed men.*

JASON: Put out the fire! Get hold of her!

MEDEA (*appears at the window of the wagon and shouts*): Do not come closer, Jason! Forbid them to move!

JASON (*stops*): Where are the children?

MEDEA: Keep asking yourself so that I can see your eyes really well.

She shouts.

They are dead, Jason! Both of them were slaughtered, and before you take a single step I will be struck by the same sword. Now I have found my sceptre again. My brother, my father and the fleece of the golden ram are given back to Colchis. I have found my country again and the virginity which you tore from me. I am Medea at last and for ever! Look at me before you are alone in this rational world, look at me well, Jason. I touched you with these two hands, I put them on your burning brow so they would be cool, and sometimes I put them burning on your skin. I made you weep, I made you love. Look at them. I am your little brother and your wife! I, the horrible Medea! And now try to forget her!

She strikes herself and collapses in the flames, which increase and envelop the wagon. JASON *motions his men to stop as they go towards the flames, and says simply.*

JASON: Yes, I will forget you. Yes, I will live. And in spite of the bloody trace of your passage near me, tomorrow with patience I will reconstruct my poor and fragile human edifice under the indifferent eyes of the gods.

He turns towards his men.

One of you watch the fire till only ashes remain, until the last bone of Medea is burned. The rest of you come with me. Let us go back to the palace. Now we must live, secure order, give Corinth laws, and without illusions rebuild a world befitting us, in which to wait and die.

He goes out with his men except for one who starts chewing tobacco and morosely stands guard before the fire. The NURSE *enters and timidly goes and sits down near him in the rising dawn.*

NURSE: Nobody had time to listen to me. And yet I had something to say. After the night, morning comes and there is the coffee to make and then the beds. And when you have swept, you have a quiet little moment in the sun before peeling the vegetables. Then if you have been able to gather a few coins, it's good to feel the little warm nip in the middle of your stomach. Afterwards you eat the soup and you wash the dishes. In the afternoon there is the laundry or the brass to polish, and you gossip a little with the neighbours and supper comes along without fuss . . . Then you go to bed and you sleep.

GUARD (*after a pause*): It will be a beautiful day.

NURSE: It will be a good year. There will be sun and wine. And the harvest?

GUARD: They mowed last week. They'll gather it in tomorrow or the day after if the weather keeps up.

NURSE: Will the crop be good around here?

GUARD: No need to complain. There will still be bread for everyone this year.

The curtain falls while they are talking.